Working with Sex Offenders

Forensic Focus
Series Editor: Gwen Adshead

This series takes the currently crystallizing field of Forensic Psychotherapy as its focal point, offering a forum for the presentation of theoretical and clinical issues. It also embraces such influential neighbouring disciplines as language, law, literature, criminology, ethics and philosophy, psychiatry and philosophy, as well as psychiatry and psychology, its established progenitors.

Forensic Psychotherapy
Crime, Psychodynamics and the Offender Patient
Edited by Christopher Cordess and Murray Cox
ISBN 1 85302 634 4 pb
ISBN 1 85302 240 3 hb 2 vols
Forensic Focus 1

The Cradle of Violence
Essays on Psychiatry, Psychoanalysis and Literature
Stephen Wilson
ISBN 1 85302 306 X
Forensic Focus 2

A Practical Guide to Forensic Psychotherapy
Edited by Estela Welldon and Cleo Van Velsen
ISBN 1 85302 389 2
Forensic Focus 3

Prison Theatre
Practices and Perspectives
Edited by James Thompson
ISBN 1 85302 417 1
Forensic Focus 4

Challenges in Forensic Psychotherapy
Edited by Hjalmar van Marle and Wilma van der Berg
ISBN 1 85302 419 8
Forensic Focus 5

Managing High Security Psychiatric Care
Edited by Charles Kaye and Alan Franey
ISBN 1 85302 581 X pb
ISBN 1 85302 582 8 hb
Forensic Focus 9

Forensic Nursing and Multidisciplinary Care
of the Mentally Disordered Offender
Edited by David Robinson and Alyson Kettles
ISBN 1 85302 753 7 hb
ISBN 1 85302 754 5 pb
Forensic Focus 14

Psychiatric Aspects of Justification, Excuse and Mitigation
The Jurisprudence of Mental Abnormality in Anglo-American Criminal Law
Alec Buchanan
ISBN 1 85302 797 9
Forensic Focus 17

Forensic Focus 15

Working with Sex Offenders in Prisons and through Release to the Community

A Handbook

Alec P. Spencer

Jessica Kingsley Publishers
London and Philadelphia

Grateful acknowledgement is made to Professor William L. Marshall for permission to reproduce the three tables on pp.83, 84; to *The Grapevine* for permission to reproduce Chapter 13 which originally appeared as an article in their Easter 1995 issue; and to Ruth Mann for permission to reproduce Appendix I on pp.201–205.

A version of this book was originally published in June 1998 as a Scottish Prison Service Occasional Paper

This edition published in the United Kingdom in 1999 by
Jessica Kingsley Publishers Ltd,
116 Pentonville Road,
London N1 9JB, England
and
325 Chestnut Street,
Philadelphia, PA 19106, USA.

www.jkp.com

Second impression 2000

Copyright © 1999 Alec P. Spencer

Library of Congress Cataloging-in-Publication Data
Spencer, Alec,
    Working with sex offenders in prisons and through release to the community : a handbook / Alec Spencer
        p.   cm. -- (Forensic focus 15)
    Includes bibliographicsl references and index.
    ISBN 1 85302 767 7 (alk. paper)
    1. Sex offenders--Rehabilitation. 2. Sex offenders-
-rehabilitation--Great Britain. I. title. II. Series.
HV6556.S64   1999   99-41642
364.15'3--dc21   CIP

British Library Cataloguing in Publication Data
Working with sex offenders in prisons and through release to the community :
a handbook. – (Forensic focus ; 15)
1.Sex offenders – Rehabilitation 2.Prisoners I.Title
365.6'6
ISBN 1-85302-767-7

Printed and Bound in Great Britain by
Athenaeum Press, Gateshead, Tyne and Wear

Contents

DEDICATION   6

FOREWORD BY WILLIAM L. MARSHALL   7

PREFACE   9

1.   Introduction   13

2.   Sexual Offenders and their Victims   20

3.   Creating an Integrated Approach within a Prison Service   42

4.   Other Issues for Prisons   61

5.   The Programme   77

6.   Complementary and Supporting Programmes   107

7.   Monitoring and Evaluation   114

8.   Staff Training and Support   119

9.   Information about Offending Behaviour   130

10. Bridging the Gap I – Throughcare,
     the Multi-agency Approach   135

11. Bridging the Gap II – From Prison to Home
     and the Community   141

12. Other Multi-Agency Issues   180

13. The Prisoner's Tale   189

14. Postscript   192

15. A Model for Multi-Agency Casework, Cooperation and
     Management of Information about Imprisoned Offenders
     who are Subsequently Released to the Community   194

APPENDIX I: THE SEX OFFENDER TREATMENT PROGRAMME (SOTP),
ENGLAND AND WALES   201

APPENDIX II: CASE STUDIES FROM THE STOP PROGRAMME   205

REFERENCES   233

SUBJECT INDEX   243

AUTHOR INDEX   251

Dedication

This book is dedicated in four ways:

First, to the staff at Peterhead Prison, past and present, who have turned the concept of working with sexual offenders into reality. In particular, to Bill Millar, who had the foresight to see the issues and begin useful training with staff; Philip English and his social work team, especially Val Shrimpton and Sheena Watson, who began working with offenders and joined with and supported prison staff in the groups; Jim Cunningham, Del Shannon, David McNiven, and Andy Innes,[1] the first four core workers, and Allan Boath for his support; and Robin (Bob) McConnell, who ably facilitated, managed and organised everyone and who, from my vision, cajoling, harassing and steamrolling created the STOP Programme. All of them have contributed to the development of a centre of excellence at Peterhead Prison.

Second, to Bill Marshall, such a likeable guru, who helped us to get on course and whose talks, discussions and advice I found so valuable and inspiring. I hope that in some small way this book might be seen as a tribute to his own extensive work with sexual offenders, resulting in the implementation of programmes in many countries.

Third, to Hilary Eldridge, who provided us with consultancy, training and support; Doris Aitken, Allan Boath and John Duncan, who contributed to the awareness training of staff; and NOTA (The National Organisation for the Treatment of Abusers) for their supremely useful conferences and seminars. Also, if they do not mind me saying so, to Audrey Park and Sue Brookes, who jolted me along with women's issues and made me reassess my own inaction on pornography.

Finally, and most importantly, this book is dedicated to victims and survivors. One person in particular has made me look at my duty to the public. She, herself, has shown great courage and fortitude and awakened me to the urgency and necessity of our work. So ultimately this book is dedicated to Judy and countless others who have suffered – to let them know that some of us care. Rather than just locking up offenders we want to reduce their potential to do harm in the future, reducing the number of victims. I believe that intervention programmes for offenders undertaken in prison are the least that those of us working in prisons can do to reduce the numbers of people at risk. It is not a lot – but it is something.

---

1   These seven staff members were awarded the UK Butler Trust Group Award in March 1996, having been nominated by 60 'C' Hall prisoners at Peterhead Prison for their outstanding contribution to the development of the STOP Programme and their exceptional work with sexual offenders.

Foreword

Sexual assaults of children and adults occur at a staggeringly high frequency in our societies, and these assaults seriously impair the future functioning of the victims and cause great distress to their families. Indeed, the frequency of these offences and the damage they cause are so extensive that we all ought to feel a sense of shame for having neglected the problem for so long. Although we have recently begun to focus on addressing this issue more adequately, our political leaders and the administrators of our social agencies appear determined to do no more than is necessary to deflect the censure of vocal critics. Counselling for victims and their families is too frequently left to the devoted efforts of volunteers with little financial support from government. Almost no resources are provided to determine what steps might be taken to prevent sexual abuse, and although a growing body of evidence suggests that treatment of offenders can reduce future victimisation, governments have been slow to implement such programmes. Government ministries that ought to play a role in treating sexual offenders have displayed a reluctance to offer the full support necessary to make these programmes maximally effective, despite clear evidence that treating offenders both reduces human suffering (Marshall 1992a) and is cost-effective (Prentky and Burgess 1991).

In the present book, Alec Spencer makes a strong case for implementing treatment for sexual offenders within prisons and correctly points to the need for treatment and supervision in the community once these offenders have been released. Most importantly, Spencer makes it clear that treatment for sexual offenders cannot be simply slotted into the present prison system. If treatment is to be effective, the whole prison service has to see it as a priority and restructure the way they do things. Sexual offenders are harassed so incessantly by other offenders that they become protective of the identity of their offence and reluctant to say anything that would give away their status. As a result, they either refuse to enter treatment or, if they do, they refuse to engage in the open discussion of their problems so necessary for treatment to be effective. Spencer outlines a system-wide structure and an integrated, prison-specific approach to the treatment of sexual offenders that should serve to reduce markedly the problems of client participation. The detailed advice he has to offer prison administrators is invaluable. His book should be required reading for all senior prison administrators and on-line officers working in prisons where sexual offenders are being treated.

Spencer describes the operational requirements and human resources that are necessary (and readily available) to implement and maintain a sexual offenders' treatment programme within a prison service. Not only does Spencer describe the overall approach to the intake process and allocation of sexual offenders to suitable institutions, but he also provides accounts of the treatment process and the training of staff. In describing the programme at Peterhead Prison in Scotland, where he was the senior administrator, Spencer makes it clear that prison officers can play very important roles, as either treatment providers or by offering support for the programme.

The use of prison officers as active agents of therapeutic change may strike readers from outside Britain as a radical departure from the typical practice of using only qualified professionals as treatment staff. However, having had personal experience of working with prison officers in both Scotland and England who were providing treatment for sexual offenders, I can verify that after adequate training they function at a level that is comparable to most other therapists that I have seen. Prison officers are an obviously neglected resource that Alec Spencer and his team have utilised to maximise effect.

This book should be invaluable reading for those who are contemplating implementing treatment programmes in prisons, and for those who are already operating such programmes. Prison officials and treatment staff will learn a lot from Spencer's perceptive analyses of possible problematic issues (e.g. the availability of pornography), as well as from the sensible solutions and wise use of resources that he suggests. If all prison-based treatment programmes for sexual offenders, and the prisons they operate in, were run in a manner similar to that at Peterhead, then the future for potential victims might be better than it is presently.

Professor William L. Marshall,
Queen's University, Kingston, Canada

Preface

Managing prisons is more than merely prison management. Prisons are dynamic institutions where sometimes even trying to 'keep the roof on' begins to take on the appearance of an art form. But these are the basics: to establish appropriate routines, respecting individual rights and dignity, providing proper care in safe surroundings, and so on. All of us engaged in governing prisons accept the primary building blocks upon which we operate: the requirement to keep in custody those sentenced by the courts and by so doing provide the retribution and punishment of society, knowing that while an individual is with us the public are protected from his or her particular brand of menace. However, an examination of regimes that operate in prison establishments throughout the world tells us that in many places something else also appears to be happening. There are custodial or control regimes; therapeutic regimes; prisons operating on 'consensual' models (Toch and Grant 1982; Toch 1995); those that give opportunities for prisoners to exercise personal responsibility; prisons working on 'treatment' and/or 'training' models; and prisons based on the principle of education. In some systems there are discussions about the level of 'intervention' that is considered appropriate, and there have been studies on types of correctional management (Jacobs 1977) and those who run the systems (DiIulio 1989). And still the discussion rolls on.

The reasons for all this diversity and discussion are the secondary issues facing prisons – those being what we do to, or with, prisoners once they have been incarcerated. This debate has been with us as long as imprisonment itself, and there is a wide range of literature to explain the foundations of our current ideas on punishment (Foucault 1977; Garland 1985, 1990; Ignatieff 1978). Rehabilitative and reformative ideals have also coexisted for as long as this, and in some jurisdictions the requirement to contribute to crime reduction and prevention is as important as the custodial function itself. So, for many of us working in the penal system, there has always been that secondary purpose, that calling or vocation, whether driven by individual pathology to treat, cure, save or improve the individual through direct intervention or facility, or because we are aware of the wider context of crime reduction, harm minimisation and concern for our fellow law-abiding citizens – or indeed both.

Of all offenders admitted to prison, those convicted of sexual offending currently present us with the greatest challenge. For many years prison systems themselves hardly recognised the specific problems sexual offenders brought – apart from the need for protection. All through the 1970s and for much of the 1980s we tended to isolate and protect sexual offenders, leaving them to their own devices. In retrospect, it was short-sighted to treat in this way groups of men who did not mix with the rest of the prison and who therefore spent most of their days in and out of each other's cells, perhaps discussing crimes, sharing fantasies and exchanging information on victims or potential targets. In particular, this presented paedophiles with a rare opportunity to network.

In those days we did not understand them and their method of operation. This is hardly surprising, since work on understanding the nature of the problem and devising appropriate programmes was only in its infancy during the 1970s. We were still addressing the constitutional theories of crime causation and the nature or nurture dichotomy. Whereas we had come to terms with 'ordinary' criminals and could provide them with education and training, we still did not know what to do about sexual offenders. In many ways, the fact that we did not know what to do with sexual offenders and did not really understand the processes of their offending meant that it was easier for us to sweep them under the carpet, hide them in a corner of the prison and forget about them. To that extent, prisons (and society in general) *denied* the issues and *minimised* the risks.

In 1977, the English Home Office published *Prisons and the Prisoner*. In this 188-page book, the only reference to sex offenders was made in relation to the usage of open prisons:

> ...the Department has usually had, at the planning stage, to give pledges restricting the type of prisoner sent to each particular prison; for example prisoners convicted of sex or violence are debarred from some open prisons (even though experience suggests that *some* such offenders could be transferred without risk to open conditions after a period of observation in a closed prison). (Home Office 1977, p.117)

The concepts of sentence planning and looking at personal development plans only began to be discussed in the 1980s (Spencer 1982):

> I would suggest that an individual programme is tailored for each long-term prisoner, mapping out the objectives that he must expect to face and achieve over the period detained. This is not meant to be purely a 'treatment model' – the objectives will vary according to the individual and his stage in sentence, but the important departure from the 'treatment' model is that the prisoner is not an object *to* whom a form of 'treatment' is given, but a person *with* whom a programme is devised and who, himself, strives for its achievement. (pp.27–28)

In Scotland this led to the development of sentence planning with self-analysis packages for prisoners to work through (Scottish Prison Service 1990):

> If the prisoner is to relate the opportunities in the penal system to his own personal development then he needs to have a greater awareness of his own situation and problems... Areas likely to be covered include any problems the prisoner may have in relation to his offence, family, work and personal skills; what ambitions the prisoner has; and an opportunity to address what needs to be done to help the prisoner deal with his problems and meet his ambitions. These

issues will then be linked to a sentence plan prepared with the prisoner's involvement. (pp.30–31)

So the language of the 1990s has changed to addressing offending behaviour and offence-specific work. It is the delivery of such concepts which now presents the problems and challenges. Marshall, Laws and Barbaree (1990) urge us never to forget 'The bottom line', our reason for undertaking such work:

> Sexual assaults have devastating effects on innocent victims, so that any reduction in the rate of offending should be viewed as beneficial. In fact, an often neglected aspect of offering treatment to offenders is the real reduction in suffering that occurs when even a few of these men are prevented from reoffending. The rate of reoffense among sexual offenders is known to be very high; it is known that in some subgroups the majority of offenders eventually reoffend. Whenever treatment, no matter how unsophisticated, reduces reoffending by *any* degree, it saves innocent victims much suffering. (p.6)

I make no apology for repeatedly underlining this *raison d'être* throughout the book. It gives us our balance and perspective.

This book, which had the seeds of its origins in a paper presented to the Scottish Prison Service (Spencer 1994b), therefore seeks to position the delivery of prison-based, offence-specific programmes within the broader context of how sexual offenders are managed by the criminal justice system in custody and in the community. But I hope it does more. If there is one thing I have learned, it is that upon entering this area one is stepping into a minefield. However much goodwill there is, however much training and support exists for staff, the sexual offenders themselves are initially the least willing, most suspicious and most manipulative group imaginable. They want to have the label of being 'cured' without undergoing change. They want to retain rights to receive visits and return home to their families without accepting their dangerousness, the possible impact on the local community and the very real probability of the abuse continuing. Until *they* understand the nature of the damage done to others, and *those working with them* – both in prison and in the community – understand the sexual offender's propensity to continue abuse and guile at denying the truth, the possibility that we will miss the signals or even collude makes each step through the minefield ever more perilous.

Alec Spencer
Edinburgh, April 1999

Introduction

WHY THIS BOOK?

I recently heard of a prison where they had undertaken work with sexual offenders. From what was told to me it seemed that anything which could have gone wrong did. Sexual offenders are people, perhaps like you or I. It is their *apparent normality* which often allows them to go on offending undetected, sometimes for lengthy periods. You certainly would not be able to pick them out in a crowd. But what often marks them out is their guile and cunning, their manipulativeness and their ability to distort the truth. These acquired skills make it difficult to begin work with them and puts those around them at some risk. Without adequate training and support, without establishing ground rules for the way things should proceed, the staff involved are as likely to be at risk of being manipulated as their former victims.

Some of the things that went wrong at that prison are summarised below (Gallagher 1994). If this list sounds like it has potential resonance or parts of it feel familiar, then this book is for you.

1. Staff involved in the programme immediately became alienated from other staff and regarded themselves as an élite.

2. Prisoners found it very difficult to cope with the groups, as did some of the tutors doing personal officer work; indeed, some of them found it easier to opt out of the group work and collude on a one-to-one basis.

3. There was a lot of public reaction, generally along the lines that these characters ought to be punished. Staff felt quite threatened by that.

4. Uninvolved staff became very negative and either actively got in the way or were unable to offer appropriate support.

5. There was a lot of family pressure on staff with individuals getting confused and disorientated about attitudes to sex and sexual behaviour. A number of tutors experienced psychological problems. Sexual relationships developed between prisoners and also between staff and prisoners, and there was an unusual degree of marital breakdown among staff involved in the programme.

6. The local branch of the Prison Officers Association were wholly bemused by the matter.

7. Other people in the prison who had previously been involved in what they perceived as high-quality programmes became jealous, and there were squabbles over territory.

8. Specialists also began to fall out with one another and with mainstream staff.

9. Management had a very hard time. Middle managers and supervisors opted out and a lot of dirty washing was hung out in public.

10. A lot of smart, manipulative prisoners were in the sex offender group. They were highly intelligent, indeed; many of them were more intelligent than the staff. They got hold of the agenda.

11. The work was very complicated, more so than the staff had thought. There were all sorts of sexual undertones in staff/prisoner relations; among the prisoners the more vulnerable ones were under a lot of pressure and many of them cracked.

12. Real or imagined breaches of confidentiality were used to undermine the project by those who were not very keen on it.

13. The project demanded changes in shift systems and working patterns which the prison did not manage to achieve.

14. A number of staff became over-involved in morbid case histories.

15. There was some contact between inmate families and staff, not all of which was useful.

16. There was an unprecedented outbreak of religion among prisoners and that was a problem because it was supported by the clergy. The implication was that the prisoners were using conversion as a way out of addressing the real issues which underlay their offences.

17. There developed a big problem around the issue of censorship and the use and availability of pornography within the prison, particularly material for paedophiles.

18. Prisoners manipulated training in their own interests and for their own purposes; in particular, they wanted to get on sports and games courses so that once they got out they could claim to be qualified in that area and thus have access to young boys. Bizarrely, some wanted to learn spoken Portuguese because they had heard that the age of consent for homosexual relationships was lower in Portugal than in Britain!

This book provides a cohesive strategy for the management of sexual offenders in prisons and its interrelationship with other correctional agencies. It is also intended to highlight issues which need to be addressed if such programmes are to stand a chance of succeeding in a penal setting. There are so many potential pitfalls and hazards facing those delivering such programmes that it is worth spending a little while examining some of these issues before embarking upon them.

If assumptions based on Scottish and European figures are correct, then sexual offenders provide us with at least 10 per cent of our 'customer' group within prisons. As practitioners, many of my colleagues and I were for too long unaware of the issues and tended to ignore this aspect of our work. I am pleased that within the Scottish Prison Service a cohesive policy is now being developed for this group.

Since 1992, as the nature of its population has changed, Peterhead Prison has set itself the task of identifying a new role. I believe we have now developed a quality service for sexual offenders which is second to none. All the evidence seems to suggest that the staff are delivering an intervention programme to a very high standard.

As for myself, I have had to acquire a whole new area of knowledge – a field about which I should have known much more in the past and, as a consequence, done much more about in the past. I have spent a lot of time learning about sexual offenders and trying to comprehend the enormity of the effect such people's actions have on their victims. In the process I have come to realise that prison services *can* do something about reoffending (Andrews *et al.* 1990; Marshall and Barbaree 1990; McGuire and Priestley 1995), and that perhaps, through positive programmes, we can actually reduce the level of relapse and consequently reduce the number of victims. This handbook uses the early experience of the STOP Programme at Peterhead Prison and the information we have about working with sexual offenders, the process of sexual offending and a number of related issues as a starting point from which to examine the issues in a broader context and see how we can best manage sexual offenders within prisons.

Peterhead (which is a maximum-security prison) takes long-term prisoners and at present accommodates about 200 prisoners in the main part of the prison. It is primarily a prison for offenders who are considered to be 'vulnerable' in mainstream prisons, nearly all of whom are sexual offenders. However, even holding 200 long-term sexual offenders (or 300 when all accommodation is used) and providing intervention programmes will not meet the demands of our own prison service, for two reasons: first, there are significantly more sexual offenders in the system than Peterhead caters for; and second, short-term sexual offenders are not provided for at Peterhead.

It would appear that within Scotland some work is being done with short-term sexual offenders in other prisons (e.g. Barlinnie Prison in Glasgow and Edinburgh Prison), and with long-term prisoners (at Shotts, Lanarkshire); we have also received enquiries from a number of other penal establishments, including young offenders institutions, keen to develop their own programmes. While clearly such advances are to be welcomed, I do, however, have a number of reservations about isolated programmes which are detailed under the heading 'The general prison environment' (p.55) in Chapter 3. More importantly, unless a solid programme challenging attitudes to a whole host of issues is embarked upon and relapse–prevention work undertaken, and unless this is supported by effective communication of information between prisons and receiving agencies (usually social work departments), there is a likelihood that mistakes and assumptions will be made, and victims and the public put at risk.

It seems to me that in the management of sexual offenders five discrete phases can be identified. These provide the framework from which a successful programme can be run. Anything less and the work undertaken at any stage becomes less meaningful and effective. The stages are:

1. Assessment of risk, focusing on decisions about the appropriate intervention or 'treatment' options (depending on the dangerousness of the prisoner and the timing of programmes within the length of the sentence) and looking at what complementary work should be undertaken in support of offence-specific programmes.

2. Offence-specific intervention programmes, providing the core residential group work (Level 1) – at Peterhead some 200 hours (minimum) over one year.

3. Maintenance programmes to sustain the core work undertaken and keep relapse-prevention strategies updated. Maintenance programmes can be undertaken in conjunction with (Level 2) programmes for offenders assessed as being of lower risk.

4. Supervision and support in the community, including post-release arrangements and parole conditions, attendance at offence-specific groups, integration into the community and family reunification where appropriate.

5. Post-supervision support: voluntary and informal arrangements made with social workers and/or family and friends to provide long-term support for the offender.

These five stages generate a number of issues which need to be addressed *within the prison system*, and a further set of issues which have a wider impact *between prisons and other agencies*. In particular, they focus upon the relationships between staff of the various agencies and the need for both good communications and methods of conveying information about the offender's patterns of offending behaviour and his response to the 'treatment' interventions made. These are detailed in the following chapters.

Summary of key points

- Before embarking upon establishing intervention programmes for sexual offenders it is worth spending some time planning to avoid the potential pitfalls and hazards which face those delivering such programmes since the client group is at times unwilling, suspicious, manipulative and vindictive.

- Sexual offenders are likely to comprise at least 10 per cent of the prison population and require special attention.

BACKGROUND NOTES

In this book I have tried not to use the term 'treatment' to describe the work undertaken in prison. 'Treatment', as a medical model, implies two things: first, that having diagnosed some malady, there is a *cure*; and second, that *something can be done to the patient* to provide the cure. Sexual offending, like other behavioural problems, addictions or obsessions, cannot be cured. That is, there is no guarantee that undertaking a course of 'treatment' will have the desired effect. Whatever is done, it is the offender who must come to internalise inhibitors, understand the harm he causes victims and learn about his cycle of offending so that he can intervene before his lapse leads to relapse. The work delivered is thus a programme of *intervention*.

Our first thoughts on the naming of our programme were positioned around the intention to deliver a Sex Offender Treatment Programme or SOTP. But SOTP was not a useful acronym, so we juggled with the letters to come up with the word 'STOP'. Bearing in mind the comments above, we also came to realise that we were in the business of delivering an intervention programme designed to break the pattern of offending behaviour exhibited by sexual offenders, not a 'treatment' programme. STOP, therefore, is not an acronym but represents the *aspiration* of preventing reoffending behaviour.

Throughout this book the offender is referred to as male. Overwhelmingly, statistics show that more than 90 per cent of sexual offenders are male. In the Waterhouse, Dobash and Carnie (1994) research on 501 Scottish child sexual abusers, only three (0.6%) were female. Although sexual offenders are predominantly male, there are female sexual offenders and abusers and it is estimated that 5–10 per cent of offenders are female. In some cases the motivational issues are different from men, in some cases the offences are perpetrated with men – but they too impact on their victims. When such individuals are identified, work should be undertaken with them. A fuller account of female sexual offenders is given in Chapter 2.

Peterhead Prison embarked upon the Sex Offender Intervention Programme (the STOP Programme) in order to reduce the reoffending of sexual offenders when they return to society. I know that the staff's primary motivation is to reduce the number of victims and lessen the damage done to others in the community. Management also tried to play its own small part by attempting to ensure that the environment in which such work is carried out is appropriate and pornography-free. We developed a simple *vision* at the prison, focused both on our staff and our client group: to become recognised as a centre of excellence through the valuable work undertaken by our staff with sex offenders.

As the number of sexual offenders in its population increased, Peterhead Prison set itself the task of responding to the new situation. We were particularly fortunate with the calibre of our social work staff, who from an early stage realised the importance of the work that needed to be done, and began the processes of group works and training – vital prerequisites of a more formalised programme. As the role of Peterhead Prison changed, it was important to get staff to see for themselves that if we were to have a viable future we must provide a quality service – and that this service had to be focused on our sex offender group. I must add that the staff responded by gradually changing the emphasis of their work, making the intervention programmes central to our purpose. We planned to open our refurbished hall, 'C' Hall, as a place dedicated to these programmes. Notices were published for the attention of both prisoners and staff and selections made from those who volunteered. Interestingly, a large number of staff expressed a desire to work with sexual offenders in 'C' Hall, which opened at the beginning of 1993.

Prisoners were required to agree to certain conditions before they were selected and these included the following: that they be willing to address their offending behaviour; that they participate in sentence planning and the personal officer schemes run by the Scottish Prison Service; and that they maintain a pornography-free environment. The management of 'C' Hall also decided that they would try to run the hall on community-based lines, with prisoners taking far more responsibility and having some say in the running of the regime.

We were also fortunate to have Professor W.L. Marshall of Queen's University, Canada with us for a few days in 1992. As one of the world's foremost experts on sex offender programmes he spent time with staff as part of our staff training process. After visiting a number of prisons in Scotland he indicated the progress which could be made at Peterhead (Marshall 1992b). He has been back on three further occasions, the first being in 1993 for a month as a visiting consultant. His assessment, advice and training input has been immensely valuable to our progress (Marshall 1994). More recently, in both 1995 and 1996, he twice spent a further week looking at our programme and providing developmental guidance and teaching.

In my view, what is crucial to the programme at Peterhead, and will be for other prisons considering such a programme, is that it is run primarily by basic prison staff. The reasons for this are detailed later on. Each group (we started off with two groups) is run by two prison officers and one social worker. They have with them up to ten sex offenders. The group meetings take place in a purpose-built set of rooms. They comprise of a larger group discussion or meeting room, adjacent to which is a smaller studio housing audio and visual monitoring equipment. Communication between the studio and the meeting room is by a one-way mirror, behind which one of the three group workers watches and comments to the leader via an infra-red sound link. These tasks rotate. The third member of staff, in the observation room, provides an element of supervision and a degree of learning, and also watches and films what happens so that issues can be discussed by the staff later. The prisoners are aware of the process and know that a member of staff is behind the mirror. Prisoners are also free to inspect the studio and try out the video camera.

These groups are now achieving a very high standard, in which prisoners are breaking down their barriers of denial, challenging opinions and values, and are prepared to reveal their deeds and innermost feelings to other members of the group. The groups also make great demands on the skills and emotional stamina of the staff involved. However, we must not delude ourselves that all will succeed. Without some form of help, perhaps more than half of our sexual offenders will reoffend. Even with our programme, and support on the outside, one or two from every group might still reoffend. So we will have to be resilient when the one or two do let us down and the press picks up their story. We cannot allow the staff to blame themselves. No matter how hard we try *it is the offender who has responsibility for his actions*. The success of the staff will be the extra one, two, three or four from each group who do not reoffend, or those whose pattern of offending is delayed or diminished.

Summary of key points

- The work undertaken with sexual offenders is not 'treatment' in the medical sense. Sexual offenders cannot be cured but can be helped to understand their problems and learn coping mechanisms to minimise the chances of relapse.

- It is the offender who has responsibility for his actions. Staff should derive satisfaction from those they have helped to succeed, and consequently the victims saved, rather than feel culpable for any failures.

CHAPTER 2

Sexual Offenders and their Victims

SEXUAL OFFENDING

A question often asked is whether the incidence of sexual abuse cases is on the increase. There is no categoric answer, but what is evident is that the incidence of reporting such cases to the police and social work departments has increased. I think there are two reasons for this. First, improved education in schools and media reporting of such cases, and the associated publicity, makes it *easier* for the victim to disclose (as the victim believes someone will listen) and *more acceptable to declare* such experiences; and for some it perhaps *identifies* behaviour which, as isolated victims, they were uncertain was deviant. And second, society may be becoming more intolerant of such types of offending.

However, this does not help us to understand whether sexual abuse is on the increase or not. In fact, a number of the cases which have come to light relate to behaviour which occurred many years before. Numerous studies have indicated that sexual abuse and offending has affected up to one-third of the population (see p.68). This is not merely a problem – it is an epidemic. (See, for example, Anna C. Salter's (1989) study 'Epidemiology of child sexual abuse'.) In a Lothian Crime Survey carried out by Edinburgh University, Richard Kinsey (1993) found that there was vast under-reporting of crimes against children, who often accepted violence and sexual offences as everyday occurrences. Nearly one-third of girls aged between 14 and 15 reported that they had been the victims of some kind of sexual offence by an adult male in public within the previous nine months. The offences ranged from indecent exposure to attempted abduction and rape and in 40 per cent of cases the girls knew or recognised the man involved. Kinsey related:

> The girls would say to us: 'Why is it, mister, that these men want to put their hands inside our shirts?' By the time they are 15 this is taken for granted as part of becoming a woman in our society. (*The Glasgow Herald* 1992, p.5).

I use that example because it is Scottish, recent and comes from a general survey, not one looking specifically at sexual offending.

What do we mean by sexual offending?

Different jurisdictions define sexual offences in differing ways. However, they appear to fit into a broad set of criteria: a sexual act committed by one person against another, either against the will of that person (lack of consent) or when such consent cannot validly be given (such as by a child). Offences such as forcible or violent rape and incest with a young child are obvious examples of the above categorisations. However, sexual offences are harder to prove when the circumstances point to differences in power between the offender and the victim, and thus the implied power of one over the other.

O'Connell, Leberg and Donaldson (1990) discuss the principles of how sexual offending could be defined. The following construct can be derived from their discussion: *A criminal offence involving sexual behaviour occurs when one party does not give, or is incapable of giving, fully informed consent or where the difference in power between the two parties is such that one is not in a position to make a truly free choice.*

Sexual offending can be committed by both male and female offenders upon both male and female victims but, as we saw earlier, the preponderance of offences both reported and researched involve male offenders and adult female or child victims (Finkelhor 1982). Where shorthand is required, the offender will therefore be referred to as 'he' and the victim as 'she'.

Why do sexual offenders commit offences?

It may seem somewhat simplistic to say that sex offending occurs because the offenders like doing it. However, sexual offenders commit sexual offences because it makes them feel good, even though that feeling may be only short-lived and they know that after the act they might experience shame or fear of being caught. According to O'Connell *et al.* (1990), sex offending is therefore likely to be driven by a number or combination of factors:

1. attraction to the behaviour because of the pleasure derived

2. a perception that there are no other available means of obtaining pleasure

3. a lack of concern about or understanding of the damage that results from this behaviour

4. insufficient controls to prevent the offender from acting on a desire to seek pleasure in this way.

As with the causes of crime in general, there is no single definitive causal explanation of why individuals become sexual offenders. In order to commit their first offence the offender has to cross strong legal, social and ethical boundaries. For most of us these boundaries and controls are so strong that we give little serious thought to crossing them and react with revulsion and incomprehension when we hear about those who do so. In one way or another offenders do not have those controls operating in their lives.

Sometimes offenders simply have a strong preference for a particular type of pleasure seeking that happens to involve victimising others. Often, however, offenders feel themselves to be faced with limited choices; they see few ways to glean a meagre bit of comfort in what they perceive as an unrelentingly hostile world. In either case, offenders usually have some understanding that the sex offending behaviour is wrong or could get them into trouble (offences are generally done in secret). They do not, however, have a strong enough reason *not* to offend when compared with the perceived pleasure to be derived. There are not enough controls, either internal (recognition of the harm to victim, wanting to do the right thing, and so on) or external (fear of getting caught, concern about what others would think if they knew, and so on). Offenders have some combination of overpowering attraction to the behaviour (compulsivity) or lack of control (impulsivity). (O'Connell *et al.* 1990, p.13)

Recently, however, there has been a shift of emphasis in how we might view sexual offending. With the emergence of the feminist movement, a number of feminist scholars (Brownmiller 1975; Dworkin 1979; Rush 1980; Russell 1984) have emphasised the commonalities among various forms of sexual aggression previously viewed as separate phenomena, and have linked, for example, predisposing factors in the sexual abuse of children with that perpetrated on women. Their argument is that although the sexual drive is important, the patriarchal nature of our society and the culture in which we develop means that other factors are equally important. Thus, sexual offending can be used by men to fulfil non-sexual needs such as the expression of power, anger, and the need to control, dominate and, through that, humiliate women.

Even in non-overtly feminist sociological literature it is recognised that for work with sexual offenders to begin to take on contextual meaning, often unresolved issues from childhood will have to be addressed. In acting out, sexually offending males are expressing non-sexual needs for power, affection, and affinity, negative attitudes to women and the reinforcement of aggression. In beginning to tackle such issues and examining the cognitive patterns these behaviours represent, the sociological and feminist viewpoints begin to merge. In trying to understand the aetiology of male sexual offending we are driven to accept the explanation that it is the cultural and societal values which we experience in our upbringing that lead to the male desire for the expression of power over females.

Juliet Darke (1990), in her paper on sexual aggression, goes further and asserts:

It is proposed, here, however, that *all* sexual assaults are perpetrated to satisfy the aggressor's desire for, and to enhance feelings of, power. (p.58)

Her argument runs that a sexual assault represents a blatant attempt to control another person physically and emotionally. In the socialisation process, women are encouraged to develop characteristics of dependency, emotionality, weakness and passivity, and these are seen as less desirable than the masculine traits of strength, logic, aggressiveness and independence. Female socialisation has traditionally suppressed the qualities of intelligence, strength, physical prowess, competence and achievement orientation and, therefore, can be seen as training in the abdication of personal and social power. While men, on the one hand, are considered to be sexually dominant (i.e. exercising leadership and control, particularly over women), women, on the other hand, are considered to be submissive, particularly towards males, with displays of patience, caution and restraint. This cultural process reflects and maintains the power differential between men and women. Sexual assault represents a gross personal invasion and an extreme violation of bodily integrity. Men sexually assault in order to control, dominate and humiliate their victims. This is accomplished from a position of power, with forced sex as the vehicle for such humiliation. The enforcement of sexual activity upon another represents the ultimate in power and control. To be powerless to stop such abuse must be the ultimate humiliation. (Paraphrased from Darke 1990, pp.58–59.)

Humiliation of women is reinforced through the non-verbal and verbal actions of sex offenders. They cover a range of behaviours, from anal penetration, ejaculation and urination over the face to abusive comments which suggest that the victim likes the actions of her assailant or what she is being forced to do, is a whore, or is totally worthless as an individual.

FEMALE SEXUAL OFFENDERS

Although this book is primarily concerned with male offenders, who we now understand a good deal about, it is useful to consider female sexual offending. In comparison with male offending not a lot has been written on the subject, perhaps reflecting the growing interest in this problem and the fact that society itself finds it difficult to accept the reality of female violence and aggression. We are still less certain, feel greater unease and find it harder to comprehend female sexual offending, and feel abhorrence when we uncover abuse against children by females. Why should this be? We used to describe male sexual offenders as 'beasts' or 'monsters', but gradually we have come to recognise such offenders as people. Now we have transferred our fear of the unknown to a subset of sexual offenders – females – who are the archetypical carers, the protectors and nurturers of children, and who provide a deep-rooted emotional context in our subconscious, in our culture and in our evolutionary genetic make-up – that of 'motherhood'. In the normal schema we have created, in our perception of the world, women are seen as caring, 'softer', trustworthy and mothers. The courts and professionals – compounded by popular disbelief that it can actually happen – have been slow to recognise the issue of female sexual offending. Yet in many ways it should be no less unexpected than its male equivalent. We have identified extreme cases, such as Myra Hindley, and turned them into images of people none of us could be. By redefining such people we run the risk of shifting our attention away from ordinary abusers and offenders.

> Women who then deviate from the stereotype will be seen as monsters, rather than people who offend, and who, like other offenders, may have good and bad reasons for doing so. Anger and aggression may be as much part of femininity as of masculinity. The stereotype is harmful to men and women in general, but especially to victims of abuse by women, who know better. (Adshead, Howett and Mason 1994, p.54)

Prevalence and characteristics of offenders

It is probably the fact that very few women are actually convicted of sexual assaults that has resulted in little research data being available in this area. Approximately 3 per cent of convicted sexual offenders are female and in about half of these cases they have been involved with male offenders (Eldridge 1998). It is estimated that between 5 and 15 per cent of all perpetrators coming to public attention were female (Watkins and Bentovim 1992). Of the 8663 children who contacted ChildLine in 1990 and 1991, 9 per cent said they had been abused by a woman (Harrison 1993). In two studies looking at the histories of convicted male prisoners and rapists, over 40 per cent of those who disclosed they had been abused said they had been abused by a woman (Condy *et al.* 1987; Groth and Burgess 1979), although the figures were significantly lower for non-criminal populations. From the statistics available (including Condy *et al.* 1987; Finkelhor and Russell 1984) it is clear that boys are more likely to be abused by female offenders than girls (by a significant factor). Why male children are more frequently targeted is uncertain, but enough is known of the backgrounds of these women, their motivations, cognitive distortions and offending behaviours to give us some good insights. It is generally held that female sexual offenders have a higher rate of past victimisation than males. Studies have put the prevalence as high as 60–90 per cent (Adshead *et al.* 1994), and in looking at comparisons between female and male juvenile perpetrators Mathews, Hunter and Vuz (1997) found that the developmental histories of juvenile female offenders reflected more extensive and severe maltreatment, the majority having suffered sexual and physical abuse from an earlier age:

> The juvenile female perpetrators tended to have experienced more severe victimization experiences, as evidenced by a higher average number of molesters, a younger age at first victimization, and the more frequent report of having been subjected to offender aggression. (p.191)

It is also widely held that females tend to internalise the impact of such abuse (i.e. there are more self-abusive behaviours in their histories) and males externalise (i.e. there is a higher incidence of delinquency and acting out). This may account for low self-esteem, an inability to form healthy relationships, and an increased likelihood of victimisation. However, like male offenders, women who sexually abuse children can be of any age, intellectual ability or marital status, come from all walks of life and do not have characteristics and personality profiles that distinguish them from other women. They too develop distorted thinking patterns which legitimise, minimise, justify and excuse their behaviour. Motivation for abusing is variable: in some cases there is a clear primary sexual motive; others use sexual offending to satisfy a whole range of emotional needs (e.g. for intimacy, love, or company); yet others engage in sexual abuse of children as an exercise in power or revenge (e.g. to gain control over another person, particularly a male, or inflict pain to get back at men for the suffering they have caused); or a combination of these factors, may lead to offending in circumstances in which the female feels in control and less vulnerable.

Women choose the children they abuse. Where the perpetrator is the child's mother it is also probable that she is the sole carer. The child's father may have little or no contact and thus there is no non-abusing parent who could attempt to protect the child and take on the role of primary carer. The mother is then in an intimate authority relationship with the child in which close contact such as bathing, play, cuddling and expressions of love, and taking the child to bed with her are natural activities which provide opportunities for abuse under the guise of normal parenting behaviour.

Although many female abusers offend in isolation, some offend with male offenders and are frequently coerced by them into this behaviour. Coercion can take the form of threats to hurt the mother or the child, which may make her feel too frightened to escape. Some of these women cease to offend when separated from the male offender, but others then go on to continue to offend themselves. This category is described by Mathews, Matthews and Speltz (1989) and Saradjian (1993) as the 'male-coerced' offender. Mathews *et al.* devised a typology to categorise women sexual offenders as:

1. offenders who are seen in the role of either teacher or lover (victims are often adolescent males)

2. offenders who are coerced by males

3. 'predisposed' offenders (i.e. offenders who have been the victims of sexual abuse themselves as children)

4. psychologically disturbed offenders (i.e. women with a mental illness which may be related to their offending behaviour).

In her earlier work Saradjian (1993) described five categories:

1. women who target pre-pubescent children
2. women who target adolescent children
3. women who are coerced by men to offend
4. women who co-offend (with women or men)
5. women who are involved with ritual abuse groups.

But more recently Saradjian (1996), whilst acknowledging the less typical categories of ritual sexual abuse and psychotic states, has refined the three main groups (which echo the first three types of Mathews) as follows:

1. women who initially target young children
2. women who initially target adolescents
3. women who are initially coerced by men.

The predisposed offender has usually been extensively abused herself. She acts alone and initiates the abuse. She usually chooses her own very young children. She may use aggressive tactics to control the child but does not use seductive techniques. Women who target older children use grooming tactics similar to those used by male offenders (i.e. implanting thinking errors to make the child believe they are responsible). The teacher/lover targets adolescent or pre-adolescent boys, not usually their own children. Many of these women have been sexually abused by an adult male partner and perceive the boys they abuse as lovers who are less threatening and will hurt them less than adult men.

Victims of female sexual offending

As society in general does not perceive women as sexual aggressors, the harmful effects on the child victims of female offenders are often regarded as minimal or in some circumstances even denied. Finkelhor (1984) conducted a survey which showed that members of the public perceived acts by females, whether on male or female victims, to be less abusive than the same acts by male perpetrators. In fact, however, victims of female offenders feel every bit as traumatised as those of male offenders. Children may well feel that they will not believed, especially since women are not seen as likely offenders. Victims also suffer because of society's confused attitude towards adult women introducing younger males to sex. The perception that a younger male (e.g. 12 years old) is 'lucky' to be initiated into sexual activity with an older woman may result in the child not identifying himself as a victim or feeling guilty and confused about any fear or pleasure that he may have felt. Saradjian (1997) considers that the effects on male victims are particularly compounded:

> For victims of female offenders the social construction of women as carers, nurturers and asexual beings, particularly if the abuser is the mother, given the link for the child between care-getting, care-giving and sex is likely to be even

more distorted. The confusion for the child in sexuality and sexual norms, when the abuser is a woman, that is, an ostensibly non-sexually aggressive being, is likely to be intensified and more complex. Some victims, particularly boys, protect the image of the mother as sexual by construing themselves as the sexual aggressors or at the very least equal partners. This statement was made by a male who was sexually abused by his mother from infancy until his teenage years: 'My mother was just loving me, in the only way she knew how. She would never have done anything to hurt me, she was my mother. I could have stopped her if I had wanted to but I kind of liked it … It was always me who had the real say in whether we did it or not.' (p.6)

The victim may feel stigmatised as a result of experiencing guilt and responsibility for implicating their 'good' mother, and this is exacerbated by the belief that they are deviant or different from others. They may minimise and rationalise what has happened, saying: 'I must have misunderstood her way of showing affection.' Children feel powerless to do anything and betrayed in such situations. Because of the closeness and intimacy of the relationship with a sole carer, these child victims sometimes feel a loss of their own independent identity. Even after the abuse has ceased such victims are often so emotionally enmeshed that they find it difficult to break free of the abuser. One of the consequences of abuse is anger in the victim. Curiously, whether the primary abuser was a male and the mother was not able to protect the child, or whether the abuse was committed with a male even when overtly coerced by violence, or whether it was perpetrated only by a female, the victim invariably feels more anger towards, and betrayal by, the female. In stereotypical terms the male is expected to be aggressive and as an offender to be abusive; the female is expected to be there to care and protect. When she does not or cannot protect them, the victim feels more hostility to the non-abusing mother than to the sexually abusing father. In 'Jill's story' (Elliott 1993) these feelings were expressed:

> The abuse by my father was part of my normal life. It was something I grew up with, a weekly event. The abuse by my mother is still something that I am trying to come to terms with … It's odd that the abuse by my father was not so awful as the abuse by my mother. There's something about a mother. (p.138)

Although the mother may be blamed for not protecting her child from male sexual abuse, the reverse situation does not occur, because when a woman sexually abuses a child it would be rare for the child to have any expectations that his father would be available as a primary carer; thus the anger is directed solely towards the female offender. In a study by Bowlby (1988) it was noted that many young male victims became very physically aggressive towards mothers who had sexually abused them, or very passive in relation to their mother and aggressive to others, particularly women, whereas female victims often tended to direct their anger inward on themselves.

Interventions

It is probably too simplistic to think that an intervention programme designed for male offenders will be equally suitable for female offenders. Female sexual offenders share the same kinds of cognitive distortions, belief systems, justifications and transferences of blame that male offenders demonstrate. Indeed, in general they also perpetrate the same types of offences as their male counterparts. Kaufman *et al.* (1995) found some gender differences such as more anal abuse by males and a greater use of foreign objects by females – explainable by obvious biological differences. However, 'male and female offenders did not differ in their use of pornography, threats, and coercion during the sexual abuse. Nor did males and females differ in the extent to which they used force to make a child either have or watch sex' (p.327). Therefore, in principle, the main difference is not between the male and female genders but between individual offenders. However, there are gender differences, and females learn their value systems within society in a context of female socialisation. These value systems reflect a society in which females are expected to be more vulnerable and passive, and as a consequence female offenders tend to rationalise from a victim stance. Certainly, if female sexual offenders have experienced severe abuse and maltreatment in their own childhood, it brings into question whether the approaches and programmes developed for sexually assaultive males, which may be confrontational in nature and which focus on accountability and behavioural changes, are appropriate for female offenders. Mathews *et al.* (1997) suggest that in the light of the 'reports of more extensive maltreatment, high levels of familial dysfunction, internalized negative self-image, and impaired capacity for healthy attachments, a treatment approach which includes a developmental perspective and victimization treatment components appears to be more appropriate' (p.197). These offenders are often of the 'predisposed' type. They can have the most horrendous backgrounds and the most damage to repair. They have few coping skills and few positive associations. Matthews (1998) details their therapeutic goals:

> The primary goal is to build the self-confidence of these women. Their self-esteem must be elevated and they must start believing that people can care for them. Their affiliation needs must be met by someone other than their children. The most important therapeutic goal is for these women to voice their own childhood pain and sort out all the conflicting emotions of their chaotic experiences. They may both love and hate their parents, hate the parents for their abuse or nonsupport, and at the same time desperately hope that their family has changed and can finally offer love and support to them. These offenders often want but fear an adult partner. They can be rejecting and clinging in regard to their own child, and they may vacillate between confidence and withdrawal. (pp.263–264)

Whilst the impact of their trauma has to be addressed, so too has their offending behaviour. Since relatively few female sexual offenders come to notice in an area at any given time, it may be difficult to bring together enough women at any one time to form a group. It is possible that the prison environment may present the only realistic opportunity to bring together sufficient numbers of female sexual offenders to enable such groups to function. The work will then have to deal with both their trauma and offending. Although some joint groups focusing on socialisation and early offending (such as date rape) have been run in America for male and female juvenile offenders, it is usually inappropriate to include women offenders in groups with their male counterparts, if for no other reason than to prevent the continuation of abuse and its consequential trauma. Eldridge (1998) lists three reasons why 'mixed' groups are inadvisable:

1. Because of the small numbers, the women offenders would probably be in a tiny minority within a group: maybe even just one woman per group. This could lead to major problems in group dynamics.

2. Women offenders are often current victims of male abuse and hence being with a group of males may not feel like a safe place for them to share difficult material.

3. Male offenders are particularly inclined to use the existence of female offending to excuse their own!

Therefore, it is likely that most work with women offenders, at least in the community, will be undertaken on an individual one-to-one basis. Individual work can be very effective provided it is done by an experienced worker who has knowledge of the field and experience of working with female offenders. As with their male counterparts, good support mechanisms must be in place for those working with female sexual offenders. Workers, who are not divorced from our society with its values and social constructs, sometimes find female sexual abuse, especially offending by mothers, particularly emotionally demanding and may be more likely to collude with or reject the individual than when dealing with male offenders.

MENTALLY DISORDERED OFFENDERS

When deemed to be mentally disordered as defined in the Mental Health Acts (England and Wales 1983, Scotland 1984), sexual offenders are dealt with by psychiatric services either in the community, on an outpatient basis, or in regional secure units (England and Wales) and special hospitals. The special hospitals are of higher security and tend to take the more serious and intractable cases. To be detained in a hospital or secure unit patients have to suffer from a mental disorder (defined as mental illness, psychopathic disorder, mental impairment or severe mental impairment) and require detention for their own health or safety or for the protection of others. In the case of psychopathic disorders the individual must also be 'treatable'.

Prevalence and characteristics

Only a small proportion of convicted sexual offenders receive a psychiatric disposal in court and less than 8 per cent of such offenders have a psychiatric illness (Barker and Morgan 1993). However, there has been an increase in the number of sexual offenders admitted to psychiatric hospitals over the last decade. In 1994, sexual offenders accounted for a fifth of all patients admitted to secure hospitals in England and Wales under restriction orders. This increase is mainly accounted for by transfers of remand prisoners to hospitals under the Mental Health Act 1983. A similar picture exists in Scotland. Approximately 80 per cent of restricted sexual offender patients are detained in the legal categories of mental illness and psychopathic disorder; the remainder suffer from mental impairment (a form of mental handicap). If the category of 'sex offender' is broadened to include those offenders in whom sexual behaviour contributed to the commission of a non-sexual index offence, e.g. manslaughter or attempted murder, and those with histories of sexual offence, then between 50 and 70 per cent of offender patients in special hospitals may be regarded as sex offenders (Butwell 1996; Fisher, Grubin and Perkins 1998).

Research has failed to identify significant distinctive features in sexual offences committed by the mentally ill. As with most sexual offences, it is likely that those committed by the mentally ill are multifactoral in origin. There are few reports in the literature of offences in which the psychotic phenomena of a mental illness are thought to have played a part (Jones, Huckele and Tanaghow 1992). The difficulty thus presented for those treating mentally ill sexual offenders is whether to consider sexual offending as part of the 'illness'. Those admitted to hospitals and secure units range from the sexual offender who has a psychopathic disorder, who might be equally suitable for a prison environment and benefit from a cognitive–behavioural approach (such as a group programme for sex offenders), to those with psychotic delusions (such as those suffering from schizophrenia), who commit offences due to illness and where the first priority lies in getting the illness under control. The question that is then asked is whether they are sex offenders as well, or conversely, whether they would have offended had they not been mentally ill. These are questions with which psychiatrists must wrestle; they raise complex issues relating to mental health, tendencies to sexual offending and, in some cases, the impact of brain damage.

Treatment

This confusion may have led to a lack of clarity of purpose with hospitals naturally tending to treat disease rather than the propensity to offend. Then there is a second problem. In assessing patients for release, psychiatrists have to consider not only the health and safety of the individuals concerned but also the risk they may pose to the public. Thus, even when a sexual offender has been 'cured' of his mental illness, his psychiatrist will have to make a judgement as to whether he continues to pose a threat in relation to sexual offending. This double criteria makes psychiatrists reluctant to admit offender patients, as it may be difficult to feel comfortable about releasing them later. The effect of such dilemmas has led Fisher *et al.* (1998) to criticise British psychiatrists for displaying 'a good deal of ambivalence in relation to sexual offenders'.

> At one level, they show little reluctance to provide reports to the courts in which they assess risk in individual cases, and on occasions they will recommend that an offender should be dealt with by way of a hospital order rather than a prison sentence. They are also frequently involved in assessing suitability for release from prison when sexual offenders come up for parole and they sit on the national boards that make parole decisions. Similarly, they assess and make recommendations about the relatively small group of sexual offenders who are compulsorily detained in hospital for treatment; they always sit on mental health review tribunals, which determine whether such offenders are treatable and whether they are safe enough to be released. However, when it comes to actually providing treatment for sexual offenders psychiatrists are often much more reticent, particularly when treatment is associated with compulsory admission to hospital... there is a legitimate concern that too judicious a use of mental health legislation in relation to sexual offenders may lead to the risk of detaining obviously dangerous men in hospital for whom treatment is either inappropriate or ineffective. In addition, if and when the release takes place of compulsorily treated sexual offenders, many psychiatrists feel particularly vulnerable to criticism should their patients then reoffend. (p.192)

Fisher *et al.* argue that in the United Kingdom, training for psychiatrists has focused on mental illness and, to some extent, on dysfunctional behaviours that lead to personal distress. Assessment and treatment of sexual offenders does not fit easily into this framework. With the exception of those who are attracted to psychoanalysis and psychotherapy, psychiatrists in general are unaware of modern thinking on sex offending and effective, cognitively based treatment programmes. This divide needs to be bridged. In a book review, Robertson (1998) expressed frustration at the two separate approaches: 'The cursory dismissal of psychodynamic theories betrays an unwillingness, I suspect, to frame early life experiences within any particular theory' (p.36). It is claimed that apart from forensic psychiatrists, who themselves do not encounter more normalised offenders and deal only with a small number of the most serious cases (e.g. sexual murders), psychiatrists working in the community do not ordinarily come across sexual offenders. They deal with sexual counselling for couples and occasionally treat exhibitionists or voyeurs who come to them as voluntary patients. Lewis and Perkins (1996) also argue that while

> psychodynamic psychotherapy can play an important part in the treatment of the sex offender it cannot be the sole mode of treatment since there are defects and deficiencies in the development of thinking, feeling and behaviour which frequently require additional complementary and supplementary therapeutic and educational inputs to enhance changes in the areas of cognition, emotion and conation. (pp.245–246)

Pfäfflin (1996) asserts that 'instead of playing off the behavioural against the psychodynamic approach, or *vice versa*, it seems much more useful to integrate both approaches' (p.265). Lewis and Perkins also recommend that 'collaborative strategies in the context of multi-disciplinary work, with psychiatric, psychological, nursing, social work, occupational and educational input, are imperative in the diagnosis, clarification and resolution of the difficulties that underlie sexual aggression' (p.246).

The initial decision as to whether a sexual offender receives a hospital disposal from the court on the grounds of psychopathic disorder depends on chance variables, including whether or not a psychiatric report is requested and the therapeutic optimism (or pessimism) of the reporting psychiatrist (Chiswick 1998). While in hospital, psychiatrists have responsibility for offender patients in terms of their management and eventual release but are unlikely to be involved in their treatment, leaving this to psychologists or nursing staff. The exception is the case of the psychotic sexual offender, in which the psychiatrist takes an interest in the treatment of the psychosis. 'Even here, however, the behaviour associated with the sexual offending will either be ascribed to the psychosis and effectively ignored, on the assumption that the risk disappears with the symptoms of mental illness, or dealt with by another member of the clinical team' (Fisher *et al.* 1998, p.193).

There are also general difficulties with working with mentally disordered offenders: they may be on high levels of drug therapy which can affect their thinking and responsive capacities; they may become distressed or angry when confronted with their offending acts; and they may be poor communicators, have little motivation to address the issues or simply not wish to co-operate. Like other non-mentally ill offenders, they are also likely to deny, minimise and rationalise their offending behaviours if they actually start addressing them.

Within special hospitals it is likely that those mentally disordered patients who have sexual motivation associated with their offending will be treated in wards specially tailored to offer psychotherapeutic treatments, both individually and in groups, providing non-specific psychotherapy or sex education. In the last few years there has been a growth of the multi-disciplinary approach, with some recognition given to the value of cognitive–behavioural components. Mentally disordered sexual offenders are likely to be viewed in two ways: those with a *psychotic illness,* who may be viewed in a more sympathetic light by staff taking the view that the individual would not have offended had it not been for his mental illness, and that controlling his illness will prevent further sexual offending; and those with a *pyschopathic personality disorder,* who are seen as being difficult if not almost impossible to treat. This is a simplified view and conceals other issues. For example, some offenders with psychotic illnesses may well have committed sexual offences whether they were mentally ill or not; and, in both groups, assessment of suitability for discharge or transfer to a less secure setting is a major problem, particularly where there does not appear to be a close causal relationship between the mental disorder and the sexual offending. In particular, there is great reluctance among regional and less secure units to admit sexual offenders suffering from psychopathic personality disorders, because of the fear of their reoffending and the difficulty of accurately assessing whether it is safe to discharge them into the community.

Finally, pharmacological therapy may play a part in treatment. There is a role for libido-reducing drugs such as cypoterone (an anti-androgen chemical) but they do not provide a simple solution to the problem of sexual offending. Patients need to understand and agree with the aims of such treatment, and compliance in hospital does not guarantee compliance within the community. Also, there is no drug that acts selectively on deviant sexual drives while leaving ordinary non-deviant drives unaffected.

Because of the range of problems and concerns faced by psychiatrists, mentally ill or disordered sexual offenders have tended to be a neglected group within the mental health system. Recently, however, with the success of programmes based on the cognitive–behavioural approach within prisons and the community, mental hospitals have begun to develop similar programmes for patients who are also sexual offenders. This multi-modal approach is to be welcomed.

OTHER ISSUES – PORNOGRAPHY AND RIGHTS

One of the spin-offs of trying to establish a programme for sexual offenders is that we have all had to re-examine our own attitudes to women in society. Sexual offending by men against women and children (which represents the overwhelming majority of such offences) is the social by-product of a society in which women do not have equal rights and in which they are perceived to be dominated by men. Another form of offending against women, and for that matter against children, is the use of pornography.

Pornography represents an assault on women and children on several counts: *for what it is* – a form of exploitation; *for what it does* – which is to reduce relationships to processes and to objectify its subjects, leading to attitude change and distortion, and in some cases to sexual offending; also *for what it underpins* – as it is a significant factor in the subjugation of women and is, therefore, on its own an immensely important human rights issue. In relation to its effect on the young the Council of Europe Committee on Crime Problems (1993) viewed this matter extremely seriously and recommended to

> make the public aware of the devastating effects of sexual exploitation which transforms children and young adults into consumer objects and urge the general public to take part in the efforts of associations and organisations intervening in the field. (p.9)

Abuse, male domination, battering, pornography and sexual offending have been critically important issues for women throughout the ages. But changes in social attitudes begun in prisons have little chance of succeeding unless similar changes also occur within society at large. Although prisons can have an impact on the wider community, greater influence is exerted by the major institutions of society, the media, advertising, politicians, the academic, industrial and commercial worlds, and so on.

In relation to sexual offenders there are important issues surrounding the availability of pornography within prisons. These are discussed further in Chapter 4.

VICTIMS – A BRIEF INSIGHT

This book is about the management of sexual offenders within prisons, but without some awareness of the huge impact such offending has on victims our work would be undertaken in a contextual void. It is therefore important to understand what it is like to be the victim of sexual offending. Both women and children (and even a few men) are the victims of male adult offending, but the principal focus of this book is on the effects of sexual abuse of children by adults. The majority of the prisoners held at Peterhead have committed sexual offences against children either in the context of their family homes (incest or familial offending against a stepdaughter) or against children in general (non-incest paedophilia). Women, of course, also experience violation, humiliation, degradation, feelings of vulnerability and many of the impact issues listed below, but it is right that we focus on one specific group to illustrate the nature of the damage that can be done.

The problems for many children lie in understanding what has happened to them and attempting to think back to earlier events. In order to survive children will adopt coping mechanisms which may allow them to minimise or rationalise what has happened or even to deny or forget it.

> Children often cope with abuse by forgetting it ever happened. As a result, you may have no conscious memory of being abused. You may have forgotten large chunks of your childhood. Yet there are things you do remember. When you are touched in a certain way, you feel nauseated. Certain words or facial expressions

scare you. You know you never liked your mother to touch you. You slept with your clothes on in junior high school. You were taken to the doctor repeatedly for vaginal infections.

You may think you don't have memories, but often as you begin to talk about what you do remember, there emerges a constellation of feelings, reactions, and recollections that add up to substantial information. To say 'I was abused,' you don't need the kind of recall that would stand up in a court of law.

Often the knowledge that you were abused starts with a tiny feeling, an intuition. It's important to trust that inner voice and work from there. (Bass and Davis, 1988, p.22)

To those of us who have not been abused it is difficult to realise that the victim may herself be unsure of what has happened and find it difficult to define what has occurred. In *The Courage to Heal*, Bass and Davis (p.21) provide a checklist.

How Can I Know if I was a Victim of Child Sexual Abuse?

When you were a young child or teenager, were you:

- Touched in sexual areas?
- Shown sexual movies or forced to listen to sexual talk?
- Made to pose for seductive or sexual photographs?
- Subjected to unnecessary medical treatments?
- Forced to perform oral sex on an adult or sibling?
- Raped or otherwise penetrated?
- Fondled, kissed, or held in a way that made you feel uncomfortable?
- Forced to take part in ritualised abuse in which you were physically or sexually tortured?
- Made to watch sexual acts or look at sexual parts?
- Bathed in a way that felt intrusive to you?
- Objectified and ridiculed about your body?
- Encouraged or goaded into sex you didn't really want?
- Told all you were good for was sex?
- Involved in child prostitution or pornography?[1]

'All sexual abuse is damaging, and the trauma does not end when the abuse stops. If you were abused as a child, you are probably experiencing long-term effects that interfere with your day-to-day functioning' (Bass and Davis 1988, p.20). To help us understand the range and magnitude of the actual problems generated by sexual abuse, and highlight the *raison d'être* for working with sexual offenders

1   Between 500,000 and 1,000,000 children are involved in prostitution and pornography in the US; a high percentage of them are victims of incest (Dellacoste and Alexander 1987).

(both in prison and in the community) to prevent future victimisation, listed below are some of the commonly identified impact issues and treatment strategies.[2]

Impact effects on the child victim and issues to be considered with some treatment strategies:

1. *Victim feels like 'spoiled goods':* The child feels violated and dirty and believes she is 'tarnished' when compared with others. She begins to hate herself and feels bad. Workers need to ensure and reassure her that she is OK, help the child not to feel a 'freak', and work with her and others not to perceive her as 'damaged goods'.

2. *Feeling set apart and stigmatised:* The child experiences feelings of worthlessness and feeling different from other children. She feels that there is something wrong deep down inside. She must be a bad child as she knew what she did was wrong – didn't she keep the secret? If people really knew her they wouldn't stay friends. The child begins to isolate herself and in some cases this can lead to drinking, drugs, running away and acts of self harm.

3. *Feelings of guilt and shame:* The child feels guilt for her actions and shame about what she has done. There is a need to reduce the guilt felt: she has to learn that the abuse was the perpetrator's responsibility; keeping secrets (what he wanted) was wrong and disclosure was right. She needs to hear that the consequential family disruption was not her fault and that it was right to tell and this protects other siblings.

4. *Feelings of fear:* The child experiencing abuse, violation and the inability to prevent the actions of an adult creates feelings of powerlessness and helplessness and often leads to phobias. The child will need help to identify her rational and irrational fears, and the provision of protection and a safe environment. She will require to build 'trusting' relationships, or rebuild old, damaged ones e.g. with her mother, if she feels her mother has let her down.

5. *Depression:* There is a requirement to acknowledge, accept and not minimise the child's feelings; reassuring her without giving false promises. Workers should build on positives but be alert for signs of depression including suicidal feelings. The child may feel self-destructive or just wants to 'hide and die'.

6. *Repressed anger and hostility:* The child should distinguish between rational and irrational anger, acknowledge rational anger and re-focus it into

---

2   I am indebted to Jenny Still (1990) of the former Gracewell Clinic for her initial classification of these issues. This provided the basis for my own work, which I have developed, adapted and enlarged, taking account of some of the issues identified in Bass and Davis (1988), pp.33–54.

non-destructive, not self-blame which is correctly attributed to the perpetrator.

7. *Low self-esteem and personal power:* When abused the child's boundaries, her right to say no and control are violated. She feels powerless and the abuse makes her feel worthless. To help her regain self-esteem she can, for example, share experiences with other victims to relieve the sense of 'I'm the only one'; and those around her can emphasise good qualities in the child and help her 'own' them.

8. *Poor social skills:* The child may have been told she was useless, a waste of space, stupid and only good for sex. These messages only perpetuate the status quo. In addition to enhancing her self-esteem there is a need to improve social skills; develop assertiveness – her ability to say 'no', 'tell', 'shout' etc. to prevent further victimisation.

9. *Inability to trust, and having feelings of betrayal:* Someone who they trusted and depended upon caused them harm. The family may have been unable or unwilling to protect, or listen to disclosure. If she reported events to an adult she was probably ignored, told to forget it or she was told that she had lied. Her reality was thus denied, distorted and she may have felt that she was losing her grip on reality. She may feel abandoned and more likely to latch on to others/anyone creating even more risk. There is an important need to help build or rebuild trust: rebuild damaged relationships e.g. with her mother; build new trust/caring relationships; identify 'safe' adults who she can 'tell'; and learn how to give and take and help others.

10. *Blocking out feelings and pain:* Children cannot afford to feel the full extent of their terror or pain as the agony would be devastating. Since love and trust have been betrayed the child learns not to rely on feelings. If you raise the issues of adults' feelings, to the child this could mean violence, anger or beatings. This process also applies to physical pain which is blocked out. The child may not want to give the abuser the satisfaction of seeing the child cry and has not done so. 'Getting in touch' with one's feelings is a long and painful road to recovery.

11. *Blurred boundaries and role confusion:* To minimise role/boundary confusion the child needs to understand what has happened, and what are acceptable patterns of behaviours for adults. The perpetrator must take complete responsibility for the abuse and acknowledge to the child that it was wrong. Positive role modelling needs to be put in place by family and professionals.

12. *Inability to experience normal intimacy:* The foundations of appropriate intimacy are learned throughout childhood – in the two-way mutual processes of giving and receiving, caring, trusting and loving – which nurture relationships. Abuse ruins trust, distorts reality and provides

confused messages about the relationship between sexual activity and love. The child has to re-learn about healthy relationships and the supportive value of appropriate intimacy.

13. *Pseudo maturity and artificial sexuality:* Inappropriate sexualisation of a child for her age leads later to dysfunctions. Sexual arousal becomes linked to feelings of shame, disgust, pain and humiliation. Sometimes the child can be used in pornography or for prostitution. A focus of rewarding the child for her sexual favours creates confusion in the child between sex and love and caring – and she learns that the way to obtain approval and attention is to be sexual. The child needs to be helped to relinquish inappropriate adult responsibilities (sexual and domestic) and let the child in her become (or revert to being) a child. She will need biology and sex education. There is a requirement to modify the child's posture and learned sexual behaviour to appropriate behaviours for her age.

14. *Poor self-mastery and control:* There will be a need to help the child behave responsibly towards herself and others, and to assist her develop independence from her immediate family and background (to break generational cycle). This will contribute to developing the freedom to make choices.

15. *Forgetting, denying, minimising and rationalising:* The child tries to cope and survive as best as she can. In order to do so she will often adopt similar techniques to that of her abuser – but for different reasons. She will try to repress what has happened and put it to the back of her mind and forget. That is perhaps why so many adult survivors are superficially unaware of the fact they were abused. Children also deny it is actually happening to them, perhaps hoping by so doing that it will go away, or it may be easier to deny reality than to try to tell others and face further rejection and lack of protection. The child may attempt to belittle what has been done to them and shrug it off as a way of coping, 'doesn't every father do that?'. Or they may try to justify it for the abuser and rationalise events – 'he can't help himself', 'he doesn't get on with mum and looks to me for comfort', or 'what can you expect when he's drunk'. Helping children to fully understand what has happened to them is a slow and painful business. It should only be undertaken by experienced therapists.

16. *Additional problems created for other siblings:* Other children (in the family) may experience confusion as to 'why him/her and not me?' Feelings of jealousy, rejection, exclusion, guilt, blame, social stigma, fear of abuse, secrecy and silence may occur. (Many of the problems created are similar to those of the actual victim).

Some possible post traumatic effects which can be experienced by the abused child:

Acute, prolonged and/or delayed:

- Sleep disturbance and/or nightmares.
- Flashbacks and re-experiencing of abuse.
- Emotional flatness, memory impairment, poor concentration.
- Hyper-alertness; anxiety, irritability, mood swings, general unhappiness.
- Detachment and isolation.

Longer term:

- Regression, bed-wetting/soiling.
- School failure, poor self-care.
- Running away from home, child prostitution, addictions to drugs and/or alcohol.
- Self-mutilation, overdosing, suicide attempts, eating disorders (anorexia).
- Isolation; poor relationships/social skills.
- Sexually provocative behaviour; blurred behavioural boundaries.
- Risk of becoming an abuser to younger children and/or becoming an adult offender later on in life or anxiety that this might happen.
- Persistent 'victim role' pattern.
- Feeling 'spaced out'; not being there all the time as the mind wanders.
- Living fantasy life to escape past; gambling.
- Being perpetually busy or a workaholic to repress thinking about abuse.
- Develop various forms of mental illness.
- Dysfunctional development for many years: isolating self from feelings, rage and blankness.

The effects listed above can last for many years – one case recently reported to me was of an 80-year-old woman who had been admitted to hospital for a para-suicidal event. During post traumatic counselling it emerged she had been the subject of child sexual abuse which had affected her to the present day.

It is also worth looking at the extent to which some sexual offenders have involved victims. For example, in Abel *et al.* (1987) 153 non-incest paedophiles who targeted male victims were able to identify 43,100 separate acts involving 22,981 victims, whereas 224 who targeted females had 4435 victims. In the case of female victims of incest, 159 offenders perpetrated 12,927 acts on 286 victims (an average of about 45 incidents per victim).

Sexual offending and abuse is damaging to victims and can cause substantial and, in many cases, long-term problems for the victims, be they children or adult women. That is why intervention programmes, whether in the community or within prison, are so important. But assessment and work designed to challenge offending behaviour can only really be effective in an environment which understands about victims and the impact offending has on their lives. In the chapters which follow we look at how appropriate intervention programmes might function within a penal setting.

VICTIM TO ABUSER?

There is the belief that once you have been bitten by sexual abuse then it follows that you will become an abuser and offender yourself. As Michael O'Brien put it, beware of the 'vampire syndrome' (address to NOTA Conference, Dundee, 1992). Not only does it not hold good for all offenders (as some who offend have not been abused and, indeed, many who have been abused do not offend), but the motivation for disclosure could be suspect. Offenders might lie about having been abused to provide some justification or excuse, and they might use their claims of having been the victims of abuse to gain empathy and support, or to secure less challenging interventions. In the Waterhouse *et al.* (1994) Scottish study into child sexual abusers, of 209 cases in which background information was known, only 17 per cent of the abusers were reported to have been sexually abused themselves (this includes 5% on whom the abuse was both sexual and physical); a further 6 per cent were reported to have been physically abused only (23% in total). (The authors express a degree of caution given the limited number of cases in which sufficient background information was available (209 cases from the sample of 501). However, assuming the figures are indicative – even just for that group – then the 'vampire syndrome' is certainly not borne out by the statistics.)

Society seems to want an answer to the question: 'Why do men sexually offend against others?' The notion of a *cycle of abuse*, of going from being a victim to victimising others, seems to be a relatively simple and easily understandable explanation. However, in the most recent research, Hanson and Bussière (1998) use meta-analysis to examine predictors of sexual offence recidivism, and state: 'Contrary to popular belief, being sexually abused as a child was not associated with increased risk' (p.353). So where does this leave us? The association between a sexual offender's own past abuse and his becoming a sexual offender is more than a simple cause-and-effect relationship, since there must exist a whole host of factors which may influence and intercede in whether a victim of sexual abuse will go on to offend against others. Although being a victim as a causative factor is intuitively appealing, empirical studies of the actual incidence of abuse in the histories of offenders suggest that it is much less than popularly assumed. In a review of all studies reporting histories of sexual abuse in adult sexual offenders, Hanson and Slater (1988) indicate wide variations in reported rates, ranging from 0 per cent to 67 per cent depending on whether narrow or broad definitions were used, with an average of around 28 per cent. Although this rate is higher than the rates for general community samples (one in six, or about 17% for the male population as a whole, Hunter 1990), it also suggests that many offenders are not abused. Hanson and Slater point to problems with studies of child sexual abusers who were sexually victimised when they were young, noting that the rates of victimisation may be overestimated because such offenders have more reasons than non-sexual offenders to identify an event in their history that explains their offending.

Two recent studies (Cooper, Murphy and Haynes 1996; Dhawan and Marshall 1996) have examined samples of sexual offenders and non-sexual offenders to see what could be learned about the aetiology of offending. In Cooper *et al.* (1996) the researchers examined and compared the cases of about 300 abused and non-abused adolescent sexual offenders. The results indicated that those offenders who were sexually abused had begun their offending at a younger age, had more victims and were likely to abuse both males and females, and tended to show more psychopathology and interpersonal problems. The study did not explain why either group had begun to sexually offend. Dhawan and Marshall (1996) looked at a prison population of sexual offending and non-sexual offending inmates. They found that the prevalence rate of sexual abuse in the whole sample was very high, about 46 per cent, when compared with the general population, and that reports of sexual abuse were much higher among the sexual offender group (58%) than the non-sexual offender inmates (20%). They also found that a large percentage of the abused sample (42%) reported experiencing a high subjective impact on their lives as a result of their abusive experience. They were also more disadvantaged in terms of family background than the non-sexually abused group. 'The non-abused group reported better family support, which included getting along well with their families, being told that their caregivers loved them, and being shown physical affection ... [and] also reported more support from people outside their immediate families' (p.14).

Since not all victims of sexual abuse go on to become sexual offenders, there must be a number of intervening factors that influence the outcome. According to Langevin, Wright and Handy (1989), sexual experiences in early childhood do not necessarily lead to maladjustment. It is therefore important to look at other factors associated with these experiences such as the gender of the perpetrator, their relationship to the victim and whether force was used, as well as the family as a supportive structure. Seghorn, Prentky and Bouchier (1987) believe that it may be difficult to infer a direct relationship between being a child victim of abuse and later sexual offending, since it is likely that sexual abuse typically occurs in the presence of many other important childhood stressors.

It therefore appears that while a proportion of the population are victims of childhood sexual abuse, only a small number of these go on to offend. Why the others do not (because of personal resilience, family support, societal norms or whatever) has yet to be fully explored, as indeed does the question of why those who do not suffer early sexual victimisation become sexual offenders.

CHAPTER 3

Creating an Integrated Approach within a Prison Service

WHY BEGIN THE PROCESS IN PRISON?

Nothing would suit many sexual offenders better than for the prison authorities to forget about their crimes while they served their sentences. However, by ignoring their offences we tacitly collude with them and allow them to reinforce their own self-perceptions and fantasies, thus contributing to a continuation of their distorted value systems.

It is important, therefore, that the offender accepts that he has done something wrong. All the anecdotal evidence suggests that once the offender has been released, and there are few controls over him, he becomes reluctant to accept that he has done anything at all or, alternatively, considers that as far as he is concerned he has done his 'time', taken his punishment and does not need to do any more to address his offending behaviour. As a consequence, he is still a significant threat to the public.

In prison there are some controls and, depending on the type of sentence, may be some incentives. Ideally, all sexual offenders should undertake offence-specific work. However, prisoners cannot be compelled to engage in such work. If they could, the work would be meaningless. But we do need to try to get all prisoners to engage. Perhaps incentives such as the promise to reduce the security classification once staff believe that he has become less of a danger to the public, or the opportunity of gaining parole, should be available only to those prisoners who have shown a willingness to address these important issues.

It is important that the offender accepts and understands the nature of his offending and how it harms the victim. This is the first step in a long process which tries to bring about a change in attitude and ultimately to reduce the propensity to relapse.

From this follows the vital work, if appropriate, of working towards some family reconstruction, but with a host of safeguards (discussed later) against the possibilities of relapse, revictimisation, and continuation of the abuse.

Clearly, the important issue from the criminal justice perspective is reducing the number of victims in the future. In prison we have the opportunity to work with the offender. Many victims sustain long-term psychological damage which can result in the need for clinical and psychiatric support. The existing child protection procedures often result in the child being removed from the abusive situation, that is, taken from home. This can be perceived by the child as a further punishment and may reinforce the child's sense of being in the wrong.

Finally, working with the offender, at times, can provide valuable information on how he manipulates his victim, who often feels the guilt; this information can help free the victim from feelings of responsibility for the abuse. Therefore, there is a need to share such valuable information gained in the prison setting with relevant agencies so that others can benefit.

Summary of key points

- It is important to get sexual offenders to begin addressing their offending behaviour in prison, otherwise they will feel that they have served their sentence and need not engage in offence-specific work on release.

UNDERSTANDING THE SCALE OF THE PROBLEM

Not all sexual offenders are easily identified as such. Some are convicted of less obvious crimes such as assault or breach of the peace – which could be for indecent exposure – and are therefore often missed in the penal setting. We do not always realise the range of acts and offending that lie behind a 'simple' conviction of murder. Non-specific index offences are available, and the use of plea bargaining makes it possible to reduce offences such as assault with intent to ravish to simply assault. Often, by their very nature, sexual offences are difficult to prove. In using the evidence of one person's word against another it is only natural that prosecutors will be tempted to settle for accepting a guilty plea of some reduced or simplified charge rather than putting victims, be they women or children, through the ordeal of a trial. On the other hand, offenders often choose to plead guilty to something 'they did not do', stating that they are taking this course of action only to spare the victim (usually a child) a court ordeal. The real motive may be less sympathetic, as the offender still denies that he has done anything, and in such cases it is known that there can be a high rate of abuse continuing on release.

Of course, this state of affairs is desired by the offender, as not only would he have a harder time in prison if identified as a child sexual offender, but he might also reap a series of other consequences including more social work involvement and even having to face up to his offending! For managers of the prison system, not only does it take some probing to find out which long-term prisoners are sexual offenders, but there must be prisoners serving comparatively short sentences for such offences of whom we do not know.

From the general evidence available and from comparisons with other systems, it appears that at least 10 per cent of the Scottish prison population might be sexual offenders. In Scotland, that figure represents something in the order of 500 to 600 prisoners. In March 1992 it was estimated that there were some 450 sexual offenders in the system (Walker 1992). Indeed, it is likely that the trend will be for an increase in numbers, both as a proportion of the total prison population and in absolute terms. On the basis that the general trend will be to reduce imprisonment for those least requiring it (lesser property and fine-default cases), then the proportion of offenders convicted of violence against the person and received into prison may rise. Additionally, there has been a raising of public awareness about what constitutes sexual abuse and the need to protect the equal rights of women and children. In the short and medium term it is likely that the response by the criminal justice system will outstrip any cultural changes within society which may lead to a modification of behaviour.

We therefore need to have better information from the police and courts about the nature of the charges for which the offender is convicted. Prisons have recently begun to receive copies of the judge's notes from High Court cases and this has improved the position. In Scotland, the introduction of the new computerised prisoner records system in 1994 under the Scottish Prison Service Information Network (SPIN) project is facilitating the development of an integrated approach to information within the Scottish Prison Service. However, it may still be necessary to try to tease out this information from social work departments and other agencies when the index offence is of a non-specific nature. In Scotland there is a need to share information with the police, Crown Office, Scottish Courts Administration and social work departments if such offenders are not to slip through the net. At some point in the future all the agencies involved in the delivery of criminal justice will need to have a unitary, computerised system of sharing the same information. There are now signs that this matter is being considered:

> The absence of a statistical data base based on behavioral offence descriptions, as well as variations in the completeness and availability of behavioral offence descriptions in inmate files, has deleterious consequences. It makes sex offenders difficult to identify in the system; this problem is exacerbated when one considers that the propensity to offend sexually is related to the offenders' *history* of sexual offending and not just the nature of the admission (index) offence itself. The index offence of an inmate, who should be considered to be a sex offender for the purposes of management and treatment because of his history, may or may not be sexual in nature. Similarly, an inmate's history may contain sexual misbehaviors that did not result in criminal charges but rather in some other disposition (such as

commitment to a mental institution): Such nonlegal information is directly relevant to treatment and supervision decisions. (Quinsey 1990, p.18)

Quinsey argues that in addition to information about the index offence, prison management should have access to the data which builds up a case history of the individual. Such background information would certainly help to build up a picture of the offender and determine whether his offence was sexual or otherwise.

Summary of key points

- An effective prison system must understand the scale of the problem and then manage sexual offenders appropriately. To do so it needs accurate information on the nature of their index offences and other details which would contribute to building up a case history on each prisoner. There are now signs that within the criminal justice system in Scotland consideration is being given to ways of improving information flow.

A SYSTEM FOR THE MANAGEMENT OF SEXUAL OFFENDERS

An effective prison service needs to develop a cohesive and holistic policy which:

1. identifies sexual offenders on admission and, where possible, receives information on previous sexual offending and other relevant misbehaviour

2. identifies suitable locations for work with such short-term and long-term prisoners

3. develops adequate risk assessment procedures

4. allocates sexual offenders to appropriate prisons

5. integrates sexual offenders with sentence planning initiatives and provides scope for movement within the system

6. integrates sexual offenders with offence-specific intervention programmes at its various locations and phases, so as to provide consistent and incremental packages for each

7. integrates the work of the prison service with the requirements of social work throughcare and the protection agencies

8. provides a relapse prevention strategy for each offender to take with him into the community for use by social workers and/or family/friends

9. informs the Parole Board about the issues, progress and risks surrounding such prisoners

10. and, only where appropriate, begins family reunification processes, always giving priority to the needs of the victim.

Most (known) sexual offenders require some form of protection from their mainstream peers. We have tended to lock them away in little enclaves and this has only reinforced their own self-perceptions and, if anything, contributed to a continuation of their distorted value systems. In some circumstances, merely housing sexual offenders together has led to the learning of new offending behaviours, the sharing of names of victims or targets and future networking, particularly among paedophiles.

Prisons should set up systems which identify sexual offenders on admission and subsequently cater for both short and long term prisoners in appropriate locations with proper offence-specific programmes. Because of the 'vulnerability' of many sexual offenders to attack from ordinary prisoners, a progression system based on the usual mainstream options is not always likely to be appropriate. In any event, once sexual offenders have participated in the STOP Programme or other intervention programmes, any onward movement within a prison system should be accompanied by a transfer of information and a maintenance process to sustain the relapse prevention work already undertaken.

In Scotland some thought is being given to the setting up of a national induction centre for sexual offenders at a single prison. Wherever the location of such a unit, this proposal has great merit. The unit must be accessible to social work agencies so as to allow for the sharing of information, the progressing of throughcare and, in a number of cases, the processing of statutory child protection matters, particularly in relation to offenders convicted of offences against children, known in Scotland as Schedule One offenders – that is to say, those offenders covered by Schedule One of the Criminal Procedure (Scotland) Act 1975, as amended by the Sexual Offences (Scotland) Act 1976, which defines a range of sexual (and related) offences against children.

Assessment is primarily intended to establish two things: first, the risk of reoffending; and second, the individual's (intervention) needs. It makes sense for the assessment process to begin at a national induction centre. Indeed, the process of engaging the individual offender in offence-specific work begins at the assessment phase, when the issue of the offender's responsibility for his acts is discussed as part of a wider assessment. Assessment may be particularly important in quantifying the element of risk where shorter sentences are concerned and decisions as to timetabling and allocating the offender to programmes are involved.

The assessment phase is a multi-disciplinary process, requiring the use of prison-based social work, psychology and prison officer skills. In addition, useful information can also be gleaned from education staff and, on occasion, psychiatrists. Supplementary information is sometimes available from external statutory and voluntary agencies, and caseworkers involved with the family and victims. A fuller account of the assessment procedures is given in Chapter 5.

The whole programme, when up and running, will require monitoring and evaluation. The best place to start this process is at the entry stage of the programme – the induction unit. Assessments can thus be used to provide baseline data for future evaluation and research into offence-specific programmes.

Movement within the prison system

It is likely that following an initial phase of assessment in the national induction centre, the offender will be put on an offence-specific programme. If long-term prisoners start at the induction centre and then, for example, move to Peterhead (or a designated prison) for the core programme, they may require further onward movement after having undertaken the programme if they are not to stagnate. Although Peterhead is now a reasonably 'safe' prison because, in the main, it only houses this type of prisoner, onward movement will have to be supported by the provision of equally 'safe' accommodation elsewhere, be it at the site of the induction centre, a hall in a mainstream prison offering an enhanced regime, or in an open prison. Some prisoners may want to move back to prisons which are more accessible to their families, and which may also allow for improved throughcare contact, but the environment would have to be supportive and non-threatening. In such places it should be possible to continue the lower-level work of 'maintenance' for higher-risk prisoners who have undertaken the core work on 'low-risk' programmes for those lower-risk and shorter-term offenders also requiring offence-specific programmes.

> The idea of movement from Peterhead to a Central Belt prison, for those offenders who satisfactorily complete treatment, is that their relapse prevention and release plans can be refined, and that contacts with their community of release can be established or re-established. It is quite easy to unify a programme for these men with the limited programme for the low risk offenders. (Marshall 1992b, p.23)

Timing of intervention

There is no 'right time' to commence an intervention programme. Ideally, it should be ongoing throughout the sentence. However, judgements will have to be made about when it is most appropriate to deliver such a programme. It makes sense that such work is most effective and best undertaken prior to release or potential release on parole. Such decisions should be discussed while the offender is in the induction centre and taken as part of the sentence planning process, taking account of individual circumstances and the options available. This should not undermine any other proposals for work to take place from the start of sentence, and can be tied into a broader programme examining other issues such as anger management or cognitive skills work. According to Marshall (1992b):

The timing of treatment for the long-term offenders is important. There is no point in involving them in extensive treatment early in their sentence since when they are finished the benefits will likely be eroded during the long wait to release. It is far better to have them enter treatment when they have a reasonable prospect of release soon after treatment is complete. However, this does mean they will have to spend a good deal of time waiting to enter treatment and this could present problems of loss of interest, cynicism, and the adoption of criminogenic attitudes. To offset this possibility a self-help group, guided by a successful graduate of the programme who is awaiting transfer or release, should be provided. This group should meet once a week and the focus should be on maintaining optimism and dealing with denial and minimization issues so as to prepare these men for treatment. (pp.24–25)

Since the programme at Peterhead has only begun to create 'graduates' comparatively recently, only now is it possible to follow the suggestion made by Professor Marshall. The programmes comprise a *maintenance* group for 'graduates' who have completed the core STOP Programme, a *low-risk* group for those offenders assessed as presenting a lower risk, and a *pre-intervention* group for those requiring some degree of preparation before entering the main programme. We have also been aware of the need to run a complementary programme which helps prisoners to examine their own attitudes and is a useful 'taster' for the subsequent STOP Programme groups. To this end a *reasoning and rehabilitation* group (Ross, Fabiano and Diemer-Ewles 1988), designed to develop cognitive skills among offenders and already pioneered in Canada, was established with specialised training provided by the Scottish Prison Service. The SPS subsequently established its own cognitive skills programme as part of a service-wide initiative. In 1995 the Scottish Prison Service embarked on developing and training for its own accredited programme with the support of Elizabeth Fabiano and Frank Porporino. Such cognitive skills programmes have become widely available in Scottish prisons.

Short-term prisoners

Additional provision will have to be made for short-term prisoners. There is a need to begin work in earnest with such offenders on two counts.

First, they have only a short sentence and time is of the essence. They may also have received a supervised release order or an extended sentence, and so it will be necessary to undertake the groundwork prior to supervision in the community. (A supervised release order may be made under the Prisoners and Criminal Proceedings (Scotland) Act 1993, Section 14(1), 'Where a person is convicted of an offence and is sentenced to imprisonment for a term of not less than twelve months but less than four years, the court on passing sentence may, *if it considers that it is necessary to do so to protect the public from serious harm from the offender on his release, make such an order...*' (my italic). Section 4 of the Crime and Punishment (Scotland) Act 1997 further extended the maximum period of supervision for serious offences to ten years. An extended sentence may, under the Crime and Disorder Act 1998, Sections 86 and 87, only be passed in indictable (i.e. serious) cases. However, the court can pass short-term sentences (under four years) with a period of supervision of up to ten years. Exceptionally, in indictment cases, the courts can order a supervised release order where the sentence imposed is less than 12 months in order to protect the public.) Undertaking work with short-term prisoners is always preferable before release on any type of supervision or parole.

Second, such short-term prisoners might well be more serious offenders not yet caught or in the making. It may be appropriate to consider the option of using a small prison or separate part of a larger complex for such a clientele. For this group, in particular, developing links with agencies in the community takes on a greater degree of urgency, and there is a special need to ensure that the appropriate preparations are made and that information about the offender and his offence-specific work accompanies him on release. A recent development for short-term offenders, the Creating Control Programme at Barlinnie Prison, is to be welcomed. In this programme the work begun in prison is continued in a group outside.

Marshall (1992b) advocates a three-step process for incarcerated sexual offenders. Long-term prisoners would appear to fit into step one and short-term prisoners into step two (the third is community based):

1. extensive and intensive treatment for those deemed to be at moderate to high risk to reoffend and who have, therefore, a broad range of problems or at least reasonably deeply entrenched deviant propensities;

2. a less extensive and intensive programme both for the lower risk offenders who have less extensive problems and a less well-entrenched deviance, and for the graduates of the more extensive programme; and

3. treatment in the community upon release, associated with supervision by a parole officer designed to ensure implementation of the offender's relapse prevention plans. This, as I noted, is optimal and should be worked toward, but cannot be expected to be implemented immediately.

However, the first two steps can be, and these require the identification of particular institutions to meet these needs. I should note that offenders going to the first level programme should be serving sentences of at least two years, otherwise there will not be sufficient time to get them effectively through treatment. (pp.20–21)

The second level of treatment (i.e. for graduates of Peterhead and for lower risk offenders) should be implemented at one of the Central Belt prisons... [However,] how could they accommodate sex offenders in an environment that

freed them from the hassles and the restrictions imposed by the close proximity
of nonsex offenders? (pp.22–23)

Summary of key points

- Prisons identify sexual offenders on admission from the courts.

- A national induction centre for sexual offenders would be the ideal place
  to begin the process of working with such offenders.

- Assessment procedures initiate the process of forcing the offender to
  address his offending behaviour.

- There is a need for monitoring, evaluation and research. This should
  commence at the assessment stage.

- The sentence planning process provides a basis for consideration of the
  timing of the offender's participation in intervention programmes, and
  judgements about his movement between establishments. Cognitive skills
  programmes can be used to begin the processes of enabling the prisoner
  to think through a range of issues and familiarising him with group
  intervention programmes.

- Two types of programme can be established for sexual offenders
  following the induction/assessment phase. Level 1 is for sexual offenders
  who are serving long sentences and have been assessed as high risk. Level
  2 is for short term/low risk sexual offenders and for those Level 1
  offenders who have already engaged in a programme and require
  maintenance work.

DEVELOPING A TEAM APPROACH

Within prisons it is necessary to integrate the various players delivering
offence-specific programmes to offenders, principally prison officers, social
workers and psychologists. They have to begin to share common values and train
as a team. They must receive consistent management support for a team approach.
The programme will only succeed if the team can work in harmony and is focused
on the output. There is much anecdotal evidence to show that a number of
specialists are somewhat protective of their own area of operation. In an article
from the Prison Reform Trust magazine, *Prison Report*, Angela Brown (1994)
supports this view:

> The programme was 'owned' by the psychology department, which was
> determined to go it alone. Briefing sessions for other disciplines allowed little
> input about what was to happen. (p.4)

Staff must learn to trust each other and share necessary information between
departments and between prisons, on both casework issues about offenders and

their backgrounds and more offence-specific details. There has to be an acceptance that the concept of confidentiality includes and involves a range of staff (officer and specialist) who are all in the business of delivering a professional service.

However, in my view, a sex offender intervention programme is only sustainable on a large scale if delivered by core staff, i.e. prison officers. There are a number of reasons for this:

1. Sex offender work *is* part of a prison's core business, and work undertaken by specialists is often seen as marginal or as an appendage to the main work.

2. Initiatives are more likely to succeed if they are delivered by staff who have a vested interest in their success or who have the power to diminish their chances of success.

3. The staff who deliver such programmes require the active support of their colleagues and other staff.

4. Those delivering the programmes need to acquire a range of skills; where specialists are the main providers of the programme, their skills are not transferred and are lost when individuals move on.

5. The volume of delivery would be determined by the number of specialists employed and hence would be limited by their availability. Specialists should instead be used to support the work of core prison staff.

6. Specialised work improves the job quality and satisfaction of staff.[1]

Using prison staff, therefore, enables the STOP Programme to develop in an organic and self-sustainable way.

Our experience is that staff are dedicated to the goal of reducing the reoffending of sexual offenders when they return to society. Their prime motivation is to reduce the number of future victims and lessen the damage done to others in the community. Experienced prison officers who have trained in these specialist areas have proved to be very effective in the delivery of such programmes.

Summary of key points

• Management must ensure sustained support and guidance for a team approach to the delivery of offence-specific programmes. All staff

---

[1] In the recent SPS paper *The Third Prison Survey* (Wozniak, Dyson and Carnie 1998) it was reported that 'the vast majority of staff still supported programmes for addressing offending behaviour and were in favour of extending their own involvement in such programmes', p.123.

involved in the delivery of this work should feel confident in sharing information.

- The sex offender programme is best sustained when delivered by prison officers as part of a prison's core business. Staff will require appropriate training and opportunities so that they can experience delivering therapeutic work in groups.

THE GROUP APPROACH

There are a number of reasons why it is best to deliver intervention programmes within a group work setting:

1. It is less resource-intensive to run groups of between eight and ten prisoners than to engage in one-to-one offence-specific work.

2. The real experts on sexual offending are the offenders themselves, so it therefore makes good sense to let them challenge other offenders who are trying to deceive themselves or those around them.

3. Groups are not always comfortable for those offenders being challenged, but one-to-one therapy depends on a degree of rapport being built up between the therapist and offender which, out of a desire to progress issues, may become too cosy or even collusive at times (Beckett *et al.* 1994). Offenders may therefore use one-to-one situations as a way to avoid tackling the real issues, and there is a danger that the offender may start to manipulate, target or groom the therapist.

4. Groups should be heterogeneous (including a range of offending behaviours) so that challenges are made from differing viewpoints and sustained. Whether specific (homogeneous) groups should be held for specific types of sexual offenders is a subject of current discussion. Waterhouse, Dobash and Carnie (1994) suggest as a method of classification 'RAPID', the acronym standing for the four types of sexual abusers identified in their study: random abusers, paedophiles, incest and deniers. However, it is known that many abusers offend against more than one victim type, e.g. many incest offenders also offend against non-familial children (Abel *et al.* 1988). It has been argued that as a group, incest offenders need lower levels of intervention, but 'risk' is based on individual characteristics and some such offenders are high risk. The RAPID classification also includes deniers. These could perpetuate any type of offending. It is my view, first, that since many offenders display a number of paraphilias, singling out one form may not be all that useful. Second, the challenges within a group come from offenders of differing viewpoints. As a group, offenders are more likely to be less collusive and present greater challenges when their distorted cognitions and value systems differ, i.e. a heterogeneous group of sexual offenders.

5. Groups contribute to the resocialisation of their members, helping to develop interpersonal skills and cognitive processes.

6. By joining a group a sexual offender publicly acknowledges his need to change.

7. Group members can provide 'out of group' support for other members who are going through a difficult patch and can, where necessary, help resolve issues before the next session.

Waterhouse, Debash and Carnie (1994) found that some offenders initially had reservations about participating in group work.

> One of the most contentious issues discussed with the offenders was the use of group work. The views expressed were quite varied, on balance men appeared to prefer individual sessions and seemed unaware of the potential benefits of addressing and challenging offending behaviour in a group context … Some men had reservations about the confidentiality of group work. They point to the problems inherent in conducting group work in a prison setting where the intimate details of their lives would be shared and possibly used by others. (p.198)

The issues concerning the value of groups and the individual's ability to feel comfortable within them are important ones, supported by a wealth of literature. Confidentiality and trust are also important issues which are discussed further in the following paragraphs.

For the delivery of group work to be effective, there needs to be a suitable *internal environment* to facilitate the process. At Peterhead the group meetings take place in a purpose-built set of rooms within the Victorian accommodation. They comprise a larger group discussion or meeting room in which there are comfortable chairs, a flip chart, notice boards, etc., adjacent to which is a smaller studio housing audio and visual monitoring equipment. Communication between the studio and meeting room is by a one-way mirror, behind which one of the three group workers watches and comments to the leader via an infra-red sound link. These tasks rotate. The third member of staff in the observation room provides an element of supervision and a degree of learning; they watch and sometimes film what happens so that issues can be discussed later by the staff and occasionally by the prisoners. The studio room provides an ideal training facility. When only two staff are involved, the room need not be staffed. This facility also can be operated by specialist staff trainers, but for any person to be in the studio room there must have been prior agreement from the group. To dispel any anxieties, group members are also free to see what is going on in the other room and operate the video camera.

There are, however, considerations to be borne in mind when video cameras are used. Even with reassurances, some prisoners remain nervous and frightened by their presence. Their fears can include the worry that a tape might be spirited out of the prison and ultimately find its way to the media. Videos of sessions are useful aids for staff training but, like any method of recording what happens, cannot show everything. Staff therefore must not rely solely on such material. In fact, it is probably better for all three core staff to sit in on the majority of the sessions where possible, leaving video recordings to be made when specialist trainers/consultants are present.

One particular use to which the video camera can be put is the filming of *snapshots* – statements made by offenders in the group, at particular stages or regular intervals. By comparing them with previous statements, we can monitor the progress of offenders. It might be possible to link such video evidence to submissions made to the Parole Board, discussed later in Chapter 12.

Ground rules have to be established when the group commences about what will be done when 'new' information is revealed to the group. Information relating to the index offence or of non-specific, general or vague nature will not be transmitted out of the group because that would serve no purpose. However, specific information which enables other past offences to be identified, information about other named offenders (such as those in active paedophile rings) and details about further victims will be passed on to the appropriate authorities (principally, the police and/or social work departments). All participants are made aware of this condition, which is agreed before the group commences.

Summary of key points

- Offence-specific work is best undertaken in groups held in dedicated accommodation.
- All group members understand that 'new' information given about other offences, offenders or victims may be passed on to the appropriate authorities.

PROGRAMMES IN THE WIDER CONTEXT

Whilst this is not the place to examine the role of programmes within the Scottish Prison Service, the belief that cognitive-based programmes can contribute to the positive rehabilitation of offenders has gained ground both within the SPS and in the wider criminal justice arena. Programmes have been delivered to substantial effect in North America (Wozniak 1996), and the public rightly believe that the prison system has a part to play in reducing recidivism. The Crime and Punishment (Scotland) Act 1997 envisaged (in Section 34) that prisoners could earn early release by participating positively in programmes. In the debate on the bill the Scottish Prisons Minister stated that:

…the earning of early release should be about more than simply not breaching prison discipline. Prisoners should be required to demonstrate positive good behaviour and that they are making constructive use of their time in prison to address their offending behaviour. As appropriate, that might mean participating in a programme… (House of Commons Official Report, Parliamentary Debates 1996b, col. 294)

…the Scottish Prison Service already challenges prisoners to participate in programmes to correct offending behaviour. That applies to all offenders, whatever their age and whatever their offence. There are a number of programmes across the prison estate, including programmes on drugs awareness, alcohol misuse, sex offending and anger management. (1996a, col. 130–131)

The provision of programmes first appeared as a 'Key Target' in the 1996–99 SPS Corporate Plan (1996). The agency agreed the following performance measure with the Prisons Minister:

The amount of available opportunities for prisoners' self development: to ensure that 400 prisoners have completed a cognitive skills programme and 100 prisoners have completed a sex offender programme during 1996–97. (p.33)

Thus the delivery of programmes for sexual offenders, which had been pioneered within Scottish prisons at Peterhead, became recognised as part of the wider duty of the service to make available a range of programmes to enable prisoners to address their offending behaviour.

THE GENERAL PRISON ENVIRONMENT

The sex offender intervention programme is not an easy one to introduce in a prison. In my view it will not be successful if undertaken in isolation: it has to be central to the work of the establishment and form part of its culture and core business. Therefore:

1. All staff must be aware that the programme is central to the work of the prison and support it. It is a demanding job and is an emotional drain on the staff who work in groups. They need support, not cynicism, from their colleagues, and sustained support must come from the top of the organisation down through all levels of management.

2. Prison management has to organise manpower and resources to facilitate, not hinder, the intervention programmes. If group meetings are to be regular, old traditions have to go and the work of the core group staff come before other rostering or 'emergency' needs. Similarly, the prisoners' attendance at groups has to have priority over other work. Thus the organisation of the prison has to revolve around and serve the needs of the programme, and not vice versa. Staff cannot be pulled off for other types

of duties and prisoners must not be kept back for 'someone' to see them. Without this absolute commitment, the programme is doomed to fail from the start. (The work of the groups should remain sacrosanct. In Peterhead, between 1993 and mid-1995, all 480 sessions were held for the first six groups. Staff, with management support, readily agreed to roster their days off, holidays and night shifts so as not to interrupt the STOP Programme.)

3. In order to implement a successful programme staff have to receive training in the nature of offending and the purpose of the groups, and they must support the work. All staff have to be aware of the nature of the programme and undergo 'awareness' or 'attitude' training intended to raise their consciousness and harness their support for those directly involved in the group work. For some this will provide a different perspective from that which they may have held previously, and focuses on women and their rights and role in society. They learn about sexual offenders and their victims – women and children – and explore the relationship between offending and the attitudes, values and beliefs of offenders, so that they become supportive of the work their colleagues are doing and do not inadvertently collude with sexual offenders and their belief systems. This training provides an opportunity for staff to explore their own attitudes, values and beliefs, and how these impact on their work, and also supports the equal opportunities policy of the prison service – we have a number of female prison officers in all our prisons as well as female participants delivering the programme. (I have had a number of interesting discussions with staff on such courses, particularly in the area of pornography. Sometimes the view is expressed that magazines such as *Playboy* are healthy male pursuits. When, at the start of a line of questioning, I asked them if they would purchase them openly if I or their wife were present, they became a little sheepish! It has an impact on staff if their bosses demonstrate appropriate values.)

4. The general regime of the prison has to be consistent with the sex offender work. We have to train and encourage staff to act as personal officers and we must encourage prisoners to become involved with the sentence planning initiative which provides a method of developing self-awareness over a range of personal issues. Over many years within the Scottish Prison Service, from time to time, specific officers have been assigned to individual prisoners to be 'personal officers'. These staff have been a consistent point for counselling and support. With the introduction of the Sentence Planning scheme in 1992 for prisoners serving over four years the process became formalised. On induction to a prison the prisoner is allocated a 'personal officer'. The officer is expected to get to know the prisoner, and undertake regular sentence planning reviews with him. The

officer provides support and can act as a facilitator to the prisoner self-awareness package of the Sentence Planning Scheme. Staff should also undertake counselling and welfare work, where necessary, with support from the staff of prison-based social work units.

5.   Good staff/prisoner relationships are essential. In particular, the prison staff involved with the core work of delivering the intervention programme must have established trust with the prisoners. The discussions of the group will need to remain confidential to the group, and this places pressures on both the staff and prisoners who might otherwise turn elsewhere to discuss some of the issues raised. Boundaries must be established between group sessions and informal discussions which can take place at any time or location. In addition, the rest of the prison staff must be made aware that the offence-specific discussions of the group remain confidential to the group and the core group workers. There is a natural desire to try to find out what is going on and to find excuses for coming in and looking at the proceedings. Staff will initially want to pop in to check numbers or ascertain which prisoner is where – supposedly for security reasons, of course! But this must not be allowed to happen. The groups will need strong support from their managers to ensure that interruptions are eliminated. Instead, the core staff should establish good 'public relations' with other staff to let them know the type of work being undertaken, demystify what is going on and dispel notions of elitism.

6.   The environment must be made conducive to such work and must be comfortable and supportive, have dedicated facilities (not merely a number of chairs round an ashtray) and be pornography-free (at least in the part of the prison where such intervention programmes occur). In general the regime should be one in which staff work with offenders in a 'non put-down' environment which is supportive but not collusive. This milieu is difficult to achieve without an approach that values our clients as individuals. In the absence of such an approach, any attempt to undertake therapeutic or cognitive group work with individuals who suffer from low self-esteem is unlikely to make much progress. The need to develop an approach that will enhance the self-esteem of the offenders cannot be overstated. Marshall (1995) states, 'We have found that increasing the offenders' sense of self-worth is critical to changing all other features of them' (p.3).

7.   Other parts of the regime should work to contribute to the programme. The education unit can provide a range of supporting classes and groups, improving communication skills through, for example, discussion groups or dance and drama classes, examining gender issues in women, men and society groups, and teaching basic competencies through life and social skills classes.

8. Specialists and prison staff should deliver a range of other (not necessarily offence-specific) groups on subjects such as anger management and substance and alcohol abuse, and promote other groups which develop cognitive skills that will assist offenders in examining their own attitudes and offence patterns. Prisoners on offence-specific programmes may require additional, non-offence-specific support from time to time: this should be offered by staff, psychologists or social workers but should not replace or provide an excuse to avoid the challenges of group therapy work. Staff should not offer to provide individual offence-specific work (see above). It is worth noting that it should not be the intention to provide round-the-clock, seven-days-a-week intervention programmes and therapy. Other staff who also deal with these prisoners should ensure that they clarify the role of the core worker and distinguish it from the very different but also supportive role of the residential or personal officer. The other staff can deal with a whole host of personal and situational issues but should be careful not to stray into the offence-specific work or attempt to continue the work of the core groups. There is therefore a need for continuing good liaison and discussion between both types of staff.

In this way, and by continuing the training of core workers and other staff, and also by providing a range of support for regime activities through a supportive culture within the establishment and a degree of networking, it should be possible to develop a sustainable programme.

My own view is supported by Professor Marshall (1992b) who puts it succinctly:

[Group work] is best conducted in an institution with sound peripheral security that exclusively houses sex offenders. In this way a therapeutic environment can be created where the offenders can effectively carry on the treatment-initiated changes and can discuss treatment issues openly with other offenders and staff without fear of retaliation from nonsex offenders. If sex offenders are integrated with other offenders, treatment benefits are typically slow in coming and are frequently eroded by the hostility from other offenders. Also, staff typically find it difficult to manage sex offenders who are in treatment when they must mingle with, or be located close to, other nonsex offenders. On-line staff have a very important role to play in therapy and their job in this regard should be made as easy as possible. (pp.21–22)

We therefore need to examine closely the physical layout of the establishment, its culture and the support mechanisms available before deciding where such programmes should be located. We should also examine the potential use of accommodation in establishments or complexes where it is possible for prisoners to live and work in separate areas from their mainstream counterparts. Any attempt to integrate sexual offenders into ordinary prisons would present a huge challenge. However, as increasing numbers of prisoners become involved in sentence planning and the requirement of facing up to real-life issues, including their own predispositions to offending behaviour, the climate might change so as to allow for some improved integration with sexual offenders. Indeed, in the future, a measure of the success of the cultural and civilising changes in prisons might be the ability to integrate non-sex offenders with sexual offenders.

Summary of key points

- To develop sustainable offence-specific work, prisons need to ensure that the culture and operation of the establishment has changed to accommodate the programme. Management and staff should be supportive and see this work as part of their core business.

THE RESIDENTIAL SETTING

At Peterhead, both prisoners and staff were trawled and selections made from those who volunteered. A large number of staff expressed a desire to work in 'C' Hall, which opened at the beginning of 1993. It is important that staff who work in a hall where offence-specific work is undertaken are supportive of their colleagues delivering the programme and supportive of, but non-collusive with, sexual offenders.

Prisoners were required to agree to certain conditions before they were selected for transfer to the hall and these included the requirements to:

- be willing to address their offending behaviour
- participate in sentence planning and the personal officer schemes
- maintain a pornography-free environment.

The management of 'C' Hall also decided that they would try to run the hall on community-based lines, with prisoners taking more responsibility and having some say in the running of the regime.

For groups to have the best chance of succeeding, their members have to be able to feel safe. In working with sex offenders, who are considered 'fair game' by other types of offenders for threats, assaults, extortion, and so on, it is vital to create a safe and non-threatening environment. In reality, this is only likely to be possible when such offenders are segregated from mainstream prisoners. Similarly, the staff themselves have to ensure that they do not use 'put-downs' in their relationships with prisoners. We have already seen that great importance is placed on the need to enhance the self-esteem of offenders, and they must be supported to allow for the development of self-worth. It is only when sexual offenders can feel that they are really human beings, capable of having value and worth themselves, that they will open up, talk to others and begin to internalise the normative values and controlling inhibitors that their group workers and others of us around attempt to portray as what is 'expected' or 'normal'. The hall, wing, unit or block in which the work is undertaken, and where possible the whole prison setting, should be safe and non-threatening. This means that not only should sexual offenders feel free from fear of violent attack, but also that the regime itself should challenge attitudes and values and be non-collusive.

Peterhead Prison was built in 1888 and juts out into the North Sea. A Victorian edifice, it was constructed to house convicts brought to Peterhead to break granite rock in the local quarry and construct a harbour of refuge. It can be a cold, bleak place and the cells retain their old and solid feel. Thus, when we talk about a comfortable environment for group work, what is meant is a place which is pleasantly decorated, appropriately furnished, and feels non-threatening and supportive. The comfort does not come from the nature of the intervention programmes undertaken. Many offenders have spoken about the fear, even terror, that they face when contemplating group intervention programmes. For them, offence-specific work does more than open up a can of worms: it forces them to come to terms with their worst fears and nightmares and with their darker side. In fact, it is reality that sexual offenders fear. That is why they deny. Prisons have to be able to create an atmosphere in which these offenders can feel able to tackle such difficult issues.

Summary of key points

- The residential (hall or unit) environment needs to be supportive and non-threatening, and where possible, staff working in the hall should be volunteers. The aim must be to create an ethos of making prisoners feel safe, avoiding 'put-downs' and being supportive but also challenging.

CHAPTER 4

Other Issues for Prisons

PROBLEMS WITH VISITORS

The act of visiting a prisoner is, or should be, voluntary. Yet sexual offenders, like no other type of offender, create turmoil and trauma within the family by their actions. If the offence is non-familial, such as the rape of an adult female, huge tensions are created between the offender and his partner which may never be resolved. If the offence occurred within the family, for example on a child, then not only does the non-offending mother blame herself for allowing it to happen, but all trust is destroyed, and the offender may not be suitable for return to the family home since contact with the victim, their child, is likely to perpetuate the abusive offending. Contact with the offender may be the last thing that the family wishes – yet pressures to retain contact through letters, telephone calls and visits exist.

This is clearly, therefore, a problem area, and if the victim is permitted to visit the offender special precautions must be made. Otherwise, these visits, if not properly managed, might give the offender the opportunity to perpetuate the abuse and victimisation of the child, and, equally harrowingly, transfer feelings of guilt and responsibility to the non-offending mother. Whatever arrangements are put in place, the visit has to be managed carefully, and priority must be given to the victim's situation. Such visits should take place only in the presence of a counsellor or social worker monitoring what is being said, and only after support has already been provided to the victim. It should also be remembered that it is possible for the offender to continue the process of grooming other children even if the primary victim is kept away. Prisons have, I think, tended to ignore these aspects of visiting and have been content to allow arrangements to continue in the normal way unless information is received to the contrary from the family or legal constraints are imposed. Perhaps the time has come to examine whether we should not first consider the nature of the offence and the victim before we automatically grant the right for visits without checking who has been 'invited' to attend. Through the use of the telephone and letters, sexual offenders, if so motivated, can still exert undue influence and perpetuate the fear of abuse.

Also, family contact, which is normally improved by the availability of play facilities and crèches, can be abused unless those facilities are properly managed.

Because of the range of problems associated with family contact and visits, close co-operation and good communication must be maintained between the prison and social work authorities. As indicated above, it may be appropriate to start with the assumption that sexual offenders are not allowed child visitors unless it can be shown that the child is not put at risk by visiting. However, it is to be remembered that not all sexual offenders are identified as such, because their main offence may not have a 'sexual' connotation, or the sexual offence may be from a previous conviction.

Before children are brought to visit their father in prison it is worth taking the time to consider a few issues *(these should be read in conjunction with family reunification issues in Chapter 11):*

1. In any decision being made whether to visit, it must be asked in whose interest is the visit and whose needs should be taken into account and given priority? Can we assume the offender's love for his child is genuine and does it matter if he states that he misses his child and the rest of his family and longs to return home? The interests of the child must always be put before the emotive appeal of the abusive parent. Children need to feel safe. These considerations are further complicated when a child expresses the view that she or he misses their father. This is a natural reaction but would a visit be in the child's best interest.

2. Fathers usually perform a parenting and developmental role. However, can a sexual abusing parent still be allowed to perform such a role?

3. If the child who it is proposed to bring is a victim, has she received support, counselling, therapy and is she willing to visit the offender?

4. It is important to realise that only the child has experienced the abuse and only she may know the rituals of how it begins, the cues (verbal and non-verbal), symbols, whispers and what is being implied that can retrigger the abuse and its traumatic effects. Such cues and signals can be given even when adults/social workers are around and supervising the visit.

5. Physical contact with the adult, being kissed or sitting on his lap can be part of the grooming or targeting/selection process, seeing how far the abuser can go (without complaint), desensitising the child and building up 'casual' physical contact, i.e. grooming for further exploitation. Therefore, physical contact with an abuser should be avoided during visits.

6. Other non-abused siblings who visit may either know of the abuse/power cues or the start to the abuse process or understand that it is their turn next. They may also be at risk of being traumatised.

7. Will a visit interfere with the healing process of the child victim or sibling, who also feels range of emotions? Children need to feel safe.

8. Before the visit the non-offending mother must have accepted it was not her fault, nor her child's, otherwise she may be full of guilt and self-blame about not protecting her child.

9. The non-offending mother needs to know the process of sexual offending, cognitive distortions, grooming and manipulation by offender to understand the past, their responsibilities, and how to survive and protect her children in future.

10. Has the offender already sent a letter expressing remorse, acknowledging the harm and hurt caused and accepting full responsibility?

11. If the visit is held too soon (e.g. before the impact of an intervention programme has been internalised) the offender may project blame back on to the victim and/or non-offending mother.

Therefore, before a visit takes place the offender should have undertaken an intervention programme and there should have been work with victim, sibling or vulnerable person.

Some guidelines are offered for during the visit:

1. There should be no pressure on child to forgive or excuse some of the responsibility of the offender as this allows him to deny the act and continue the abuse and victimisation.

2. The discussion at the visit should not focus on offenders needs.

3. The offender should not try to impose his will or his thoughts on the child, which continues his control over the victim.

4. The offender should never be left alone with victim/child.

5. The chaperone (if not the mother) should be someone who child/victim is comfortable with.

6. The offender must never be responsible for the supervision or disciplining of child during the visit.

7. No physical or affectionate contact must be initiated by offender. A hug/kiss at end of the visit by the child may be allowable if the child wishes this and if supervised to ensure appropriate behaviour on the part of the offender.

8. In general, physical contact between any child and a sexual offender is to minimised. He should refrain from tickling, horseplay, and having the child sit on his lap, etc.

9. There should be no secrets between the offender and the child.

10. The offender should not make displays of emotional need, conveying that he wants care or affection from the child.

11. There should be no discussion of 'sexual' matters.

In England and Wales the prison service issued guidelines (Prison Service 1998) to support child protection measures, introducing a range of measures to minimise the risks that prisoners involved with sexual offences against children might present to children whilst in prison. The measures are primarily focused around communications (i.e. letters and telephone calls) and also seeking prior information and clarification about children who propose to visit such prisoners.

Prison services have been developing their family contact policies on the assumption that children have a right of access to a parent who is imprisoned and that quite apart from the benefits to the prisoner of visiting, or indeed to the prison system itself (through more contented prisoners), enhanced family contact and access has to be based in part on the recognition of the needs of children and families in general. Peart and Asquith (1992) emphasise this point:

> By adopting an approach based on the rights of the child, the needs of children and families can be differentiated from the deeds of the imprisoned parent. The danger otherwise is that children and families may themselves be punished in a variety of ways for what the imprisoned father or mother, or partner has done. (p.7)

However, the United Nations Convention on the Rights of the Child, Article 9 (3) states:

> States Parties shall respect the right of the child who is separated from one or both parents to maintain personal relations and direct contact with both parents on a regular basis, except if it is contrary to the child's best interests.[1]

There are clear indications in this Article, and Article 3 (on the best interests of the child) and Article 19 (on protection from abuse and neglect), that the rights implicit in *the best interests of the child* should also be respected. Thus both child protection laws which enforce separation from the abuser and action taken by prison authorities to restrict access at visits would conform to the UN convention.

These are difficult issues for prison management, who must attempt to balance the needs of their own prisoners with the rights and sensitivities of the victims, especially when they are children. Prisoners can often fail to take into account the difficulties their demands place on families. In particular, sexual offenders who deny or who have made little progress do not understand the harm they have done and continue to see their victims as objects. Paradoxically, those offenders who have gained insights into their offending behaviour and who, as a consequence,

---

1   *The United Nations Convention on the Rights of the Child,* adopted by the UN General Assembly on 20.11.1989 and ratified by the UK in December 1991.

may be less of a danger to their victims, are more likely to be sensitive to the damage done and the continuing impact they have on the child.

Summary of key points

- Caution needs to be exercised over visits to sexual offenders. It may be appropriate with this group to begin with the assumption that child visitors should not be allowed unless it can be shown that they are not put at risk through visiting.

PROBLEMS ABOUT HOME LEAVE AND HOME VISITS

Similarly, enhancing family contact through prison staff-escorted home visits or home leave requires particular attention. Such consideration needs to be more rigorous when applied to sexual offenders than to other types of offenders. Even in terms of ordinary pre-release home leave given to offenders as preparation for their release, we have to give serious consideration to family circumstances and the proposed location of the home leave, so that there can be no contact with the family unless it is the opinion that they are not going to be placed at further risk.

In this book reference is often made to *incest offenders*. This is not because of their prevalence – in Peterhead Prison probably only about one-third of sexual offenders have offended against children in the home. There are at least an equal number of non-familial paedophiles. But using familial offenders as examples brings into sharp focus most of the issues concerning the problems of the victim–abuser relationship. Returning home or to the home area affects the families of all sexual offenders. For those paedophiliacs who have non-familial victims, knowledge of their presence in the neighbourhood could well bring concern and anxiety, even outrage, from the parents and the child victims, and the fear of them may rekindle memories of former abuse. If the offence is one of rape (of an adult female victim outside the family), there may be concerns in the community about a rapist 'being on the loose', and his going home may be no less problematic. There will be a range of emotions felt by the offender's partner and serious questions to resolve about their own relationship. His return may not be desired or appropriate. In fact, the offence of rape could well be part of wider distorted cognitions in which the male abuser believes it is acceptable to abuse all women, and his own relationship with his partner could well have been abusive with violence and/or an abusive or coercive sexual relationship.

The same issues may arise even if the sexual offender is no longer considered to be a risk to the public and is classified in the lowest security classification, as fit for open prison (security category 'D'[2]). This is because some more subtle forms of abuse can continue to be perpetrated by the offender on the victim even though the physical side of the abuse has ceased. It is therefore important to know the progress that such offenders have made in any form of therapy and also the progress victims may have made in the intervening period. Before making arrangements prior to release or following a request by the prisoner for home leave or a home visit, the balance of priority must always be placed, firstly, on the professional opinion of social workers or case workers who are working with the victim and family, and secondly, on whether the family and victim themselves feel that it is appropriate for the offender to return, albeit for a short while, to the family home. (A fuller account of the issues and processes involved is given in the section on family reunification in Chapter 11. The procedures outlined in that section should be followed particularly where it is thought that the offender will meet with a child victim. However, the principles described in that process are equally applicable to situations where an adult victim may feel at continuing risk from the offender.)

In addition, many of the longer-term prisoners serving sentences for sexual offences have committed crimes that horrified the localities in which they lived (and where the victims and their families may continue to live), and therefore we should be sensitive to the likely impact upon local communities of any proposed visit or leave, however brief.

These are crucial issues for prison managers, who have to balance the requirement to keep in custody prisoners sent by the courts with the need to help prisoners adopt a more responsible approach to others in the community. Part of that development involves considerations about a programme of reintegration into the community – but this process can be especially hazardous for sexual offenders. The public rightly expect such dangerous criminals to remain incarcerated until the end of their sentence and are horrified at the thought of such people in their midst at any time, let alone while still serving their sentence. The victim and family are given respite from the imprisoned offender, whose return could shatter the feelings of safety which have developed during his absence. Thus any considerations about visiting home must take into account the impact such a visit is likely to have on the victim and her family in particular and the wider community in general. Such visits must be closely managed and should

2　　Security Category 'D' is defined in The Prisons and Young Offenders Institutions (Scotland) Rules 1994 (at Rule 14A) as: 'A prisoner who is considered not to be a danger to the public and who can be given the opportunity to serve his sentence in open conditions.'

be allowed only when these issues have been taken into account and given the most careful consideration.

Summary of key points

- Contact with families must be handled carefully and sensitively, especially where offences have been committed against members of the family (and/or young children). Close involvement needs to be maintained with the appropriate social workers and priority must always be given to the feelings of the victim. Where visits to the home are being contemplated, additional consideration has to be given to the likely effect on the family home and the expected impact on the community.

LIMITATIONS ON 'TESTING SITUATIONS'

In prison systems we often use opportunities such as outside work, study and voluntary community programmes to place prisoners in situations which present them with chances to demonstrate that they can act as responsible citizens. These activities are considered as part of the way in which prisoners might be trained for freedom. While such opportunities are generally welcome, they are not always appropriate for sexual offenders, and tell us little about the risk that, for example, a familial offender will pose, not to the community at large, but to his own family. Because the act of sexual offending is part of a longer cycle which involves stages of fantasising, targeting, grooming and planning, it is unlikely that such offending will occur on an occasional visit outside. For some sexual offenders, then, these activities are unlikely to provide real opportunities to prove that they have changed and, although such events tend to ameliorate the harmful effects of imprisonment, the positive advantages gained by the individual are often outweighed by considerations of our duty to the public. In addition, some sexual offenders are intelligent and careful enough not to become involved in any overt offending during such temporary periods outside, but may often begin targeting and grooming victims well in advance of behaviours identified as sexual offences. Opportunities for offending, coupled with a reduced risk of being found out, are likely to increase after release, but such outside work placements can allow offences to be planned well in advance.

We should also be aware that an offender's level of dangerousness is likely to remain much the same throughout his sentence of imprisonment, and he should be classed as someone who is likely to remain a danger to the public (a category 'B' prisoner[3]) until such time as he has completed an appropriate intervention

---

3   Category 'B' is defined in The Prisons and Young Offenders Institutions (Scotland) Rules 1994 (at Rule 14A) as 'A prisoner who is considered likely to be a danger to the public and who must

programme and the staff are of the opinion that the desired changes in approach and attitude have been internalised. Even then, caution should be the guide when the prisoner has moved on to a reduced-security category regime.

Despite the concerns expressed above about temporary release into the community, there may be some exceptions if value can be gained by creating appropriate links with community-based programmes for sexual offenders. It would be useful to establish links with support groups prior to release. This would help ease the transition from prison-based offence-specific work to community-based work and support. Such outings would have to be managed carefully as part of the wider pre-release programme for the prisoner.

Summary of key points

- 'Testing situations' in the community are likely to be of limited value with sexual offenders.

AVAILABILITY OF PORNOGRAPHY IN PRISON

This book is not the place for a full discussion on the range of issues to do with pornography (and human rights); there is, however, a conflict between achieving change in offenders and allowing access to pornography. As indicated earlier, numerous studies tend to indicate that sexual abuse and offending has affected at least one-third and possibly up to two-thirds of the population (Salter 1989). The fact that such offending is so widespread does not confer on it some 'justifiable' or 'natural' status, and it cannot be defended in any way. The magnitude of the problem is culturally based, and is reinforced by pornography and the depiction of gratuitous violence and sexual offending in a range of media, which objectifies the victim and encourages the consumer not to empathise with the suffering that is caused.

Those of us working within prisons do not have to deal with the whole problem but only that small fraction known about and sent to us by the courts. However, the culture of our society, its role models, advertising, semi-nude models in tabloid newspapers and proliferation of pornographic videos, makes it easy for many people, mostly men, to make the jump to distorted thinking, in the process denying the rights of women and children, their victims. So our task seems an uphill one. We must not only show prisoners what is unlawful, but also what is wrong – how pornography offends and affects others and negates their rights as human beings – because as we know, unlike other types of offending, sexual assault and abuse violate, hurt, degrade and damage the individuals they are perpetrated upon. And the harm done is not transitory. Some of the effects of

be kept in secure conditions to prevent his escape'.

abuse can be seen even two or three decades later. It may take years to work through the emotional scars, and many victims, although they survive, bear with them the gruesome memories for the rest of their lives.

It seems to me that sexual offending by men against women and children is a consequence of a society in which women and children are not perceived to have equal rights and in which it is considered acceptable for women to be objectified by men. Another form of offending against women, and for that matter against children, is the use of pornography. We also know that pornography is used by some offenders as part of their offending cycle. It may temporarily satiate the offender, but he gradually requires greater stimulation and turns to *real* objects, i.e. human victims.

More recently, we have become aware of the growing trade in child pornography. Most people will never encounter hard-core child pornography. The images of helplessness, degradation and assaults by adults are beyond our imagination and understanding. This is easily condemned – yet soft porn, with images of children being used as sex objects, overly made-up and posed in provocative ways, is creeping in. Children are being used in advertisements, posters and cards and, although not overtly pornographic or erotic, the images are sexualised in order to sell the product. The messages they convey are that children are cute, sexy, knowledgeable, and available or 'asking for it'.

The Council of Europe Committee on Crime Problems (1993) put it this way:

> The media, which sometimes encourage the commercialisation of children's bodies by means of semi-erotic advertising, are urged to realise its trivialising and harmful effect. They should contribute to the generation of public awareness of the devastating effects of sexual exploitation and shoulder their responsibilities by adopting a relevant code of ethics.
>
> The committee noted that children's pictures and even voices could be used to create an erotic atmosphere for various purposes. 'Lolitas' (both male and female) seem to have come back into fashion in the cinema and show business, appealing to the unwholesome taste of a certain section of the public.
>
> Advertisers, in particular, have recently begun to rely on the impact of juvenile seduction, using it in the same way as 'conventional' erotic advertising. In so doing, they may have the effect of encouraging those who wish to widen the choice of sexual partners by means of overtly paedophile propaganda. Without criticising the use of children in advertising *per se* or advocating an over-strict interpretation of artistic freedom, the committee recommends discouraging and preventing any abuse of children's pictures and voices in an erotic context (for example, commercials, photographs and posters). (pp.27–28)

Paedophiles not only target children because they might be easy or vulnerable and because they can assert power over them, but also because they find them sexually arousing, their softness desirable and their innocence exciting. Yet they will try to justify their acts by claiming that children are wicked, wanting and waiting for sex, and throwing intolerable temptation their way!

The Council of Europe Committee define child pornography as 'any audiovisual material which uses children in a sexual context' (p.31). So why is this an important issue? Because even soft 'kiddie porn' contributes to the problem of child sexual abuse. It condones the use of children in inappropriate sexual contexts and conveys the message that they are available. It desensitises the public. In a powerful article on images of children, Michele Elliott (1992), founder of Kidscape, concludes:

> It is strengthening the argument of paedophiles that children are asking for sex. It is exploiting and dehumanizing children without their informed consent. It is glamorizing children as sexual objects. It is saying to children that adults agree with the idea of them being sexualized. It is suggesting to other children that this is a desirable way to be portrayed. It is undermining the fabric of childhood: children should be protected, loved and nurtured, not used and abused. (p.220)

The definition of pornography in the UK has its origins in morality, the law describing pornographic material as that which tends 'to deprave and corrupt'. This definition is subjective, being at the mercy of those experts called as witnesses who attempt to circumscribe what may have a corrupting effect. A more objective and criteria-based approach is to look at *harm-based* definitions. These have been developed and applied in the USA, Canada and New Zealand, and advocated by the Campaign Against Pornography (CAP). NOTA (*NOTANews 13*, April 1995, pp.5–6) supplied the following definition:

1. Pornography is defined as that which is graphic, sexually explicit and subordinates women (or people). It must contain all three characteristics.

2. It must also contain one or more specific conditions of harm in the form of sexual objectification or sexual violence.

3. Although this definition of pornography has been based on sexualised subordination of women and eroticised violence against women, it has been and can also be extended to include the use of men and children in the place of women. Clearly any depiction of children in a sexually explicit way, whether or not all three elements (graphic, sexually explicit and subordinating) are present is directly harmful and pornographic.

Specifically this means women presented:

- Dehumanised as sexual objects, things or commodities, and/or
- As sexual objects who enjoy humiliation or pain, and/or
- As sexual objects experiencing sexual pleasure in rape, incest or other sexual assault, and/or

- As sexual objects tied up or cut up or mutilated or bruised or physically hurt, and/or
- In postures or position of sexual submission, servility or display, and/or
- Being penetrated by animal, and/or
- In scenarios of degradation, humiliation, injury, torture, shown as filthy or inferior, bleeding, bruised or hurt in a context that makes these conditions sexual, and/or
- Women's body parts – including but not limited to vaginas, breasts or buttocks and anuses – exhibited such that women are reduced to those parts.

In this definition, pornography does not include sexually explicit materials premised on equality, or sex education materials. Such a definition seeks to provide guidance for practitioners and managers in relation to the use of sexually salient materials and pornography in work with sexually abusive offenders. This echoes the earlier work of Catherine Itzin (1992a, 1992b).

Work with offenders in a community setting is not held in an environment which displays pornography. The same should apply in a prison setting, otherwise one type of message is given during the offence-specific group-work programmes and the opposite message simultaneously presented when prisoners return to other areas, such as their cells, where they see pornography with its messages of objectification, dehumanisation and submission.

I am pleased that at Peterhead we made 'a pornography-free environment' a condition for entry to the programme. Indeed, the focus on pornography as an issue heightened the awareness of staff and prisoners in other areas of the prison and, as a consequence, quite a number of other sexual offender prisoners felt more comfortable in making the break with pornography. It therefore does appear possible to do away with pornography in prisons and this should give some hope to writers such as Cowburn (1992) who, in concluding the article 'Pornography in Prisons', wrote:

> Before the presence of pornography in prisons can be restricted, changes in the attitudes of staff are required. If the presence of pornography is deemed to be undesirable it will only disappear with the co-operation of prison staff. Mere censorship would drive the materials underground. Ideally the presence of pornography and the values it presents should be openly challenged by staff, and prisoners persuaded to stop using it. Such a radical change in consciousness may not be possible throughout the prison system. However, if the Prison Service wishes to focus attention on helping sex offenders not to reoffend, it cannot ignore sexism and pornography within the institutions in which it intends to work with sex offenders. (p.46)

It is interesting to note that in the recent national survey of Scottish prisons (Wozniak *et al.* 1998) almost three-quarters of all staff (73%) were in favour of pornography-free zones for prisoners. Predictably, more female staff (88%) than male staff (71%) were in favour of such zones.

Background note on the growing concern about the problem of the sexual exploitation of children

The Council of Europe Committee on Crime Problems (1993) specifically examined the issues involved. It was their concern that

> sexual exploitation of children and young adults for profit-making purposes in the form of pornography, prostitution and traffic of human beings has assumed new and alarming dimensions at national and international level. (p.7)

In an interesting insight into the evolution of a social problem, they considered that the issues could be put forward as a case study in the following way:

The recognition of the problem

1. Sexual exploitation and abuse of children and young adults, often for profit-making purposes, has only recently been recognised as a social problem which calls for urgent action on both national and international level. In fact, with respect to this issue all the stages in the evolution of a social problem, identified by social scientists, were followed.

2. First came the stage of denial or minimisation of the problem. During this stage people believed – and in certain countries some people still believe – that sexual exploitation and abuse of young people is a rare, inconsequential phenomenon. It has taken much time for people to recognise that the problem has reached considerable dimensions and that national and international attention is cogently needed. The minimisation of the problem resulted, among other things, in the paucity of reliable statistical data in this area.

3. The problem passed through the second stage: the attribution of sexual exploitation and abuse of children and young adults to a few deviants. When these forms of sexual offences first came to public attention they were analysed as extremely pathological types of behaviour. Offenders were often seen as 'degenerates or feeble-minded freaks'. Now that the media have uncovered many cases of young people who are being used in the sex business, it is no longer easy to believe that those who organise this business and profit from it, as well as its customers, are mentally disturbed.

4. The third stage was characterised by blaming the victim. Victims of sexual exploitation and abuse 'were seen as seductive and flirtatious to such an extent that they brought the sexual abuse on themselves'. They were,

irrespective of their age, considered as being 'extremely aggressive and provoking and if it had not been for their waywardness they would not have been abused'.

5. At last, in some countries the final stage has been reached: the emergence of pressure groups and social movements campaigning against sexual exploitation of children and young adults. They largely contribute to raising awareness of the legislator, the law-enforcement agencies and the public at large. (pp.17–18).

Summary of key points

- Intervention programmes for sexual offenders are undertaken in a pornography-free environment

DEVIANT SEXUAL AROUSAL, FANTASY AND THE USE OF PORNOGRAPHY IN CLINICAL 'TREATMENT' WITHIN THE PRISON SETTING

Although there is a growing body of literature (Barbaree and Marshall 1989; Murphy and Barbaree 1988) which discusses the use of various techniques in the measurement of deviant arousal, and various clinicians use fantasy in masturbatory satiation processes, I would argue that the use of pornography in these processes is inappropriate within a prison setting. I would therefore suggest that the use of pornography is limited for the following reasons:

- Even when the images are of a less deviant type, the use of pornography is wrong in principle since it objectifies women and children and supports inappropriate values and cognitive distortions.

- It prevents the establishment of pornography-free areas.

In addition, a number of generalised problems emerge:

- It is possible that the use of the penile plethysmograph (PPG) in assessment to measure penile arousal is limited in some cases by the capacity of the offender, mostly in denial, to avoid responding to inappropriate stimuli.

- Those sexual offenders who become bored/satiated by masturbation to some inappropriate fantasies may in fact move on to more severe examples and, if this is not recognised and tackled, may indeed present a greater risk; alternatively, if the deviant fantasies are not fully satiated, then the offender may be conditioned to act out such behaviours on release. However, if properly used and managed, there is clear evidence that such techniques can have positive consequences.

- Programmes are most effective and sustainable when delivered by prison staff and, in my view, it would not be appropriate for custodial staff to become engaged in such clinical and physical contact issues. These elements could, however, be undertaken by psychologists if necessary.

Nevertheless, it is worth briefly looking at these processes although, in my view, they do not blend easily with the work of ordinary prison staff and, if considered appropriate, should only be undertaken by specialists.

Arousal

A significant number of sexual offenders display some degree of arousal to deviant stimuli and are also more aroused by deviant sexual stimuli than they are by more 'normalised' or appropriate sexual clues. Part of the 'treatment' process therefore involves attempting to identify the existing stimulus and arousal patterns and undertaking an investigation into the sexual fantasies and imageries of the offender. Clinicians advocate that a baseline of deviant sexual arousal should be established for each offender early on in the assessment phase. This would then provide a benchmark against which progress can be measured.

Behavioural and cognitive reshaping

A variety of methods can be employed to attempt to reshape and reduce deviant arousal and appropriate arousal. Offenders identify their sexual thoughts and fantasies, understand their feelings and behaviours and, over the course of the therapy, try to avoid doing or thinking about those things that would reinforce or sustain an interest in deviant sexuality. In particular, they are required to refrain from masturbating to deviant fantasies. In addition, by using guided imagery techniques, the therapist can guide the offenders' fantasies into unpleasant consequences, thereby putting them off such trains of thought. Fantasy can be used to encourage responses to appropriate cues and reduce the propensity to deviant responses:

> It is important to recognize that, when pursuing pleasure from deviant behavior, offenders are driven by the arousal and do not see the behaviour clearly. Masturbatory reconditioning can be used both to reinforce arousal to appropriate sexual cues and to reduce arousal to deviant sexuality by having offenders look at the behavior from a nonaroused state. Here they are directed to create an appropriate sexual fantasy and masturbate, using that fantasy, to ejaculation. Then, in the nonaroused state, they verbalize deviant sexual behaviours or masturbate to those fantasies with a flaccid penis for a preset period of time. Pairing nonaroused, unsatisfying sexual activity with the deviant fantasy helps them to see the role of that fantasy in their behaviour, resulting in their finding it increasingly unattractive. Masturbating to appropriate thoughts and scenes

encourages them to see that there are other, more appropriate, and increasingly attractive alternatives. (O'Connell *et al.* 1990, p.98)

Penile plethysmograph (PPG)

Barbaree (1990) argues that an individual's sexual preference can be identified so that 'if a man is maximally aroused by a deviant stimulus or act, his eventual satisfaction or reward will be greater than that resulting from less strong responses to normalized or socially acceptable stimuli or acts' (p.116). He offers a two-stage explanation of the process. First, deviant sexual cues or behaviours create the greater arousal in the offender, and second, the offender then expresses a preference for such cues or behaviours, being motivated by the stronger arousal response. This becomes a self-feeding process. The issue then becomes one of how to quantify the level of deviant sexual arousal. Barbaree states that the assessment can be conducted under laboratory conditions as follows:

> ...the laboratory assessment of sexual preferences has become an important part of a complete clinical assessment of sexual offenders. The laboratory procedure involves presenting sexual stimuli to men while monitoring their erectile responses. Stimuli take the form of still pictures of nude males and females of all ages and audio- or videotaped depictions of sexual interactions, including consenting acts between adult partners and nonconsenting forceful acts. In the assessment, when the man shows significant arousal to deviant cues, it identifies him to the clinician as a sexual deviate. (p.116)

These laboratory assessments have shown different arousal patterns in, for example, rapists and child molesters. There have been discussions on the validity of such methods since some offenders are able to suppress erectile responses at will or when instructed to do so, and some non-sex offenders are able to produce erectile responses to non-preferred stimuli. Some offenders try to distort the findings by trying to avert arousal physically through, for example, tensing muscles; others try to avert their eyes to the stimuli or concentrate on other thoughts to avoid being aroused. Clinicians have become alerted to these possibilities and studies have been undertaken to combat faking the results in the laboratory. However, given the caveats above, PPG results do give information on the nature of stimulus controls concerned with sexual arousal. Discovering each individual offender's pattern of arousal may begin to assist the clinician in understanding the man's sexual offending, and thus assist with devising the most effective 'treatment' programme for the offender. It has also been recognised that phallometric measurement of sexual deviancy, particularly in relation to sexual interest in children, provide the strongest predictors of sexual offence recidivism (Hanson and Bussière 1998) and is therefore a useful assessment tool. The prison service in England and Wales have also begun to use the PPG for phallometric assessment of sexual deviancy. Research is again being undertaken to examine the veracity of phallometric assessment (see, for example, Yolanda Fernandez's study, ATSA, 1998a).

Recently, non-PPG techniques using slides depicting both sexes with the subjects clothed or partially dressed, not posed pornographically and without genitalia being displayed, have been used with success. The Abel Screen does not employ plethysmography. The dependent variable is the amount of time for which the 'assessee' observes each slide (Osborn, Abel and Warberg 1995).

In my view it is inappropriate to use pornography in prisons for the range of phallometric measurement and masturbatory conditioning techniques discussed above. It is worth considering whether it is unacceptable to subject the 'operator' to such material. Also, it sends a strange message to offenders – that such material is wrong in principle but allowable for 'treatment' purposes. Neither can one overcome the ethical dilemma that material, such as child pornography, is illegal.

More recently, the Association for the Treatment of Sexual Abusers published a revision to its 'Ethical Standards' (ATSA 1997). In its appendix on plethys-mograph examination it states: 'Efforts should be made to use new technology which does not make use of human subjects' (p.50).

Richard Laws (1996) comments:

> Over the past few years many of us have grown increasingly weary of the continued rehashing of the issues surrounding the manner in which the images of children are obtained, the legal right of individuals to possess and use the stimuli, and the use to which the images are put. (p.273)

In addition, studies have shown that where PPG measurements are known to be used to provide information towards parole or other decisions, prisoners are likely to be motivated to suppress their deviant sexual arousal and thus hide the extent and form of their sexual interests. However, there is evidence to show that the use of a range of techniques has value but is more properly undertaken by trained clinicians such as psychologists.

Summary of key points

- The use of pornography in prisons for the assessment of deviant sexual arousal and in conditioning techniques, and by prison staff, is not recommended.

CHAPTER 5

The Programme

AIMS OF THE STOP PROGRAMME

The STOP Programme has three aims:

1. To engender acceptance of personal responsibility.
2. To address the consequences of offending behaviour for both offender and victim(s), including secondary victims, e.g. family and friends.
3. To develop personal strategies that will assist in the exercising of self-control and help to avoid situations likely to lead to reoffending.

THE OVERALL ORGANISATION OF THE PROGRAMME

The programme adopts a group-work approach to addressing offending behaviour, and the central part operates over a period of approximately one year. There are three parts to the programme, the last part of which is currently being developed:

Part 1. a) Assessment

Staff assess the offender through a series of interviews, using standard banks of questions to establish the nature of his offending behaviours, the pattern of offending, how he selects and views his victim, his attitude to the offence, and other personal factors. These then provide some basis for risk assessment and decisions about the nature of the intervention to be tried (see pp.78–88).

Part 1. b) Parallel and preparatory work

This is available through the STOP Programme and from other parts of the prison; cognitive skills groups and life skills classes are examples of such work (see Chapter 6).

Part 2. The STOP Group-Work Programme

The programme has two phases, each comprising 40 sessions.[1]

- Phase 1: The programme begins by focusing on issues such as cognitive restructuring, consent, responsibility, cycles of offending and the establishment of basic victim empathy. (see pp.88–103).

- Phase 2: Continues the development and exploration of the individual's cycle of offending whilst using modular work to examine other areas. This forms the basis for the development of an individual plan for relapse prevention (see pp.93–103).

Each group consists of eight to ten offenders who have been convicted of offences against children and/or adults. Groups meet twice per week and each of the 80 sessions lasts approximately two and a half hours, with additional 'wind-down' time over a cup of coffee built into the timetable. Each group is led by prison staff and social workers. Priority is given to those men who are considered to be at high risk of reoffending.

Part 3. The maintenance programme

This part is presently being developed. The groups are low level and mix two or three types of offenders: those higher-risk offenders who have already participated in the core programme and are its graduates; those low-risk prisoners who require minimal intervention programmes; and some higher-risk offenders who might have initial problems being effectively integrated into programmes, for whom the maintenance group might provide a bridge to enable their future admission to the core programme. Such a group would also be suitable for short-term prisoners.

ASSESSMENT AND RISK

Assessment

First, staff are involved in assessment. In particular, staff will have to build a picture about the prisoner's *pattern of offending* – his behaviour leading up to the offence. Does he take risks? Is he compulsive? How does he select his victims? Are the victims likely to tell on him? How does he target his victims? Is it through friends or by driving near schools in a car? How does the offender groom his victims? Does he spend time associating with children? How does he manage to be alone with children or to be alone to seek an adult victim? How does he gradually break down the physical or psychological resistance of his victims?

A picture of *how the prisoner views his victim* is also important if those working with him are to evaluate his dangerousness and the depth of his problem. What are

---

1   More recently, the programme has been extended to around 100 sessions.

the effects of the abuse on the victim, and what was the victim's reaction? Were there any weaknesses of which the offender took advantage? What is his attitude to the victim and does he recognise the harm he has done? He should be constantly reminded of the damage he has caused. In addition, if staff have victim information, they can compare the victim's statements with the account given by the offender. This will give some further insights, and the analysis of the discrepancies may help with planning for the future care of the victim.

Finally, what is his attitude to the offence? Does he deny it or minimise what he has done? Does he justify it or blame the victim for leading him on? Is he able to empathise with the victim's trauma and pain? Is he aware of the degree of force used, the resistance of the victim and the nature of any psychological coercion?

Then there is a need to understand the individual in the wider context of his personal background. Is the offender severely damaged himself as a result of his own experiences? Are there unresolved issues from his childhood? There is thus a requirement to look at his *personal history, socialisation* and *sexual activity*. In looking at the offender's personal history the assessor will need to establish whether there was a stable family background or marital problems, whether he himself and/or other siblings were subject to violence or abuse, and whether there were alcohol/drug abuse issues in the family. Does he use drugs or alcohol and is this usage related to his offending? How did he do at school in terms of academic performance and friendships? How does he view himself? Has he low self-esteem? Is he assertive, anxious or hostile? Has he formed relationships that have provided him with some stability and satisfaction, and have these relationships been intimate or does he feel emotionally isolated? The assessment will need to build up a picture of his employment, marital and social history, any significant medical problems and his previous criminal history. How does he view women, children and sexual relationships? What are his attitudes to women and what roles does he ascribe to them? In his view, are certain levels of interpersonal violence necessary in the home? How does he relate to children and what are his views on sex with them? How much use has he made of pornography and of what type? Finally, the assessor will need to gain an insight into his sexual development, behaviours, knowledge, preferences, age discriminations and partners, and then try to link that insight to his childhood sexual experiences and those he witnessed in his family, to achieve an understanding of how he became the person he is.

The above are some of the raw data that need to be obtained from the offender, although some information should also be available from social work reports. The offence and the other personal details go to make up the assessment procedures which, after interviews, enable staff to evaluate the problems that need to be faced and contribute to an *overall assessment of risk*. (A further account of risk assessment is given in Marshall's report (1992b), pp.5–8. On pp.9–20 can be found a

description of the basics of his proposed programme.) The information gained is
then analysed and might usefully be categorised as follows:

1. scale and pattern of offending and associated thinking errors

2. personal history

3. sexual history

4. social functioning and self-image

5. ability to develop victim awareness and empathy

6. perspective-taking ability and misattributions of responsibility

7. sexual attitudes and arousal pattern

8. self-control

9. verbal intelligence and ability to work in a group

10. overall measure of risk assessment (from high to low).

These interviews also begin the process of challenging denial. During assessment
interviews, a range of strategies must be adopted in order to deal with the
offender's denial. Staff have to remain *detached* while conducting the interviews
and maintain *control* of the agenda. The issues are serious ones and the interviewer
will have to remind the offender that he is likely to come back to prison again
(having harmed others) if he does not face up to the problems. The member of
staff may have to describe their experience in this field so that they can turn to the
offender and tell them: 'I've heard all that, now, what do you take me for…it's
time to tell the truth.' It might also be useful to help the offender to disclose by
describing some general experiences of what sexual offenders are like: that they
are not unique, that they virtually all deny, and so on. It can be explained that it
might do them some good to get some of their 'secrets' off their chest and
unburden themselves, and that disclosing will help when it comes to becoming
involved in therapy. In the initial stages, techniques such as accepting rationalisations and justifications as face-saving can be used to allow admission of the
offence. Empathy can be offered for disclosure but anxiety levels should be
maintained. Using small incremental steps and repeating what has gone before
can aid the process. The interviewer might lead questions, creating a 'yes set' to
which it is hard to say no, e.g. 'Do you love your daughter?', etc. The interviewer
can also offer some hope for the future by saying: 'It's hard to talk, but it's a good
thing to do so. What you have said has been helpful and will assist with the work
we are going to do with you; we can continue tomorrow.' In *Invitations to
Responsibility*, Alan Jenkins (1990) describes a range of strategies for dealing with
denial. Explaining why offenders might adopt a stance of 'total denial', Jenkins
explores the arguments which the therapist can use.

The extent of acknowledgement may be slight at this stage, e.g. *I was just holding her and perhaps my hand slipped and it might have touched her down there.* (p.120)

It should be remembered that progress at gaining information can be slow, and that getting the offender to admit is an incremental and multi-staged process.

The offender may accept the fact that he committed the offence but use a range of further denial strategies, making excuses as to why it may have happened or reasons why there really is no need to be concerned about him being a risk in the future, e.g. 'Don't worry, I will keep away from boys'; 'I now know what made me do it, so I can go back to being the local Scoutmaster without any further risk.' In both cases there is, in fact, plenty to worry about. The offender will possibly try to find reasons for his actions which relieve him of personal responsibility, and with the right cure should not present problems in the future, e.g. 'I suffered a mental breakdown'; 'I had a loss of memory'; 'I was hooked on drugs'; 'I suffered an alcohol problem'; 'My wife and family are back together now'; and so on. Indeed, the offender might want to display what I term a *sackcloth* approach: 'Oh, the shame and guilt I feel! I have destroyed the good name of my family'; 'I hope at some time they can forgive me for the harm I have done and the anguish I have caused'; 'I feel like doing myself in and ending it all.' However, in essence these may all be attempts to claim that the misery created is sufficient to stop offending and thus deny that there is any longer a problem. The interviewer must work round all these issues during assessment. As already stated, these interviews begin the process of engaging with denial, which is dealt with in more detail on pp.88–90.

The polygraph

The use of the polygraph, or 'lie detector', is already well established in North America. It has been used effectively in helping to overcome denial in sex offenders. Sexual offenders use denial and minimisation as defensive techniques. It is certainly helpful to know whether they have committed two or fifty offences and to have greater and more reliable information on what occurred. It is used best when ascertaining the types of behaviour. Anna Salter (ATSA 1998b) has discussed the best ways of countering deception among sexual offenders. In her view, and this is now supported by many other practitioners and by research, use of the polygraph assists in getting to know the truth about index offences, behaviour patterns, progress through treatment or intervention programmes, and maintenance; it can also be useful during supervision and to check on specific issues.

It is not being proposed here that polygraphs should be used for evidential purposes, but that they can assist with programme objectives by improving the openness of sexual offenders. In one study, 23 sexual offenders had already admitted to 4020 such offences during treatment; this rose to 52,939 once they knew they were going to take a polygraph examination! Heil, Ahlmeyer and English (1998) found that sexual offenders admitted to double the numbers of victims under polygraph examination.

Earle (1998) has summarised the assistance that polygraph examination can provide. It:

- provides verification of sexual offence
- helps the offender become truly honest with his therapists
- verifies compliance with treatment or programme contract
- helps identify the sexual offence cycle
- helps identify thinking errors
- can identify issues to be addressed during therapy
- verifies progress while on programmes
- elicits new information
- helps sexual offenders move out of denial
- verifies victim perception of the molestation.

Most states in the USA are now using polygraph examinations as a tool to assist in interventions with sexual offenders. In 1992 Colorado became one of the first states to pass legislation requiring standards and guidelines for the treatment of sexual offenders; these included polygraph examination of offenders undertaking programmes. It first published fully comprehensive standards in 1996 (revised in 1998), which not only include standards for the use of the polygraph but standards for use in all areas of work with sexual offenders.

Polygraph use during programmes: can be used to increase programme efficacy by providing more comprehensive information to evaluate the offender's problem areas and progress; it can also deter offenders from attempting to deceive their therapists; and the threat of further polygraph tests can help offenders control their behaviour and develop patterns of honesty in therapy.

Polygraph use in community supervision: can be used as a monitoring tool and provide more comprehensive information to evaluate the offender's risk factors and any special conditions of community placement; it is also intended to increase public safety through a deterrent effect.

It would now appear that we should be using the polygraph also as a tool to improve assessment for programmes and risk and to assist with interventions and supervision.

Risk

The following table can be used to measure risk.

Indices of risk to reoffend among sex offenders (Marshall 1995)

	Empirically derived predictors	Indications of highest risk	Indications of lowest risk
1	Prior violent convictions (sexual or non-sexual)	• numerous and highly violent	• few or none and low coerciveness
2	Prior non-sex offences	• large number, over long period • diversity (e.g. fraud, robbery, assault, drug offences)	• few or none • single type
3	Prior sex offences	• large number of non-familial child victims • diverse victims (e.g. adults and children, male and female victims) • exclusively male children victims • use of coercion	• one or none prior or an incest victim • single victim type • female children victims • uses grooming rather than coercion
4	History of adult romantic relationships	• poor quality • no prior partners • large number of brief relationships	• good quality, few and lasting
5	History of substance abuse	• addicted, long-term abuse, diverse drugs used, failed to enter treatment or unresponsive to treatment	• no such history or history of social use or uses instrumentally to 'get courage' to offend
6	Scores on Psychopathy Checklist	• high scores, particularly 20+	• low scores
7	Intelligence	• IQ less than 80	• IQ above 80
8	Deviant sexual patterns	• presence of deviance	• absence of deviance

Using the table of indices above, it is possible to calculate the pre-intervention programme risk levels as follows (Marshall 1995):

Level	Risk	Factors
1	High	is at this level if high on 4 or more empirical predictors
2	High–Moderate	highest on 2 empirical predictors and moderate on 3 others
3	Moderate	highest on 1 and moderate on 2 others, or moderate on 4 predictors
4	Moderate–Low	moderate on 2 predictors
5	Low	low on all predictors

Treatment effects (Marshall 1995)[2]

	Treatment targets	Indications of no change	Indications of modest changes	Indications of substantial changes
1	Denial or minimisation	treatment ineffective	reasonable gains but incomplete	complete change
2	Empathy for victims	remains unempathetic	some degree of empathy	strong remorse and empathy
3	Self-esteem	poor self-image or unfoundedly high	moderate improvements	normal levels of confidence
4	Cognitive distortions	unchanged	some improvements but still distorts to a degree or at times	elimination of distortion
5	Attitudes towards women and children and general crime-supportive attitudes and beliefs	remains negative and antisocial	some movement toward more egalitarian and prosocial attitudes	significant changes in prosocial direction
6	Social and relationship attitudes and skills	remains poor	moderately good	acceptable
7	Understanding of offence cycle	poor	modest	excellent
8	Development of relapse prevention plans and understanding of these concepts	poor	reasonable	excellent
9	Degree of participation in treatment	poor	effective	excellent
10	Treatment of offence-related problems (e.g. substance abuse, anger, problem solving, etc.)	poor	effective	excellent

Changes in risk with intervention ('treatment')

This necessarily requires that a subjective judgement be applied to the above table and there are no definitive guidelines. Some therapists tend to be more conservative than others and there is, as yet, no empirical evaluation of this system of deciding on the degree of change in risk status with intervention. However, by applying the above table to individual offenders, it is possible to make some judgement as to their progress or otherwise during therapy. This can then be evaluated in terms of risk by examining the options below.

2   'Treatment' is Marshall's term – I would prefer to use the word 'intervention'.

	Response to programme	Change in risk
1	If uncooperative or hostile in 'treatment'	Increase in risk level by one step (e.g. from Moderate to High–moderate)
2	When there are little or no benefits apparent from 'treatment'	No change in level occurs
3	If modest improvements occur on at least four targets	Decrease in risk level by one step
4	If substantial improvements occur in at least six targets	Decrease in risk level by two steps

Risk assessment

The issue of risk assessment will continue to present problems for practitioners. How easy is it to know whether the sexual offender is low or high risk and whether our interventions have really impacted? As we consider appropriateness for release and have to advise on risk in the community, such questions are not merely academic. Sadly, in the past we have based our judgements on myths and gut feelings. We have tended to include factors such as educational/ intellectual levels, depression, alcohol abuse, low motivation for treatment, denial, poor victim empathy, psychological maladjustment, whether currently married, prior non-violent offences and female child victims as indicators. Very simply, they are not, and in some cases these factors negatively correlate with sexual offending. Hanson and Bussière's large meta-analysis (1998) looked at 61 studies which provided information on 28,972 sexual offenders. They were able to show that unguided clinical assessments of sexual offenders, which often also gave outcome predictions, had little or no reliability value (.04 to .10), while predictions based on actuarial or statistical methods gave more accurate risk predictions (.44 to .46).

There are only a few risk assessment scales in existence for sexual offenders. David Thornton is currently developing one for the prison service in England and Wales, the Structured Anchored Clinical Judgement (SACJ) (Thornton 1997), built on the earlier work of Fisher and Thornton (1993). Early indications show that the scale correlated .33 with sexual offence recidivism. Use of the SACJ scale comprises two steps; the first is based on assigning points for offence history data; the second adds 'aggravating' factors such as: male victim, substance abuse, stranger victim, high psychopathy score, never in a stable relationship, deviant arousal as measured by PPG and a history of local authority residential care. The combined scores then determine the level of risk assigned. To this could be added or subtracted factors indicating, for example, programme drop-out or clinical improvement.

The Violence Risk Appraisal Guide (VRAG) devised by Webster *et al.* (1994) has attracted considerable attention but is better at predicting violent recidivism, including sexual offending with violence (.47), than sexual recidivism alone (.20).

Hanson (1997) has developed his own assessment scale, The Rapid Risk Assessment for Sexual Offence Recidivism (RRASOR), which gives a .27 reliability of prediction and is based on four variables:

- prior sexual offences (higher number = greater risk)
- age at risk, e.g. at time of release (younger = greater risk)
- victim gender (males = greater risk)
- relationship to victim (non-related = greater risk).

The RRASOR is based on earlier data (Hanson and Bussière 1996, 1998) which identified a handful of factors most relevant to predicting sexual offending:

Sexual deviance

Sexual interest in children (measured by PPG)	.32
Any deviant sexual preference	.22
Prior sexual offences	.19
Any stranger victims	.15
Early onset of sex offending	.12
Any unrelated victims	.11
Any boy victims	.11
Diverse sex crimes	.10

Criminal history/lifestyle

Antisocial personality disorder/psychopathy	.14
Any prior offences (non-sexual/any)	.13

Demographic factors

Age (young)	.13
Single (never married)	.11

Treatment history

Failure to complete treatment	.17

Hanson and Bussière (1998) found that of the demographic variables, only age (young) and marital status (single) were related to sexual offence recidivism, while criminal lifestyle variables such as antisocial personality disorder and prior offences were also useful. The risk of sexual offence recidivism increased for those who had previous sexual offences, victimised strangers, had an extra-familial victim, began sexually offending at an early age, had selected male victims or had engaged in diverse sexual crimes. The strongest predictors were measures of sexual deviancy, with sexual interest in children, as measured through phallometric assessment, being the single strongest predictor. The sole developmental history variable related to sexual offence recidivism was a negative relationship with the mother (.16, based on a relatively small sample size). As already indicated in Chapter 2 above, contrary to popular belief, being sexually abused as a child is not associated with an increased risk of sexual offending. One of the more interesting findings was that offenders who failed to complete treatment were at higher risk than those who completed it. This could indicate that high-risk offenders fail to complete treatment programmes, since it is known that antisocial personality, lifestyle instability and general impulsiveness are good predictors of treatment attrition.

Finally, the research of Hanson and Harris (1998) can help us to monitor risk in the community. They analysed the reports of supervising officers to identify key predictors. Three types of data were used: *static* or historical risk factors which influence the offenders' pre-existing recidivism risk (e.g. propensity for violence or IQ); *stable* dynamic factors, if present in the offender, which do not depend on the timing of problems or changes during supervision, but assumed to reflect relatively stable characteristics (e.g. substance abuse, relationship problems, lifestyle or attitudes), and; *acute* dynamic risk factors which were noticed just prior to re-offending (e.g. disengaging from supervision, change in attitude to blaming victims, pronounced mood change). By combining all three a high degree of reliabilty can be achieved.

Static

VRAG	.32
Sexual deviance	.24
IQ	−.24

Stable

Sees self as no risk	.47
Poor social influences	.39
Sexual entitlement	.37

Acute

Access to victims	.28
Non-co-operation with supervision	.25
Anger	.19

When the factors were combined, the predictor reliance rose to .40, .53 and .32 respectively, with a .60 combined total. Another factor, sexual preoccupations, was also found to be significant in case note studies. Of the three main types of risk factors, the stable–dynamic factors predicted recidivism most strongly. The research therefore provides some guidance for those interested in improving supervision of sexual offenders in the community. The dynamic risk factors should be routinely monitored during supervision. 'The results suggest that offenders are most at risk for re-offending when they become sexually preoccupied, have access to victims, fail to acknowledge their recidivism risk, and show sharp increases in dysphoric moods, particularly anger' (Hanson and Harris 1998, p.33). By careful monitoring during supervision, it might be possible to provide appropriate responses and interventions before a sexual offender lapses into offending.

However, even with an offender categorised as *low risk*, who is generally accepted as presenting a less than 10 per cent chance of reoffending within a five-year follow-up period, there must still be concern that he could reoffend and about the potential harm he could cause. After all, assessing someone as 'low' risk implies that he belongs to a group of similarly matched offenders, 10 out of every 100 of whom would reoffend. A *high-risk* offender would represent, at the very least, about a 50 per cent risk of reoffending over a five-year follow-up period, or be among a group of 100 of whom are likely to offend. Any risk, however slight, poses considerable challenges to those supervising sexual offenders in the community.

THE INTERVENTION PROGRAMME: RESPONSIBILITY, THINKING ERRORS AND DEFENCE MECHANISMS[3]

Next comes the intervention programme itself. This begins by examining with the offender what he has done. Sexual offenders often defend themselves by limiting the amount of responsibility they accept for the act. Sometimes they *deny* having committed any offence at all (*denial of behaviour*): 'The child is lying'; 'I never did anything'; 'She made it up to get back at me'; 'Her mother made her say it.' The offender may *deny his own responsibility* for the act, declaring: 'I was drunk at the time'; 'I would have stopped if she asked'; 'She led me on'; 'Nobody wears what she did unless they want sex'; 'I spent a lot of money on the dinner and drink – she owed it to me.' He may try to *minimise his behaviour* or deny the significance or seriousness of what happened, saying: 'It wasn't as bad as it was made out'; 'I didn't hurt her much'; 'I just wanted to show I loved her.' He may try to *apportion blame* by projecting some or all of the responsibility onto someone else: 'She encouraged me'; 'My wife ignores me.' In these ways he may try to *justify* or *rationalise his behaviour* by claiming: 'I was helping with her sex education – it's better she finds out from me, her father, in a loving relationship than from a strange man who might have HIV'; 'I thought she was eight years old [not six!]' 'My daughter was comforting me while I had relationship problems with my wife – at least that way the family stayed together and I didn't have an affair with someone else.'

3   I am indebted to Anna Salter whose system of classification, in her writings and presentation at the NOTA Conference, Dundee, 30th September to the 2nd of October, 1992 has been used as the basis to develop this section.

Even where the offender accepts he has done something wrong, he will usually try to evade personal responsibility or claim that there is no longer a problem: 'It only happened once and I have learned my lesson while in prison. I don't want to come back again into prison so I shan't offend again.' Instead, he will want to emphasise some explanation of why it happened and how there are no problems for the future. He might try to deny any antecedent behaviour, *denial of fantasy or planning* as part of the offence cycle, or *denial of other deviant behaviour* when in fact there have been a variety of other acts, cross-dressing, flashing, obscene phone calls, etc., other forms of abuse or attacks on victims. The offender might also engage in:

Denial of the current relevance of the problem

'It happened a long time ago'; 'I've not offended for six months'; 'Being in prison has cured me'; 'I've agreed with my family that I will treat them properly in future'; 'I was going through a bad patch, made redundant, but I have a job to go to now'; 'It was a medical problem'; 'I was suffering from stress at the time'; 'My marriage went through a bad period and I was sexually frustrated, but now that I'm in prison my wife has agreed to take me home and things will be all right in the future.'

Denial of the difficulty of change

'It was out of character for me and it's the first time such a thing has happened. I was under the influence of alcohol/drugs, so it won't be hard for me to avoid problems in the future'; 'God has forgiven me and I now have Him on my side, I'm a born-again Christian and with Jesus with me all the time I shall walk the straight and narrow path'; 'I treated her badly after we had sex, that's why she cried rape – I have learned how to treat women better.'

Denial of the possibility of relapse

'Ever since I started on meditation I have understood myself and my bodily forces, so there is no chance I could do it again'; 'I am certainly not going to miss the Scout jamboree, I know where I went wrong before and I can now resist boys'; 'What shame I have brought on my family and what guilt I feel – there's no way I could do anything like that again.'

Denial of the seriousness of the effects

'She can't have been that damaged as she still writes'; 'It was only intercourse and I was very gentle – I know it was wrong but no real harm was done'; 'She was back at work the next day – it can't have been all that bad…and look what's happened to me, I'm in prison, I've lost my job, my family don't visit and the doctor has had to prescribe me sedatives'; 'Well I'm not denying I did it but she normally sells it at the local sauna – so I'm really like anyone else – in fact, now I come to think about it, I might have got AIDS from her!'

Denial of the future problems and consequences

This is a combination of the offender's various denials of responsibility coupled with an inability to understand the impact his actions have had on others or the likelihood of achieving change. 'My daughter still loves me and asked me when I am coming home'; 'My family will support me on release and I know they will help me so that I don't offend again'; 'I have established a good business and I can pick up where I left off'; 'I have a good circle of friends who I know will support me and invite me to parties. I'm sure they have forgiven me and the shame I brought'; 'If I am given another chance, I won't abuse it. I'm not silly, as I know I am bound to be caught if I offend again.'

It is *errors in the offender's thinking* that allow him to carry on offending. Denial, minimisation, rationalisation, justification and projection of responsibility are all forms of what are called *cognitive distortions*. These, and other thinking errors (such as viewing women and children as objects to be used) need to be tackled if the offender is to make any progress.

Group treatment, undertaken in heterogeneous groups, is an especially valuable tool for enabling offenders to face up to their responsibilities, with other group members challenging what is being said.

THE INTERVENTION PROGRAMME: VICTIM AWARENESS

The victim is considered to be a central feature of the programme (and its principal justification: see Chapter 2). This element of the programme is therefore aimed at assisting participants to gain an understanding of the emotional, social, psychological and physical impact of their offences upon the victim.

The offender has to examine his *effect on victims*. He has to begin to see them as people with names, who have identities and feelings – not merely as objects for his use. He has to understand the harm and damage he has caused and to some extent internalise the pain and suffering he has inflicted on others. Only then will he understand the real reason to stop offending.

The concept of the victim is also widened to include the *ripple effect*: the effect on secondary groups, such as the family and friends of the victim, who share in the pain and trauma and give so much of themselves in support. Of course, when the offending occurs outside the context of the family, the offender's own relatives can become a tertiary group, often the forgotten victims (Blake 1990; Cooklin

1989; Matthews 1983), not of his offences, but of the consequences of his offending behaviour.

The offender is expected to do some 'homework' outside of group sessions and draft letters to the victim. These letters are not sent and there is no victim contact. The purpose is to get the offender to recognise for himself through verbalising to the victim his remorse and guilt; to take on full responsibility for his actions without apportioning any of the blame to the victim or others; and to recognise the damage that he has inflicted upon the victim. Even though in theory it sounds relatively easy for the offender to go through the motions of writing a letter, in reality it creates tension and anxiety as the offender begins to understand what he has done and internalises some of the thought processes. (Later on, if family reunification is being contemplated, and discussions have been held between the child's social worker and the offender's core worker or social worker, it might be agreed that a letter should be sent. In these circumstances, the process would begin again and the letter would not be approved until it was considered wholly appropriate.)

The process of developing victim empathy is central to any work undertaken with sexual offenders. One of the difficulties faced by those working with offenders, particularly in incest cases, is that the offender can claim to love the child and not want to hurt her. Yet it seems inconceivable that the offender would have done what he did and not realise the harm done. This dilemma can be explained by the fact that the abuser believes (he has internalised it and convinced himself) that the child also wants this type of relationship. In this way he prevents himself from seeing the harm. The child who he claims to love is transformed by him into an object that wants his sexual attention. That is why the work of challenging the various forms of denial of responsibility is so important when the agenda moves on to victim empathy. The issues surrounding denial and victim impact lie at the heart of developing self-awareness.

THE INTERVENTION PROGRAMME: OTHER SOCIAL AND SEXUAL ISSUES

A range of more general and social issues are explored during the programme. In part they build upon other elements and explore complementary areas to give a broader perspective for the work. Each group of offenders may require specific areas of work on which to focus; some of the subjects that may be usefully employed are given below.

Consent

Consent is a major issue for all sexual offenders and further develops the processes begun when dealing with denial, blame transference and responsibility. It is linked to issues of power and gender. The group examines what constitutes consent and how it is granted on the basis of equality rather than power. It will look at everyday situational examples, including date rape, to arrive at an acceptable understanding of what consent means and why it is required.

Male/Female sexuality and sexual knowledge

Offenders have a distorted view of both male and female sexuality. The programme helps participants to examine thoughts, feelings and beliefs on this subject by asking them to consider how emotional and sexual needs can be met through relationships. Many sexual offenders display poor sexual knowledge and find it difficult to understand what is acceptable sexual behaviour among consenting partners, so such behaviours in well-functioning people are discussed.

Pornography

The group discusses the use of pornography and looks at its effects. It examines how pornography objectifies women and children, and how most offenders progress through pornography (objects) on to real victims (people). Pornography tends to show men achieving their sexual aims by dominating women (and children) who appear to enjoy being humiliated. In addition, much pornographic material shows violence and coercion, and use of these materials reinforces the sexually aggressive tendencies of male offenders. The offenders have to understand through discussion of objectification, the development of victim empathy and the examination of gender issues, that such material is inappropriate and wrong.

Gender issues

Linked to both pornography and consent are issues concerning the way offenders perceive the role of men, women and children in society. These areas are explored in order to reinforce changes in values that encourage the offender to approach other people as equals. The discussions are not always easy since the culture of Western society generally supports male domination of women and children. The goal of exploring these issues is to establish the rights of women and children and prevent coercion by the male offender.

Social and interpersonal skills

The programme is not intended to become an educational or life skills course. Other complementary programmes that might achieve these goals are explored more fully in Chapter 6. However, the group will look at interpersonal issues and relationships. Offenders will discuss how they relate to each other in the group; whether what they say is what they mean; whether they can feel comfortable in relationships, and feel they can be intimate and derive benefit from such a bonding; and whether they make appropriate social responses to the situations in which they find themselves, or need more understanding of the verbal and non-verbal cues given by others.

Filling leisure time

How do they cope with their spare time? Are they easily bored and does that contribute to them turning to offending patterns of behaviour? Do they have hobbies and do these help prevent offending behaviour? Is what they do constructive or useful? Are they involved with drugs or do they over-indulge in alcohol? How do they cope with stress and can they manage it? Do they have people to turn to?

Triggers and the feeling–thought–action chain

Offending behaviour does not occur completely spontaneously, but can be triggered by events, conversations, pornography or video films, thoughts and feelings and other stimuli. So the offender begins to look at what has been called the 'feeling–thought–action' chain. What starts him off thinking about offending? This moves the programme into the work on cycles of offending behaviour and relapse prevention, the subject of the next section.

THE INTERVENTION PROGRAMME: CYCLES OF OFFENDING BEHAVIOUR AND RELAPSE PREVENTION

Cycles of offending

Next, the offender examines his *cycle of offending behaviour.* He looks at how he plans and fantasises, how he targets his subjects and grooms them, and what the triggers and thinking sequences are. Offending behaviour does not occur spontaneously, but can be triggered by a range of stimuli. The offender looks at the feeling–thought–action chain. He gradually learns that the process of creating abusive sexual behaviours is a lengthy one, and, in fact, the same process is largely repeated before and after every act. That is why it is termed an *offence cycle.*

Throughout the process of the offence cycle, distorted thinking is apparent. These distorted beliefs allow the offender to justify or legitimise his acts, excuse himself or transfer blame to someone else. There are usually stages during which he fantasises about his offending, plans, rehearses his fantasies, and targets and even grooms the victim (and sometimes others so as to prevent disclosure). These phases occur in most sex offending cycles, and the offender develops his self-delusion, eventually convincing himself that there is no planning and things just happened. The speed at which the cycle progresses varies enormously between offenders. For some there may be lengthy gaps between offending and then lengthy periods of preparation, whereas others can move very quickly from the thought to the offence.

The fundamental elements of the cycle are:

Step	Description of process
	Normality. I have included this term to describe the state of non-offending. Many sexual offenders appear to hold ordinary lives and jobs and for much of the time are not engaged in their cycle of offending. The abnormal behaviour which labels them and has such devastating consequences may only constitute a few hours in a longer period of time (e.g. a week).
1	*Feelings* of low esteem; boredom, loneliness, confusion, lack of power, etc.; offender is unable to deal with his emotional state.
2	*Fantasies* of sexual abuse (e.g. of sexual power over, and degradation of, another person).
3	*Pro-offending thinking* and/or behaviour supported by fantasies, converting into distorted thinking and the creation of rationalisations justifying their would-be acts; passive planning is often accomplished during masturbatory fantasies.
4	…but (sometimes) *Internal inhibitors* continue to operate until…
5	*Trigger* is found. This provides the excuse to move from fantasy to reality, i.e. to begin to implement fantasy.
6	*Fantasy* rehearsal increases.
7	*Target* is found.
8	*Grooming* to 'soften' victim and help prevent disclosure later – principally applied by paedophiles to children, but could be similarly described in, for example, date rape cases.
9	*Sexual offending* takes place: the plan is acted out.
10	*Fantasy reinforcement* occurs; reason for fantasy is strengthened by completed sexual attack; sometimes loops directly back to step 6 (*fantasy rehearsal*) in short-circuit.
11	*Guilt* from offence and *fear* of being caught; offenders may even feel remorse for actions and concern for well-being of victim (usually short-lived). As a consequence, offender may go into hiding for a while and desist.
12	*Bribe or threaten* not to talk (usually children).
13	*Push guilt away* and probably start again on the cycle.

Cycles are not peculiar to sexual offenders. Most people who try to cut down or give up on something they enjoy know all about selective thinking, seemingly irrelevant decision making and how on a bad day self-delusion increases and the likelihood of relapse is greater. However, although the process may be common, in the case of a sexual offender, the content, or desired behaviour, is often very bizarre, and hence in order to legitimise or justify it to himself, he has to resort to highly distorted thinking. Whatever type of offender, Hilary Eldridge (1992) believes they display one of two basic types of cycles, depending on their attitudes, beliefs and desire to offend. She has described them as *continuous* or *inhibited*. The continuous cycle would basically run through steps 6 to 10 of the above table, while the inhibited cycle could run through the whole process from steps 1 to 13.

Cycle of sexual offending

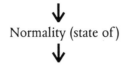

↓

Normality (state of)

↓

Feelings of low self-esteem, loneliness, confusion, lack of power;
offender is unable to deal with his emotional state

↓

Fantasies of sexual abuse

↓

Pro-offending thinking and behaviour supported by fantasies,
distorted thinking, and rationalisations justifying would-be acts

↓

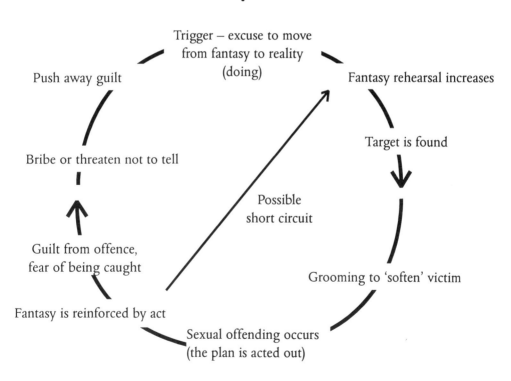

Trigger – excuse to move
from fantasy to reality
(doing)

Push away guilt

Fantasy rehearsal increases

Bribe or threaten not to tell

Target is found

Possible
short circuit

Guilt from offence,
fear of being caught

Grooming to 'soften' victim

Fantasy is reinforced by act

Sexual offending occurs
(the plan is acted out)

Hilary Eldridge (1992) describes the two types of cycles as follows:

Continuous cycles: Some offenders have a belief system which legitimises their behaviour to the point where the cycle is only interrupted by their perceived risk of being caught. For example, a date and acquaintance rapist who believes that all women say 'no' when they mean 'yes' may see his behaviour as socially acceptable and see no reason to question it. A fixated paedophile who was himself victimised as a child by someone close to him who groomed him to believe sexual abuse was not abuse at all, but an expression of love, may in his turn adopt these distorted beliefs and convince himself that he is really helping or 'loving' children. He will always seek out, or target, children to abuse. Breaks in his offending will only occur if he discovers that he has made a targeting error, i.e. he thinks that the child he has chosen may tell, and is therefore too risky to pursue. In this case he will target another child or children. Such offenders have an essentially continuous cycle, uninterrupted by worries about the way their behaviour harms either their own self image or the victim.

Inhibited cycles: Other offenders do question their behaviour. They see it as essentially perverted and worry about the way it reflects on them. They may also recognise that it hurts the victim. These offenders have inhibited cycles in which internal inhibitors operate to break the cycle. The length of breaks will depend on the strength of the internal inhibitors, of the distorted or pro-offending thinking which legitimises offending, and of the arousal or desire to offend.

Some offenders have quite lengthy periods when their cycles are inhibited and they do not offend. However, they still indulge in thoughts which legitimise offending, and they may still fantasise about abuse, thereby strengthening the desire to re-offend. They may also reinforce their own distorted thinking about abuse by, for example, fantasising about rape in which the victim resists at first but ends up enjoying it, or in which children smile and say 'please do it to me'. Such offenders may seek an excuse to offend. They may make a whole series of seemingly irrelevant decisions leading to the opportunity to carry out the secretly desired behaviour. This process enables them to avoid facing the pain and responsibility of recognising that they planned to re-offend. Other offenders may break through their internal inhibitors by indulging in self fulfilling prophesies which lead them to feel sorry for themselves and entitled to comfort. Another, who perceives rejection may indulge in revenge type fantasies about attacking and hurting others because he feels attacked and hurt.

Having begun offending after a period of abstinence, some offenders feel guilty and may not re-offend for periods of time ranging from a few days to several years. However, as their core beliefs have not changed and at some level they still wish to re-offend, they may relapse by repeating the pattern.

'Short-circuiting' the phases of an inhibited cycle

Some offenders are inclined to 'short-circuit' once they have started the chain that leads to reoffending. They feel they have failed and so give up or drown their sorrows in further fantasy and offending which temporarily makes them feel better. Alcohol can become part of the cycle, with drinking taking place before to give them courage and afterwards to drown their guilt and self-pity. In a sense they reoffend to push away the pain of reoffending. 'Short-circuiting' of various stages of the cycle can clearly be seen in incest cases. At first, there is caution and grooming of the family and victim so that the abuse is not discovered. As each subsequent event becomes easier, there is less planning, grooming, and targeting. An incest offender, for example, believes that his daughter secretly consents and goes from thought to abuse, missing out most of the cycle.

Linked cycles

It has been suggested (Eldridge 1992) that some offenders can operate both types of cycles (inhibited and continuous) at the same time. This is achieved because they respond to different victims and circumstances in different ways. Incest with one's own child, for example, might demand the inhibited cycle, while sexual activity with an older stepdaughter may be seen as acceptable by the offender, identifying only the continuous cycle steps. Sometimes these then merge.

The next step

So far we have encouraged the offender to examine his process of offending, the steps which lead him to commit sexually aggressive acts, and these are best described through the offence cycle mechanism. Interventions attempt to reduce the offender's desire to abuse, to restructure his thinking and to examine his lifestyle, which he may have used to give himself opportunities to offend. In order to be effective in helping the offender to develop strategies to prevent reoffending, programmes of intervention need to place equal emphasis on the therapeutic group work and maintenance (relapse prevention) components. In the early stages of intervention, the primary emphasis will be on 'treatment', but later, when the offender understands the need to prevent reoffending, the emphasis should shift to maintenance.

Relapse prevention

Lapse and relapse

In this section on relapse prevention the terms lapse and relapse are used. They require some explanation. 'Relapse' is easier to define – it happens when the process of self-management has failed and the offender commits another sexual offence. A 'lapse', however, can be any thought or behaviour which is part of the offence cycle, but which falls short of, and does not involve, committing any offence or inappropriate sexual act.

Thus thinking about offending, fantasising about inappropriate actions, planning, allowing himself to be in high-risk situations, deliberately choosing a route to drive past a school playground, and so on are all lapses. They are identifiable parts of the offender's process of offending which, if unchecked, would eventually lead to reoffending (i.e. relapse). If the offender recognises the 'lapse', acts upon it and shuts down on the offence cycle, he converts a potential fail situation into a successful experience of self-management.

The last element of the programme is the crucial stage of *relapse prevention*. There is a need to develop strategies to prevent lapses. The programme cannot and will not 'cure' sexual offenders. As with alcoholics, there is no cure, simply a system or routine for preventing relapse. Over time, the desire may diminish, and the knowledge about the harm created presents controlling factors. When an offender starts on a relapse cycle, he must have the ability to get off at any point. The programme aims to provide participants with the means to exert greater control over their behaviour, assisting them in identifying those internal and external factors which might place them at risk of reoffending and enabling them to take appropriate action (Pithers 1990).

> Relapse prevention (RP) was devised as a method of enhancing maintenance of change in substance abusers. As originally described by Marlatt and colleagues (Chaney, O'Leary and Marlatt 1978), RP was designed to strengthen self-control by providing clients with methods for identifying problematic situations, analyzing decisions that set up situations enabling resumption of substance abuse, and developing strategies to avoid, or cope more effectively with, these situations. Thus, as originally proposed, RP represented a method of enhancing self-management skills. Pithers, Marques, Gibat, and Marlatt (1983) modified the self-management model of RP for application with sex offenders. (p.346)

A range of factors influence whether a sexual offender will avoid committing another aggressive act. These factors, and how they interrelate, affect the probability of relapse. By entering a programme such as the STOP Programme, the offender makes a statement of intent that he does not want to reoffend. As he progresses through the programme, he gains in confidence and identifies ways in which he might survive on release. This self-assuredness increases until such time as he is faced with reality and choices, and finds himself in a high-risk situation (e.g. a child molester who goes for a walk in the park and comes across a group of children, or a rapist who is driving on business and comes across a female hitch-hiker). High-risk situations – which generate lapses – can be defined as circumstances which threaten an offender's sense of self-control and thus increase the risk of relapse (Pithers 1990). If the offender can deal with the situation in an effective way, his self-management abilities are reinforced and he justifiably feels more confident at handling the next situation. If he fails to cope with the high-risk situation (e.g. talks to some children in the park or purchases some pornographic magazines in the newsagents), he believes he is less capable of self-management, and there is a tendency to enter a downward spiral in which he just gives in when he faces the next high-risk situation. One note of caution is required. Some offenders believe that having survived their first high-risk situation they have effectively 'passed the test' and can handle all future high-risk situations. These men are setting themselves up for failure and relapse.

Although relapse prevention work is concerned with coping in high-risk situations, RP also examines the events that precede such situations. Many offenders make a series of 'apparently irrelevant decisions', each of which moves them one step nearer to a tempting high-risk situation. Deciding to go to the beach on a sunny day may seem unconnected to offending, but it is not in the case of the offender, a rapist of adult women, whose 'trigger' to offending is seeing scantily dressed women. Another example is the paedophile who visits a zoo which is popular with parties of schoolchildren. To the onlooker, the decision to spend a day at the zoo may seem irrelevant and unconnected with offending – to the offender it may not be so innocent and coincidental. The offender must recognise that each such decision contributing to lapse has to be dealt with, and he must accept responsibility for even the 'apparently irrelevant decision' if he is to succeed in controlling his desires. All too often, when an offender lapses, he begins to believe that this weakness is a personal failure. He then comes to expect further failures or lapses until he relapses and offends. While things are beginning to fail he may derive comfort from remembering some of the good feelings associated with his past offending sexual behaviours. Of course, this is selective: he forgets about being in prison or being labelled as a 'beast' by the media and remembers the satisfying feelings he gained from his sexual attack. For the more positively motivated offender, if he accepts that lapses may occur and that he should use those experiences to improve his self-management skills, and he is prepared to be honest and open with others about it, lapses can serve as useful learning experiences.

> Relapse prevention begins by dispelling misconceptions that the client may have regarding the outcome of treatment (i.e., that he will be 'cured') and describing more realistic goals. It continues with an assessment of the client's high-risk situations, which are the conditions under which relapse has occurred or is likely to occur in the future. The initial assessment also examines the client's coping skills, since situations can be considered high risk only to the extent that the person has difficulty coping with them. After high-risk situations have been identified, interventions are designed to train the client to minimize lapses and to keep lapses from evolving into a full-blown relapse. (Pithers 1990, pp.348–349)

Recognising the offence cycle, the situations of high risk, the fantasies, the targeting and the grooming, and trying to replace each step, each potential lapse, with an alternative, the offender attempts to work out for himself a strategy for an offence-free future. This process must, of necessity, be tailored to the individual needs of each offender. He will also need support on the outside, people to contact, if he feels he is entering the lapse phase of his cycle. He will need someone, perhaps a social worker, who will be able to work through his prevention strategy – his checklist – and discuss how realistic it is and whether it needs to be updated.

The Relapse Prevention Strategy (RPS) is based on two types of interventions:

1. PROCEDURES DESIGNED TO HELP THE OFFENDER AVOID LAPSES

- Identifying what leads up to offences (precursors) such as anxiety, distorted thoughts, masturbating to fantasies, and particular behaviours.

- Recognising high-risk situations such as residing with children, drinking alcohol, and driving aimlessly around streets.

- Establishing what are 'apparently irrelevant decisions'.

- Creating a list of anticipated high-risk situations and brainstorming to generate coping strategies. By repeatedly discussing these strategies, the offender begins to internalise new 'instinctive' responses.

The RPS helps offenders to realise that although strategies are created to assist in lapse minimisation, lapses may occur and these can effectively be used as learning experiences.

2. PROCEDURES INTENDED TO REDUCE THE POSSIBILITY OF A LAPSE TRIGGERING A RELAPSE

- Establishing escape strategies for when an offender finds himself unexpectedly in a high-risk situation.

- Understanding that short-term gratification is followed by negative effects (such as imprisonment) and that even if the offender has an urge, he can make a positive decision to resist.

- Aversion imagery may be used, e.g. encouraging the offender to believe he is being watched by a favourite relative.

- The offender should learn to use lapses as ways of improving his future coping skills.

- The offender should carry with him *relapse prevention cards*. These cards could contain self-help items such as:

- what a single lapse means and what it does not mean
- a caution that one lapse does not put him onto a declining path
- reassurance that he does not need to give in to deviant urges which will weaken with time
- instructions to examine what happened before the lapse (precursor) so as to improve future skills
- a list of coping responses which he feels he might need
- telephone numbers of social workers, friends or fellow group members who might give support.

The offender should also create his own *maintenance manual* to which he can constantly refer and which he can use as a refresher once the intervention programme work has been concluded. The manual can contain his reminder cards and emergency telephone numbers; the rationale behind his avoidance and escape strategies; and lists of some of his 'apparently irrelevant decisions', high-risk situations and identified precursors to offending. The manual should also contain some of his self-statements, promises and intentions, and monitoring forms which he will maintain as a log. The maintenance manual is a useful tool for an offender who leaves prison and can discuss its contents with a social worker who is providing supervision or voluntary support on release in the community. As time moves on the manual can be updated with new information and insights gained from looking at how lapses are managed. Where there is concern that an offender is beginning to lapse, the supervising officer will be able to use knowledge gleaned from the manual to work out which type of offence precursor is being acted out. Comparing that with the offence cycle table will enable the supervisor to position the precursor in the cycle – from the feelings and confused emotions at one end through to the act of offending itself at the other. The closer it is to the offence or relapse end of the spectrum, the more imminent the danger and the more urgent the need for intervention.

Perhaps it should have been said earlier that very few sex offences occur as a result of a spontaneous urge. As can be seen from the offence cycle work, which provides the rationale for the maintenance programme using RP, most are thought out, fantasised, planned and rehearsed, and sometimes the area and opportunities are checked out at first-hand. Often the victim is targeted and her movements known. Sometimes, in the case of children, grooming and familiarisation are developed over a lengthy period. I heard Professor Marshall give the following example of long-term planning. A paedophile, who wanted to create opportunities for his offending behaviour, became a medical student, studied for six years and then specialised in paediatrics in order to be able to get close to and work with, young children.

Lapse			⇒		⇒	Relapse
Thinking			*Planning*		*Doing*	
Feelings and emotions	Fantasies of sexual abuse	Pro-offending thinking or cognitive distortions	Trigger (excuse to move from fantasy to reality)	Fantasy rehearsal increases	Target identified, grooming (where appropriate) begun	Action Sexual Offending

That is why relapse prevention work is so important. Sex offending does not occur just by chance. It is planned and evolves, and what the therapist has to achieve with the offender is that he recognises the various stages when he begins to lapse and does something about it before he reoffends.

Offenders on the programme are expected to undertake *homework*, in preparation for some of the sessions. For example, as we saw earlier, they are expected to explore victim empathy through writing draft letters to their victims. Another important area for private study and thought is the requirement that they work out relapse prevention strategies through examining their offence cycles. Over a period of time, they will need to put together their maintenance manual along the lines indicated above.

New approaches to relapse prevention

Recently, Mann and Thornton in England, and Hudson and Ward in New Zealand (Mann *et al.* 1998), have been reviewing our practice and thinking about relapse prevention. RP has enabled sexual offenders to realise that lapses towards offending occur in small steps, that they can begin to self-manage and that through the offence cycle they can understand the process and can be optimistic about the future. However, often RP plans are more indicative of the therapist's ideas and suggestions, and sometimes they have vague and unrealistic strategies. Work is being undertaken to look at the pathways that people select and to develop a 'goal-oriented' approach. Goals are positive, desired states that people try to attain, and many of us structure our lives around the pursuit of goals. RP is primarily centred around 'avoidance'. Avoidance orientations create more psychological distress in individuals than positive 'approach' goals. If one focuses on failure and its avoidance, then there are inevitably many more ways to fail and it becomes easy to give up. Replacing this with positive success goals and self-learning is more likely to produce positive results. Mann *et al.* are considering ways of moving from traditional RP goals, often imposed on the offender, to 'approach' goals where the offenders set their own personally valued goals. This new review of RP will be a welcome addition to our thinking and practice in this area.

MAINTENANCE AND LOW-LEVEL INTERVENTIONS

As discussed in Chapter 3, there is a requirement to provide lower-level intervention programmes which can be used to good effect with the following types of offenders:

1. *Maintenance programme* – for 'graduates' of the higher-level core programme (STOP) as part of their maintenance routines.

2. *Low-risk programme* – for those offenders assessed as low risk and for short-term offenders.

3. *Pre-intervention programme* – for those higher-risk offenders who require support to become acclimatised to the STOP Programme.

Maintenance programme

Because of the difficulty of placing offenders on the level one (higher-level) programme at precisely the right point in their sentence (if such a point exists) many will remain in prison for some considerable time after having undertaken the core work. There is a need, therefore, to continue with the work, although not necessarily with the same degree of intensity. The focus of the maintenance group for these men is the continued development of their understanding of issues, the refinement of their relapse prevention plans and, where appropriate, their arrangements and hopes for release. Although the group would continue to be facilitated by a core worker member of staff, it could be run primarily as a self-help group. To some extent, the work of co-ordinating the group could be undertaken by a 'graduate' of the core programme, someone who displays the personal skills and confidence to do an appropriate job. Invited speakers could be arranged to address the maintenance groups and topics, for many of the sessions could be generated by the offenders. Of course, there is always the need to ensure that the work of the group proceeds in a satisfactory manner. Sexual offenders are capable of taking over the agenda for their own purposes, so therefore, an experienced member of staff should supervise the work of the group.

Low-risk programme

The initial assessment of risk provides the foundation and material for the subsequent work with sexual offenders and informs staff as to what type of intervention is required, or if intervention work is appropriate at that time. It may be that the offender is not yet ready for such a programme; alternative or parallel work (as described in Chapter 6) may be appropriate at that juncture. Among potential participants for the STOP Programme, there is a need to differentiate between those who have extensive needs and those who have lower needs. The high-level core STOP Programme was designed for offenders with extensive needs, and it was envisaged that those long-term offenders sentenced to four years or more (the entry criteria for Peterhead) would all have such needs. That has not always turned out to be the case, and it would be an unnecessary waste of resources for low needs offenders to undertake the extensive range of the core STOP Programme.

> Low needs offenders should be readily identifiable by interview as socially skilled, reasonably confident, and who display limited denial and minimization. These offenders should also be at low risk to reoffend as judged by the offence and social history. In any case, if errors of allocation do occur these are easily corrected by transfer into the other group. (Marshall 1995, pp.6–7)

The low-level group could meet once a week and focus on the following areas of work:

- eliminating denial and minimisation
- enhancing victim empathy
- increasing self-confidence
- identifying offence cycles
- preparing relapse prevention plans.

In addition, the demands placed on staff by this group are less than those required when working with the higher-level core STOP Programme group. The low-level group provides an ideal opportunity to give experienced staff a bit of a break, and prevent burn-out by moving them to the lower needs group when they indicate a need for a respite from the heavier load of the core group.

Pre-intervention programme

Candidates for this programme would be those high-risk offenders who are particularly apprehensive about group work or who have a long time to serve before imminent release. Again, this should be a self-help group in which the offender can remain until such time as he is ready for entry into the STOP Programme. The focus should be on easing the man into group work, encouraging him to participate, and challenging his pro-offending attitudes, beliefs and distortions.

LENGTH OF PROGRAMME

It should be apparent by now that where sexual offenders are concerned there can be no 'quick fix'. If the intervention programme is to be effective, it must be substantial in content and allow for all the issues to be explored. The experience at Peterhead has shown that what might have been thought to be a six-month programme has turned out to be much more. The assessment phase has lasted two to three months. The delivery of the intervention programme has taken up to one year, and staff required rostered leave (which was taken halfway though, between Phase 1 and Phase 2). In fact, in total, the programme has taken about 16 months to deliver and has been extended since its introduction.

> The speed at which one introduces key areas does not necessarily affect the length of a programme as individual group members progress at different speeds, but it does impinge upon the effectiveness of the programme. I would envisage that the programme should last for approximately a year with breaks at appropriate points. In most cases one is dealing with deeply entrenched beliefs, thinking patterns and habits. This is no quick fix: a sound programme needs to allow time for digestion and internalisation. There is a need for modules which challenge the thoughts, feelings and behaviours which support offending, and there is a need for time to develop realistic relapse prevention plans for an offence-free lifestyle. (Eldridge 1994, p.7)

From a manager's viewpoint, the policy ought always to be 'not to hurry the programme' and let the groups run at the speed dictated by the group members and their facilitators. The focus must always be on the *quality of output* and it should be understood that damage can be caused by offenders who have only a superficial involvement, having merely learned to 'talk the talk'. As one social worker put it:

> The first group that I was part of within Barlinnie ran for 10 sessions, and the most valuable thing I learned from that experience was that groups of this length do not even begin to scratch the surface. (Dempsey 1995, p.2)

The objective should not be to put through the maximum number of participants (an input measurement). Hilary Eldridge (1994) states it thus:

> At present Peterhead provides a quality programme for a realistic number of offenders. It has chosen this approach as opposed to a short programme for a larger number of offenders. In so doing it has established itself as a leader in the field. Care should be taken to ensure that this continues. A quality service run in line with current research by a well trained multidisciplinary team is likely to reduce offending rates. A service which over-emphasises throughput levels at the expense of quality may actually increase risk by teaching sex offenders simply what to say to sound as if they've received treatment! (Eldridge 1994, p.12)

Summary of key points

- The intervention programmes should be substantial enough to allow sufficient time for sexual offenders to be able to internalise the values, norms and information that they have talked about and to gradually display changes in attitude and response. They will need to demonstrate they have taken responsibility for their actions, show that they can empathise with the victim, understand the process of their offence cycle and prepare appropriate relapse prevention plans. These activities take time and genuine involvement if they are to have any chance of providing the offender with an alternative strategy on release.

CURRENT STOP GROUPS AT PETERHEAD PRISON

There are currently four *core* groups operating simultaneously at Peterhead and, at the time of writing, groups 17 and 18 have commenced. The first two were each initially run by two prison staff and one social worker, and then the social workers moved to the third and fourth groups, beginning with a higher social worker input, which gradually changed to prison staff involvement, while developing the training of these newer staff and supporting the work of the first two groups. After that, groups were run by prison staff alone or with social work involvement. In addition, the maintenance groups were begun in another hall of the prison, using further newly developed facilities. The ultimate goal is to have at least one-third of the population actively involved in core offence-specific work, with a similar number having already undertaken the core programme, and those who do not require the more intensive work also on maintenance programmes. The 'graduates' would act as ambassadors for the programme, encouraging those arriving in the prison to join in the programme.

These groups are now achieving a very high standard, in which prisoners are breaking down their barriers of denial, challenging opinions and values, and are prepared to reveal their innermost feelings and most secret memories to other members of the group. These groups are making tremendous progress – but they also make great demands on the skills and emotional stamina of the staff involved.

CHAPTER 6

Complementary
and Supporting Programmes

OTHER COMPLEMENTARY WORK

To complement the work of the offence-specific groups, other groups and classes can be established. These help in a number of ways. They create the right sort of milieu in the prison (one which is accepting of counselling and intervention work); they enable the offender to begin to look at his own attitudes and values; they begin to 'condition' him into the group and discursive environment; and they provide additional skills to improve communication, expression and reasoning. Without the offender being able to operate in the desired environment, no work could be successful. He has to feel that he can cope and is supported and valued as an individual. Below are listed some of the groups and classes which should be available to offenders. All of the suggested groups were available at Peterhead Prison in 1995.

Access to all groups is voluntary and the prisoner will have usually focused on one particular group as part of the dialogue he has with his personal officer during discussions and reviews of his sentence plan. The offender might also learn of the groups from other prisoners, education staff, residential officers or from some of the staff who run the groups and who have identified the offender as being able to benefit from a particular group.

Cognitive reasoning

This programme is designed to focus on the thinking patterns which appear to direct offenders towards reoffending. According to this model, offenders lack a range of cognitive skills: the ability to consider the perspective of others or indeed to question their own; the skills necessary to approach interpersonal difficulties in a positive, problem-solving manner; and the ability to think through from cause to effect and think before acting. The approach aims to equip offenders with the skills necessary to avoid making pro-offending choices. While this is a suitable programme to be offered to offenders as a preparation for engaging in offence-specific work, it can also be run successfully as a stand-alone programme. Specific areas addressed include:

- problem solving
- creative thinking
- social skills development
- negotiation skills
- values enhancement
- critical reasoning.

Management of emotions also plays a prominent part throughout and becomes specifically featured in the second half of the programme, when the maintenance and examination of an 'anger diary' requires participants to acknowledge the existence of emotions and examine the possibility that they might influence or control them. At Peterhead, as in other prisons within the SPS, these groups are led by specially trained prison officers. This cognitive–behavioural group work course is one of the SPS's accredited programmes and lasts for 50 hours.

Sentence planning, the personal officer and counselling

The Scottish Prison Service, as a whole, has developed a sentence planning programme which is undertaken by the prisoner with his personal officer.

> Central to our strategy for encouraging amongst long term prisoners a sense of personal responsibility for their own circumstances, are our proposals on sentence planning… *Developing the role of the prison officer as the facilitator:* Although we intend to encourage the prisoner to see himself as responsible it is self-evident that he may require some help in establishing the proper criteria for sound decision-taking. The role of the prison officer is already being enhanced in this way through existing training programmes and through the Personal Officer Schemes … We believe that their understanding and knowledge will be of considerable value in the role of facilitator to assist inmates review their situation … At regular intervals in his sentence, the prisoner will be invited to review his sentence plan. As part of the review process, the prisoner's progress will be monitored on a regular basis. A new feature will be the introduction of a system of open reporting, whereby the prisoner and officer meet regularly to discuss progress. (SPS 1990, pp.30–33)

As part of that process, discussions and reviews are held about the plan. A central feature of sentence planning is the self-awareness package, which has eight personal development modules for the prisoner to tackle if he so wishes. The first is a general introductory module which looks at the rationale for the programme and some of the techniques used. It is worth reproducing below some of the introductory comments:

INTRODUCTION In a sense everything that happens, good or bad, planned or unplanned, affects our personal development. Every day we make decisions and choices which influence our own lives and the lives of others. Often, important matters are ignored while trivial decisions take up all our time and energy. Sometimes the decisions we make prove to be the right ones … while others prove to be wrong. This file has been designed to help you recognise how to make better decisions and how these effect your personal development. The ultimate goal is that you know enough about yourself and what is important to you to shape your own future.

WHAT IS PERSONAL DEVELOPMENT? Some people find it useful to think of personal development in the same way as physical development. This involves recognising what you want to change and what effort, time and commitment will be involved in making change happen. It is essential to recognise your own strengths and weaknesses and who else can help you in making the change. (SPS 1992)

The sentence planning development files consist of the following chapters:

Introduction

1. Getting Started

2. Education and Work

   • my education

   • my employment

3. Me, the Law and Prison

   • the police

   • the court

   • coping with prison

   • prison officers

4. Spare Time

   • my leisure time

   • me and money

   • keeping fit and healthy

   • my friends

5. Pleasure or Problem?

   • alcohol

   • gambling

   • drugs

6. Knowing Me Better
- risk taking and decision making
- violence

7. Relationships
- my partner
- my children
- my parents
- my other family members
- other people.

The Sentence Planning Scheme and work by prisoners on examining these lifestyle issues are central to the whole process of the individual beginning to come to terms with who he is and what he needs to do to begin the process of change. Sentence planning, the prisoner's personal officer and the counselling work which is undertaken is central to, and supportive of, the Sex Offender Intervention Programme. Indeed, prisoners who sign up for the STOP Programme agree to a contract which includes participation in the Sentence Planning Scheme. This work is undertaken by prison officers in all SPS prisons accommodating long-term prisoners.

Aggression in the family/anger management

This programme is available for those who feel that anger and its management is an area of concern in their lives, or who are judged by staff to need the programme. It is particularly useful for those who have committed violent offences or abusive violence through anger outbursts, including those offenders convicted of 'baby battering' and similar offences. The group examines why men use violence and accept it as a normal part of their lives. They must come to recognise when violence is about to happen and learn how to put in place avoiding mechanisms. The processes and thinking distortions are similar to those of sexual offending. The thinking patterns of these offenders allow them to use abusive behaviour and see it as acceptable. They *justify* their actions: 'If she hadn't goaded me, I wouldn't have battered her.' They also experience low self-esteem, and the use of violence is related to their own needs. They believe it is their right to control the victim through violence and its threat. Like the sexual offence cycle, the cycle of violence has a pattern, with a build-up of tension, violent acts, remorse and the promise that 'it won't happen again', followed, eventually, by a repeat. Gradually, the 'honeymoon' periods between abuse become shorter until, occasionally, the whole process is short-circuited by a repetition of violence. While, from early on, sexual offenders in our STOP Programme recognise the unacceptability of abusing children, men who have had abusive relationships with women often believe it acceptable to 'batter their wife' and do not identify it as a problem. The group allows participants to develop personal strategies to deal effectively with problem solving and confrontation. The group is led by social workers.

SUPPORTING PROGRAMMES
Life and social skills

The aim of this group is to equip participants to deal more effectively with the difficulties of everyday living. Equally, they are designed to develop and reinforce a range of skills and strategies to assist men in leading a more constructive life upon release from prison. There is no set programme and group discussions can cover a variety of topics, such as: coping on your own, how to set up a flat, avoiding conflict situations, budgeting, how to use leisure time in a positive way, health education matters, diets, interviewing and job seeking skills, and so on. This group is run by the education unit, has visiting speakers, and can be supplemented with remedial and practical training as required.

Women, men and society

This adopts a social science approach to gender issues and critically examines the traditional roles of women and men in society. Attitudes and issues of power are also examined. It is aimed at all who recognise they have difficulties in the area of male/female interaction and their roles in society. It is of particular relevance to sexual offenders who have exercised distorted thinking and whose belief systems do not generally support equal gender status. The programme allows participants to examine their own values and beliefs and how these relate to other members of society. They also look at the distortions and prejudices which underpin them and acknowledge the possibility of change. The format is group based, and members are expected to contribute to the work at hand and to challenge others from their own experience. Groups are led by a teacher and a prison officer. Specific areas for discussion in the *women, men and society* group include:

- domestic violence
- issues relating to gender
- issues relating to race, colour and class
- disability and inequality within society
- relationships and breakdowns, marriage and divorce
- differing sexual orientations
- role models.

Substance abuse groups

The aim of the substance abuse groups is not necessarily to produce abstinence, but rather to develop control over behaviour when using alcohol/drugs, etc. Assistance is provided to participants to develop strategies that will link in to individual relapse prevention plans.

1. Alcohol awareness

This programme is designed for all who use or abuse alcohol or who wish to gain knowledge of the topic. Through the use of discussion groups, questionnaires, quizzes and role-play, participants are helped to gain increased awareness of the part alcohol has played in their lives. The programme aims to address the myths and misconceptions which surround alcohol, its role in society, and how it affects relationships and life in general. Participants are also given a basic knowledge of the health issues involved. In adopting an 'educative' or awareness basis, there is no intent to dictate to individuals the levels of usage they should adopt. Rather, by presenting the facts, it allows for responsible assessment of personal need for abstinence or moderation and begins the process of developing a strategy to achieve this. This group is led by a prison officer.

2. Drug awareness

This programme is designed for all who have used or abused drugs or other substances such as solvents. It gets participants to examine the role of substance abuse in their lives and identify ways in which change might be achieved. The group discussions also provide an opportunity to demystify the drug culture and provide sound knowledge of the social, health and personal issues. This group is led by a prison officer and an external drugs counsellor.

Smoking cessation

This class is designed to advise and educate those who smoke of the dangers and health implications of doing so, and to help and support them whilst they try to give up the habit. Support is also provided in the form of nicotine patches where required. This class is led by a prison officer and a prison practitioner nurse.

Dance and drama

This class is provided to improve expression, communication skills and confidence in participants. It has been particularly valuable for sexual offenders contemplating group work, since it helps prisoners to express themselves and improves their self-esteem and confidence in front of others. This class is led by a teacher.

Pre-release course

Although the topics are of a wide and general nature, relating to issues being faced on release, this course is particularly focused on the problems of sexual offenders. Modules include:

- Employment – workshop format for full week; range of inputs include form filling, interviews, disclosure of convictions and CVs.

- Benefits and entitlements – two-day workshop led by the Citizens' Advice Bureau; also includes elements on budgeting and living costs.

- Returning to the community – information and discussion; looking at how society may view them.

- Drugs, HIV and safe sex – factual information, health education and dispelling myths.

- Alcohol awareness – information about the effects of abuse, problems and health education.

Summary of key points

- Complementary and supporting programmes are essential in that they create an environment in which groups and counselling can function and provide a wide range of additional learning experiences which enhance the value and delivery of the STOP Programme.

CHAPTER 7

Monitoring and Evaluation[1]

MONITORING

Regular process review meetings focusing on each participant should take place. The meetings should be attended by key people, including the prisoner's personal officer, who might have the opportunity to witness attitudes and behaviour outside the group. It would also be helpful if a regular videotaped monitoring system was put in place in which individual offenders could make two inputs every, say, eight to ten weeks:

1. brief tapes addressing their offences, the effects and who is to blame

2. brief *breaking the cycle* videotapes identifying their cycles of offending and how to break them.

These could be available for discussion in the group if so desired, and also useful as a 'record' of how attitudes have changed, which might be of use for parole board consideration.

Steering (or Review) Group

This group should usually comprise the programme manager (prison management), the psychologist, the head of social work and the senior prison officer who has line management responsibility for, or gives support to, the core workers. It can also include, on a rotational basis, a core worker. The work of all the groups should be monitored and regularly reviewed by the Steering Group. It should supervise and direct the ongoing operation and development of the programme. The Steering Group should meet monthly, ensure proper monitoring of the programme, and develop and expand the programme as needed. The group should also provide the programme with a sense of unity and continuity. The

---

1   This book was written before announcements of the intention to introduce a central prisoner programme accreditation system in Scotland. Many of the issues concerning programme standards and internal integrity are being addressed by the Prisoner Programme Accreditation Panel, formed in 1998.

Steering Group should also be responsible for discussing any policy issues with senior prison management.

Standards, accreditation and quality

In adopting the delivery of preferred programmes as part of its core business, the Scottish Prison Service also considered the need for standards in its programmes, the examination of the integrity of work undertaken, and the accreditation of the whole programme so as to ensure quality of output. This approach was first signalled in the government White Paper, *Crime and Punishment* (1996), which stated (at paragraph 10.10):

> The Government will expect each prison to match more closely its counselling, education and training opportunities with the specific needs of its prisoner population to help reduce offending and minimise the number of potential victims of crime. We expect programmes to be effective. That means monitoring and evaluation, assessing attitude change and changes in behaviour. The Scottish Prison Service is planning work on programme accreditation and systematic assessment of the impact and effectiveness of prisoner programmes. (Secretary of State for Scotland 1996, p.44)

This development was further endorsed by the Scottish Prisons Minister during the debate on the Crime and Punishment (Scotland) Bill:

> The Scottish prison service is planning work on programme accreditation so that account can be taken of best practice and the introduction of a means of quality control. (House of Commons Official Report, Parliamentary Debates 1996a, col. 131)

The system of accreditation and monitoring, which is in the process of being developed, should provide the SPS with a robust framework to ensure the existence of high quality programmes. The accreditation process will require a group of experts and peers to provide a review of practice and establish an agreed set of standards and a system of audit. However, a word of caution is necessary. Programmes which deal with people and promote challenges and changes to belief systems can not be over-prescribed. They deal with interactive processes, relationships and feelings. If it is necessary to spend twice as much time on one module because the group is taking longer to come to terms with the issues, then so be it. The accreditation must be based on the standards of input, the integrity of the parts, the manner of delivery and the 'out-of-group' staff processes. It must never be dependent on the length of time required to deliver particular modules or sessions. It is the sequencing, rather than time taken, which is important.

EVALUATION

Evaluations can provide assessments on:

1. how well the programme is operating

2. the consistency of the programme in delivering to different groups

3. how others such as prison staff, Parole Board members, community-based social workers and offenders feel about the programme

4. the degree to which the programme meets its objectives: these include overcoming denial, accepting responsibility, developing victim empathy, understanding the offence cycle, developing sound relapse prevention plans, and other factors

5. reductions in reoffending rates on release.

Most of the first three assessments can be readily achieved by an in-house evaluation by specialist staff in co-operation with core workers. The fourth objective can also be achieved by psychologists and social workers, but a satisfactory assessment package that can be administered prior to entry to the programme and on completion will be needed.

As for the 'ultimate test', estimating the effects of the STOP or any intervention programme by measuring the rates of reoffending, this cannot be done with any degree of credibility until at least 100 offenders have satisfactorily completed the programme and have been released for a significant period of time, say five years. Before such numbers are reached, the base rates are too low to be statistically significant and, therefore, there is the likelihood of reaching false conclusions.

One of the problems of evaluating success rates, as recognised by Marshall and Barbaree (1990), is finding a matched control group who have not undertaken the programme.

> The ideal comparison group would be patients who were equally eager to enter treatment but who were refused entry on the basis of random allocation to an untreated control group. Such a control group would have to be matched with treated subjects on those demographic, personal, and offense history variables demonstrated or thought to be related to subsequent reoffending. For all manner of practical and ethical reasons, such a control group has not (and should not) be provided. Some compromise is necessary. (p.371)

The 'graduates' of the programme, if followed over a five-year period, would provide a success rate which could be compared with general (though not equally matched) rates for reoffending where known. If a programme deals with a large number of long-sentence offenders, it might be difficult to find a similar group to use as controls. There is then the added dimension of comparing a range of sexual offender offence-specific programmes to see which are most effective. Again, variations in clientele will affect results, depending on whether incest or non-familial paedophiles participate, or whether there are a larger number of rapists or exhibitionists. In general, each type of offender is known to have different rates of relapse and to be affected to differing degrees by different types of intervention programmes.

> Perhaps the most pressing problem facing clinicians in this field is the need to develop indices of treatment effectiveness. As a first step in this process, future treatment evaluations need to go beyond a simple appraisal of outcome, by providing information on changes produced by treatment on the detailed features of sexual preferences, social competence, and cognitive distortions. This information may allow predictions to be made about the likelihood of recidivism in individual cases after treatment. In addition, such data should assist in identifying why it is that different programs fail with particular types of sex offenders. (Marshall and Barbaree 1990, p.382)

Although it is far too soon to evaluate the success of the STOP Programme and, as we have seen, comparative studies are difficult to do, some early assessment by Jack and Mair (1993), of the psychology unit of the actual shift in offender attitudes using standard tests (Hogue 1992), seems to indicate that a good start has been made. It is to be hoped this will eventually translate into reduced offending. Additionally, McIvor *et al.* (1997) examined how the programme was implemented, its impact on prisoners, the attitudes of staff and prisoners to the programme and the effect such attitudes had. They found that officers involved in STOP perceived it in a very positive light, as it made their job more interesting, increased job satisfaction, provided an opportunity to learn and utilise new skills and increased their understanding of offending behaviour. Most of the officers not directly involved in the programme also identified personal benefit including greater insight into sexual offending and increased job satisfaction arising from improved relationships. Its introduction also was felt by many prisoners to have had a positive impact on the prison in general, evidenced through a change in staff attitudes, enabling them to understand and work more effectively with prisoners. The majority of prisoners who participated in the STOP programme found it to be an extremely painful experience but thought the programme had made a significant impact on their understanding of their offending and other problem areas in their behaviour.

Indications are already emerging about the efficacy of the SOTP Programme (England and Wales). The research findings (Beech *et al.* 1998) show that the programme has been successful in reducing pro-offending attitudes and reducing the level of denial of the impact that sexual abuse has upon victims. In the sample 63 per cent were judged to have shown a treatment effect, i.e. a significant change in all or some of the main areas targeted. It was also shown that the longer duration programmes had greater impact for the highly deviant offenders. Such research information is good news. It is also vital to have good follow-up data.

On the other hand, those of us working with sexual offenders are only too aware that there will be failures. By providing programmes, we can do much to provide mechanisms that will support a reduction in reoffending. But it is up to the offender, once released, as to what he does. However hard the staff try, they should never forget that it is the offender, and not the staff, who is responsible for further offending. The successes will be those prisoners who go out and do not offend.

The efficacy of SPS sex offender intervention programmes still needs to be evaluated. Given the caveats expressed by Marshall and Barbaree above, two types of such work still need to be undertaken.

1. Evaluation of the various stages of the process: a baseline assessment taken at the start of the induction/assessment process, and assessments made at significant points during the group programme phases, on completion and, where applicable, during maintenance work. These evaluations would provide the information for items 1 to 4 in the list on p.116. However, monitoring such work should not become an end in itself, with staff focused on achieving scores rather than internalised changes within the offender.

2. Ongoing research within the criminal justice system should be established to maintain statistics on sexual offenders and their reconviction rates. Comparisons should be made between offenders who have engaged in such programmes and matched control groups of those who have not been prepared to address their offending behaviour. It may not be possible to achieve such matching and consequently the data may be relatively unsophisticated, as indicated in the comments above. Nonetheless, some data is desirable.

Summary of key points

- A process of evaluation is necessary to assess attitude change at significant points during the process (e.g. induction/assessment, after four and eight months of the programme, at the completion of programme and after, say, six months or a year on a prison-based maintenance programme.

- In the longer term, statistics should be kept on all sexual offenders released from prisons and, if possible, their reconviction rates determined against a control group who have not engaged in an intervention programme.

CHAPTER 8

Staff Training and Support

THE NEED FOR TRAINING AND SUPPORT OF STAFF

Training of staff and providing effective support at all levels is crucial if the delivery of an offence-specific programme is to have any meaningful chance of success. For the core workers the training can be a lengthy process, the initial phase alone taking a number of months and being achieved through a variety of training experiences.

Staff also have to understand that they are entering an area which will present them with difficulties. The work they do will inevitably lead them to examine their own attitudes and beliefs in a variety of areas. They will question their own sexuality and motives. It will also be impossible for them to 'leave behind' their work on leaving the establishment. The images that are conveyed by offenders will remain with them, often affecting the way they view their partners and children, and sometimes impacting upon them to make them draw back from quite normal situations such as bathing their children or sitting the kids on their laps for fear of some resonance with what has been said in the group. It is important that staff understand these pressures, understand how they may impact upon them, and are able to network with other staff and get appropriate support when necessary.

In addition, the staff selected have to be personally resilient. They will need strong 'stomachs' when listening to some of the details of offending behaviours. Issues will arise which may question the very basis of their own beliefs and behaviours. Things may be said that start to stir in the staff events shut out in their own minds through time. They have to be prepared for such eventualities. Sexual offenders who deny are great manipulators of others. They will try to turn things around, score points, and prove that other people are wrong and confused, simply to turn the spotlight away from themselves and their own unwillingness to accept responsibility for their offending behaviour. And, as I have seen it happen more than once, some offenders will try to humiliate and even ruin staff. They might write anonymous letters to outside agencies and the media, suggesting that the staff themselves have been involved in abuse and offending. These *campaigns* were undertaken by offenders who did not want to engage in looking at their own offending and were therefore willing to do anything to try to destroy the whole process, and the staff with it. Luckily, these allegations (for example, of a social worker having been involved in the running of a children's home where abuse by staff occurred and where the social worker was one of those committing the abuse) were easily proved to be pure fiction. But staff have to be aware that this sort of *attack* can occur, and management at all levels (whether on a confidential basis or otherwise) have to give total support.

It is worth noting that in some ways social workers or probation staff, who are usually seen by prisoners as the more caring type of individuals, are particularly disliked and become targets of sexual offenders' malevolence, especially those convicted of offences against children. That is because these staff not only have involvement with offence-specific work inside the prison, but are involved in writing reports on prisoners which may affect their future position with their families, since they also have duties in relation to child protection legislation and access to children on the outside. Some offenders hold social work staff directly responsible for questions of access and blame them for the difficulties created with their families. Of course, in reality this should be expected, since such offenders who deny responsibility for their own actions can only turn to others and blame them for the consequences.

As we have seen, both the training and support of staff is vital. It can be given in a number of ways and to a number of differing groups of staff:

Training
1. Generalised awareness training for *all staff* so that the programme is supported, the staff who are involved in its delivery are not seen as 'different' and staff do not collude with sexual offenders.
2. Specialised training for *core staff.*
3. Generalised training for those identified as part of the *pool of potential core staff.*
4. There may also be a separate issue (for the future) of attempting to gain accreditation for the work of the core staff.

Support
1. Support mechanisms for those delivering the core offence-specific programmes.
2. Networking with other specialists and therapists.
3. Advice/support for management about issues surrounding the delivery of such programmes.
4. Management support and systems for delivery of programmes and support of core staff.

Summary of key points

- Training and support of staff at all levels is crucial for the viability of the programme.

FORMS OF TRAINING

Generalised training for all staff

It is necessary that all staff are given awareness training to understand the process and issues faced by staff and prisoners engaging in offence-specific work with sexual offenders. This examines their attitudes, values and beliefs, explores the roles of men and women in society, looks at the effects of sexual offending on victims, gives a brief outline of offenders' distorted thinking and considers the effect of pornography. In addition, all staff are made aware of the nature and difficulties of such work and reminded of the need to support staff and prisoners who are participating in the programme. Other issues which are discussed include the need to create a working environment in which 'put-downs' are not tolerated but which is also non-collusive; the boundaries between what goes on in group sessions and what can take place in informal discussions; the difference in roles between the residential officer and the core worker; and the need to maintain good liaison between the group workers and personal officers.

At Peterhead, at the time of writing, about 85 per cent to 90 per cent of all staff, including industrial, works, and administrative staff, have received such training. An input is also given at the end of the specialised sentence planning course, for all personal officers, relating the programme to the Sentence Planning Scheme. The normal three-day course, addressing attitudes, values and beliefs, has been delivered by a variety (and combination) of in-house and guest speakers and is organised by the Staff Training Unit. These generalised courses seek to raise the consciousnesses of all staff, including managers, who provide the context within which the offence-specific groups run, and harness their support for those directly involved in group work. These courses also contribute to the general ethos of the establishment, the group and counselling work and the equal opportunities policy of the prison service. Once trained and experienced, the 'core' staff also contribute to the general training of other staff.

An important message to emphasise is the priority attached by all staff, from senior management down, to the success of the programme. This will not be achieved if prisoners are prevented by other staff colleagues from attending the group work sessions, for example, by being kept back in a workshop to finish an important contract. Therefore, despite there being a high level of industrial activity in the workshops, and prisoners being required to attend education courses, turn up for interviews, or participate in physical education, and so on, the core STOP Programme must take precedence.

Specialised training for 'core' staff

As an example of the type of training that can be provided for staff working with sexual offenders, the following provides an outline of the range of training afforded to the core staff at Peterhead. In addition to the generalised training above, the first core workers were all involved in extensive training over a two-year period. They each spent two weeks on social work placements in the community, and undertook a three-day group dynamics course. They participated in a one-week course on the interviewing and assessment of sex offenders, and attended the Criminal Personality and Profiling course at Dundee University for one week. They have attended the National Organisation for the Treatment of Abusers (NOTA, the UK professional organisation which supports practitioners and promotes research and development work with sexual offenders) annual conferences, and attended other NOTA conferences, meetings and workshops.[1] They have received additional training from the psychologist in group dynamics and group work techniques to deal with offence-specific material. They attended a seminar on pornography from a member of the police obscene publications branch, which was considered to be of particular value, and have received some specialised training on paedophiles from a recognised authority.

In addition, all core workers received 'on the job' training and live supervision while engaged in the delivery of the programme for four days per month during 1993 from our visiting consultant/trainer (Hilary Eldridge, Director of Faithfull Foundation – formerly Gracewell Clinic). This was achieved using a competency-based curriculum which focused on both process and content. Training developed both use of personal style and knowledge of sex offending behaviour patterns. Professor Marshall provided additional training during his one month consultancy visit to Peterhead. The core staff were also given the opportunity to attend the Gracewell Clinic for one week and participate in the work of the groups. Two of our staff (one core worker and one social worker) were invited to work with Professor Marshall in Canada, and spent three weeks with him during May 1994. The training is ongoing and further training will be provided to develop a greater appreciation of the experiences and problems faced by victims.

Developing the skills and enlarging the numbers of core workers continues. The process is undertaken in five ways:

---

[1]   A parallel organisation, the Association for the Treatment of Sexual Abuse (ATSA), developed in the USA, NOTA and ATSA have established close links.

1. by specific training units

2. by a process of osmosis

3. through 'on the job' training and support

4. through individual reading and study

5. by developing networking with others involved in the delivery of such programmes.

1. Training programme for core staff

A basic training programme was devised by Allan Boath and John Duncan, STOP trainers, and presented on a modular basis to those staff identified for participation in sex offender group work. In particular, it gives in-depth focus to interviewing and group-working techniques. The programme content is as follows:

- *Women, Men and Society:* a societal framework against which workers can examine their own attitudes and beliefs.

- *Addressing Attitudes, Values and Beliefs:* using participatory exercises of the type used in the STOP Programme so that workers can develop issues from the first module and become familiar with their own value systems and some of the processes used in STOP groups.

- *Sex Offender Issues:* exploring the basic issues of sexual offenders and offending – where they come from; thinking processes; myths; theories of offending; offending cycles; patterns of behaviour, etc. – and examining (by making and testing) assumptions about offending.

- *Interviewing Techniques (1):* basic grounding in the techniques employed during the interview; the differences between conversations and interviews; how to structure, plan and control the interview; open and closed questioning; and styles of question.

- *Group-Working (1):* purpose of group work, theoretical models and practice issues; fundamental skills and techniques; basic exercises; use of language, body language and non-verbal communication.

- *Victim Awareness:* external trainer from organisation involved with victims gives a broad outline of how abuse effects victims and how this relates to the STOP Programme; discussions on empathy.

- *Group-Working (2):* including advanced group practices.

- *Giving and Receiving Feedback:* techniques to make the process constructive rather than destructive; allows workers themselves to become comfortable with criticism and learn from the observations of others.

- *Interviewing Techniques (2):* advanced techniques, dos and don'ts and controlling the interview – particularly focused on working with sex offenders to create productive, non-collusive interviews.

- *STOP Programme Content:* overview of Phases 1 and 2; the underlying philosophy of the programme and its aims; the availability and use for prisoners of complementary and supporting programmes; maintenance programmes and cognitive reasoning processes.

- *Team Building Exercises:* external day's training on team building and an opportunity for new members to gel with the current team – important for future relationships, networking and support.

- *Project Work:* during the training process, including two specific presentations, a single piece of research with a 15-minute presentation, and a paired project with a 30-minute presentation.

- *Review:* issues raised by participants, recap of training issues, problem identification and solution.

2. The process of osmosis

Trainee 'core' workers become involved by sitting in groups as observers and watch the processes working. They then have an opportunity to discuss these with core staff later. Much of the work of staff happens outside the group: for example, reading records of prisoners, watching video recordings of some sessions, discussing what occurred in the group and planning for future groups. The trainees shadow core staff, sit in on meetings and become involved in discussions.

3. 'On the job' training and support

This is a critically important aspect of the development of staff. At times, a consultant trainer is available to watch the STOP groups and provide advice, suggestions and training to staff. On a more consistent basis, support and guidance is provided from three sources: first, by line management, since an experienced supervisory officer (well versed in this type of work, group processes and cognitive restructuring techniques) has line responsibility for their work and provides supervision and support on an ongoing basis; second, by the head of the social work unit, who has expertise in this subject and is also involved as one of the core workers; and third, by the specialist psychologist.

4. Individual reading and study

Staff are encouraged to develop their own knowledge base, skills and competencies. The establishment's Staff Training Library has been gathering materials, and core staff are welcome to use them. Many staff display an impressive knowledge of the subject gained from reading and discussions, and it is known that they spend a considerable amount of their own time broadening their understanding of the subject.

Networking and conferences

Staff benefit considerably from the opportunity to discuss and network with other practitioners, not simply about the work but also about how they feel. It is important that they look after themselves and do not burn-out, and having the opportunity to share problems and issues with others at meetings, workshops and conferences should not be missed or its value underestimated. Also, conferences, seminars and the like provide unique opportunities for staff to learn about the work of others, discuss issues with practitioners and gain knowledge in the subject. That is why NOTA (National Organisation for the Treatment of Abusers – UK) and ATSA (Association for the Treatment of Sexual Abusers – North America) are so important. While there are a great many opportunities, for example, for doctors, psychologists and prison administrators to meet, discuss issues and network, the same cannot be said for those working with sexual offenders. One cannot just pop round the corner and chat to the local group. At Peterhead we encourage (and try to facilitate) staff to become members of NOTA and attend seminars and conferences. In the words of Marshall (1994), 'Attending conferences by people working in this field is not a luxury but an essential component to their development' (p.5).

Generalised training for those identified as part of the pool of potential core staff

With all such programmes, staff who are not involved become interested in the work and express a willingness to become involved. At Peterhead, a number of staff indicated that they too would like to be given the opportunity of delivering intervention programmes. They applied to be considered and were interviewed to assess potential, aptitude and suitability. These staff, in addition to receiving the generalised awareness training given to all staff, have received offence-specific sessions from a number of our visiting guest speakers on a number of occasions. They have also undertaken training in group dynamics, and have to comprehend the manipulative tactics of sexual offenders. They are expected to participate in exercises looking at interviewing and discussions about risk assessment. Should these staff show a continuing interest in the work, feel comfortable with it and display the appropriate aptitudes and motivation, they can then be selected for core training.

During this process, such staff have been able to use their involvement in training as a period during which they can decide to opt out if they wish. This type of work is not suited to all staff, and some find the issues involved disturbing. Yet others may, themselves, have been the victims of some type of inappropriate behaviour, and the discussions and insights gained open up for them, perhaps for the first time, very difficult areas. Finally, there may be a few staff who find the challenges to their own value systems and beliefs too close for comfort.

Gaining personal accreditation for the work of core staff

The core staff in any such offence-specific setting have undertaken a substantial amount of training and continue to develop their skills as they deliver the programme. In Peterhead, for example, according to external 'experts', the core workers have already reached a very high standard. Some staff, particularly specialists, already hold professional qualifications. An issue for the future might be consideration of whether it would be possible to gain some professional accreditation or certification for staff (particularly prison officers) who work in this area. Staff are already members of NOTA and some have participated in, or led, workshops, displaying good levels of competence and practical experience among other such (qualified) workers. Indeed, in a recent publication on sexual offender programme work in the prison service in England and Wales, Mann and Thornton (1998) refer to staff as lay therapists or 'paraprofessionals'. It may be appropriate to consider some type of professional accreditation.

SUPPORT MECHANISMS

Support mechanisms for those delivering the core offence-specific programmes

Support for those staff delivering the programmes is crucial if the programmes are to be sustained and developed. The nature of the work creates tensions and stresses, and demands a huge amount of emotional stamina. Without a range of support mechanisms in place, delivery of a meaningful programme would be impossible.

At Peterhead, support has been given in a number of ways:

1. *Debriefing* after group meetings. The team gets together for debriefing sessions. Core staff have their own office accommodation where they keep records and where they meet together to discuss the progress being made and support issues. The staff are free to discuss any issues, and problems or concerns can be discussed in a private arena. The staff also get together at other times to plan and review the work, and they function very much as a supportive team.

2. *Management support* through consistent commitment and public statements as to the necessity of the programme as part of the prison's core business. Line management support and supervision is provided by the group

manager, who has also helped by acting as a facilitator within the hall setting. First line management and support is provided by the supervisory officer (group work support/welfare).

3. *'Emotional support'* is also provided by the supervisory officer (group work support) who has regular contact and discussions. There should be regular meetings between core workers, programme manager and co-ordinator every four to six weeks for general discussion and looking at feelings and needs. Support by members of the social work team is provided as and when required – there should be an open-door policy for core workers. More professional support can also be provided by the prison's psychologist, who is a member of the Steering Group.

4. *'On the job' training and supervision support.* Some description of this has already been given above. Core workers have worked with 'experts' for parts of the programme. During the first year, a consultant was available for four days a month to review how staff worked, and was present during sessions. This provided support and training. The consultant now visits on an infrequent basis. Additional support is provided by the head of the Social Work Unit, who attends therapy groups from time to time. W.L. Marshall, who has visited Peterhead on a number of occasions as a visiting consultant, has also provided support and training at those times. It is worth noting that sexual offenders are highly manipulative and regular supervision is helpful in preventing the development of collusive relationships in groups. Finally, some training for staff trainers has been given to enable them to support core and other staff.

5. *Demands on work time.* Although staff are expected to carry out a range of duties as part of their employment, it would be unrealistic to expect them to carry out all their normal duties (as a custodial prison officer) as well as the highly intensive and demanding functions of a core worker. In fact, they must be excused such duties as night shifts and not be rostered for leave during the period of the 40 session blocks in order to avoid breaking the continuity of group sessions. With the co-operation of the unions at Peterhead, core staff have been largely disengaged from such routine work so that they can spend the time in groups, discussions, training and reviews, and on providing reports on the progress made by prisoners in groups. (In fact, with the changes in working practices introduced throughout the Scottish Prison Service in April 1995, most 'residential' officers are not now expected to undertake operational security duties such as working night shifts and taking prisoners out of the prison on routine escorts. These changes were, in part, introduced to enhance the quality of work for such prison officers.) However, they do continue to be based in the residential hall and have certain other less demanding duties. There is and always will be an inherent conflict in the relationships prison

staff have with offenders, social workers have with their clients, or, indeed, parents have with their children – that between enforcing control and exercising care, support and advice. Staff must never forget their position or their responsibilities in relation to security and good order, yet matters should be so organised that the burdens of ordinary work do not interfere with the valuable contribution they can make to the work with sexual offenders.

6. *Organisational support.* The Steering Group meets on a monthly basis to review the work of the groups, looks at problems relating to the delivery of the programme and provides future direction and development. It comprises the programme manager, senior social worker, psychologist, group work support supervisor and a core worker. As required, the group can meet with the governor in charge of the establishment and also the representative of 'outside' social work line management. There is also the facility to discuss issues at the monthly senior prison management meeting to ensure co-operation from all parts of the prison and ensure that the strategic planning of the establishment and STOP Programme developments are aligned.

Are staff able to talk?

As an organisation which values staff, and as line management, we have to be alert to the signals when staff begin to show signs of stress from this work. It may not be easy for them to disclose that they are experiencing problems and, if they believe that management will think less of them or negate their feelings, they may not even try to seek help or support (Spencer 1997). Tony Morrison (1996), in his article on 'Emotionally Competent Organisations', reworks the 'Professional Accommodation Syndrome' to show how staff bottle up their feelings and stresses (*secrecy*) and feel that the organisation is not interested in their plight (*helplessness*) and, therefore, do not complain. (The 'Professional Accommodation Syndrome' concerns the general processes of victimisation and staff stress, and is adapted from earlier work by Summit (1983), which looked at the problems of disclosure and their effects on children.) Staff are then trapped into either telling and being seen as 'unprofessional', or lying and appearing to cope (*accommodation and entrapment*). Eventually some form of disclosure occurs – distress, illness, aggression, talking, etc. (*delayed or unconvincing disclosure*). The response to the disclosure might be to ignore it or show disbelief – after all, seemingly, the member of staff has coped for a long time. In the end, the easiest way out is for the worker to ask people to forget about it: 'I'm fine now' (*retraction*). We must try to ensure that the member of staff feels confident and comfortable in talking about issues with colleagues and management before he or she begins to bottle them up.

The above process applies to a range of work-related issues and situations, not merely arising from working with sexual offenders.

Advice/support to management about issues surrounding the delivery of such programmes

Management support needs to be consistent. But management itself needs to be well informed if it is to make decisions and policies which are aligned to, and develop, the sex offender work. Management have received training about the process of creating and maintaining a therapeutic environment. Our visiting consultant (Hilary Eldridge) has provided advice and comment at Peterhead and both she and Professor Marshall have written critical and evaluative reports to advise us on how to take the programme forward. Senior staff should also try to familiarise themselves with the work of the groups and understand the objectives of the STOP Programme. They must share the values and be able to speak the language of intervention programmes. For this purpose, attending seminars and conferences is also an aid to their understanding and further evidence of their commitment to staff.

Management support and systems for delivery of programmes and support of core staff

In addition to the processes identified above, management support has been provided through an investment of management time, commitment, and giving clear and consistent signals. The feeling that 'we were in it for real' was also affirmed as a result of financial investment in equipment, rooms and training. In addition, management have been 'up front' in talking to all staff about these issues. The Steering Group was established, initially chaired by the governor, to implement and guide the programme, and clear policy lines were given with backing for the core work. Other staff were instructed that they must support, and not hinder, the work of the core staff and groups. It cannot be overemphasised that establishing a programme in any institution is not merely a matter of delegating tasks. For a new initiative to succeed, especially one in which staff require consistent support and can feel vulnerable, a clear, consistent and continuing message has to be given by top management as to the value of, and need for, the work undertaken. Anything less can jeopardise the whole process.

Summary of key points

- The provision of a range of effective support mechanisms for those delivering programmes is essential if the programme is to be sustained. Consistent support and commitment must come from management.

CHAPTER 9

Information about Offending Behaviour

THE NEED FOR GOOD INFORMATION

In dealing with offenders through intervention programmes, the therapist is helped by information about offences. The more the therapist knows, the better able he or she will be to tease out information from the offender in denial, challenge him about victim impact and look at the offence cycle with a view to relapse prevention work. Without that information, the offender could well argue that this was his first offence, that he didn't know what came over him, and that it was a one-off event never to be repeated. He may also try to diminish the seriousness of the offending behaviour that took place and the impact on, or harm done to, the victim. In fact, where the therapist works in the dark and relies basically on disclosure by the offender, little may be achieved in moving the offender from the denial stage, apart from in the one area disclosed.

Such a view is supported by Marshall (1994):

> One final comment that I repeatedly made while at Peterhead and to the people at SPS headquarters, is that the programme will be that much more effective, and far easier to implement, when information from police and prosecutors, and victim statements, are made available to treatment staff. I know of no program in North America where this information is withheld and I can see no reason, other than obstinate bureaucratic practices, why the same information cannot be made available in Scotland. (p.9)

and Quinsey (1990):

> More effective institutional and community sex offender treatment requires significant improvements in the quality of the information routinely gathered on sex offenders, together with improvements in the communication of this information. (p.18)

The same applies to social workers, who face real difficulties in preparing reports and making risk assessments when they only have partial information: in the words of the Skinner Report, 'it is wholly unsatisfactory if the only source available to the report writer is the offender' (SWSI 1997, p.19).

Different agencies hold differing bits of information which go to make up the jigsaw but, however desirable it is to maximise the information we can call upon, we also have to be aware of the potential for damage should such material fall in the wrong hands – and prosecution services are reluctant to part with statements from victims and police for this reason. In the wrong hands it provides identification of victims who could be retargeted, and also becomes a further form of pornographic material. Prosecuting authorities are naturally cautious about proposals to lessen control over this type of information, but agencies must learn to trust one another if we are to make progress in this matter. The Inter-Departmental Group on Sex Offending (1994) give this advice:

> Information should be exchanged for clearly defined purposes, as and when required. Particular care must be taken to ensure that information is restricted to those whose work properly requires access to it. (para. 3.7)

Prison services must take on board the above caution and make suitable arrangements for the safe keeping of such documentation. Information of this type, such as witness and victim statements, should be kept apart from the main administrative documentation and retained by those staff working specifically with the sexual offenders on matters relating to their offending behaviours. Nevertheless, there is an underlying need for the information and improvements to the way such information is communicated. The Skinner Report (SWSI 1997) also strongly supported moves to improve information sharing between agencies: 'The sharing of information between agencies particularly between the police, Procurators Fiscal, the Scottish Prison Service and social work services, is crucial so that full details of offences and other facts inform the risk assessment' (p.20).

Summary of key points

- Those in receipt of sensitive witness and victim information must ensure that it is only made available to those who require it for work with sexual offenders, and that the information is kept apart from the 'ordinary' information on such offenders and in secure conditions.

- Agencies should work together to share information which would inform risk assessments on sexual offenders.

THE DEBATE ABOUT ACCESS TO SUCH INFORMATION

It may be argued that the offender has human and legal rights which confer upon him protection from having used against him any unproved or untested statements made by others. Clearly, the victim's perspective might be different: they would feel that their human and legal rights had been violated and would not be unduly bothered by the rights of the offender – who was obviously not concerned about their rights and feelings. However, in terms of using the information that is already available for the purposes of attempting to reduce the offender's propensity to commit further offences, the material takes on a different status. The issue is 'What is the material being used for?' In using the material for therapeutic purposes it is not being used *against* the offender in any criminal/legal way. It is intended to be used by the therapist, so that he or she can begin to understand the modus operandi of the offender and be able to challenge his denials.

It is likely to be the view of the Crown Office that the statements held by Procurators Fiscal (prosecutors) will contain allegations in respect of which the accused is not convicted. There could also be concern that unproven statements might be used improperly by those to whom they are passed. It would clearly be wrong for prison or parole authorities to use these untested statements as further information which might affect decisions as to how the prisoner is managed within prison or as to his suitability for early release. If that were the case, then those decisions might legitimately be subject to judicial review.

However, it is suggested that there is no inherent conflict of interest. The rights of the offender are not diminished by therapists gaining access to victim and witness statements. It might be suggested that in using such information there could be a real chance that among all the statements a particular statement is erroneous and that the offender, if confronted with such information, would then naturally deny. That is to misunderstand the process used by the therapist in group sessions. The stance is not confrontational but challenging and exploratory. By using these statements, the therapist will begin to understand the nature of the offence cycle of the individual offender, and these statements may be useful in probing the offender's behaviours and fantasies. What we know from generalised information about sexual offending would lead us to believe that there are likely to be many more offences than convictions, and that these form part of the offender's pattern of offending. In addition, it is unlikely that an individual (female or child victim) would invent a statement to the police or prosecutors about a sexual offence perpetrated upon them by a named, subsequently convicted, offender. It is more likely that the incident was another example of his pattern of offending behaviour. The group worker is not trying to gain a further conviction – these statements have not been used by the prosecution and there would be no intention of holding another trial during the group sessions – but it can assist the therapist to probe further and challenge the offender when he says that he didn't know what came over him, as this was the first time such a thing has happened.

The issue is, therefore, not about the veracity of statements or the threat to the rights of the offender. It is a matter for decision on public policy. In Scotland, since the mid-1840s, the courts have recognised that witness statements taken by Procurators Fiscal remain confidential to them.[1] The question that now needs to be asked is whether such statements by victims should continue to be stored in files or be put to some more useful purpose. At the time when the case law was first developed, many convicted criminals were still subject to the death penalty or transportation. Over the following 150 years, the rules remained but society changed. Admittedly, it is only in the last few years that prisons have begun to undertake this work and realised the value of such information. However, the literature on working with sexual offenders now abounds with exhortations on the need for good information, including victim and witness statements. Since our fundamental objectives are crime prevention and the protection of the public, some further thought needs to be given to this matter:

> [there is a] need to convince Justice Department officials that Crown Attorneys should release to prison treatment staff all their pertinent records on convicted sex offenders so that treatment staff can effectively deal with these men. The first, and most critical, aspect of treatment involves having the offender accept responsibility for all aspects of all of his offences. It is well-nigh impossible to do this if the only basis of information is the offender himself. In all other countries where I have assisted in setting-up prison treatment programs (Canada, USA, New Zealand, Australia, and Bermuda, and I think also England) the Justice Department readily supply this information to prison staff as they realize how critical the information is to the effective treatment of sex offenders. (Marshall 1995, p.11)

The concern of Procurators Fiscal is not that the material is 'confidential' in the sense that it cannot be shown to others. Precognitions are statements made to them in private and remain merely unused statements unless tested in court. There may be a whole host of reasons why the statements are not used. Sometimes, these statements may be irrelevant to a case or unnecessary for the proof of a case. On rare occasions it may be that what is disclosed is so sensitive and personal that to use it would cause distress to the witness and a decision might be taken by the Fiscal that on balance, and in the public interest, the statement should not be used. In many cases involving sexual offences the Fiscal has difficult judgements to make, and may decide to protect children or other victims from the ordeal of an appearance in court. Yet, as a consequence, the information remains stored away when some of it could be of great use to therapists.

---

1   Scottish case law [Donald v Hart (1844) 6D 1255, Arthur v Lindsay (1894)1 Adam 582, and Sheridan v Peel (1907) SC 577] sustains the view that precognitions are the Fiscal's version of what a witness has said to them in response to questioning and, as such are confidential to the Lord Advocate, who can refuse to produce them on the grounds of public interest.

One way forward would be to establish that, in cases involving sexual offences, precognitions and witness statements made to the police be treated differently. The public interest would be better served by making these statements available to those working with sexual offenders. Perhaps a first step might be made in those cases where the offender is convicted of a sexual offence which is also listed under Schedule One of the Criminal Procedure (Scotland) Act 1975, and as amended by the Sexual Offences (Scotland) Act 1976, which defines a range of sexual (and related) offences against children. The courts already have a duty to mark the warrants of such convicted offenders; the next step would be for the Procurator Fiscal to pass the witness statements and precognitions to the prison authorities. Since it would not be in the interests of justice to pass on these papers until appeal procedures had run their course, in some cases this might involve some necessary delay.

However, notwithstanding the nature of the progress, progress needs to be made in this area so that vital information which already exists can inform work with sexual offenders. The same problems which face prison service group workers also cause social workers anxiety:

> Further discussions are urgently required on the practical and policy difficulties that stand in the way of ensuring that social workers preparing reports, at least in serious cases, have good information about current and previous offences. It is not clear how, in Scotland, this may best be done or from what source the information may best come. However, there is a point of consensus that fuller information should be available and The Scottish Office should take forward discussions on this basis. (SWSI 1997, p.19)

Summary of key points

- Those engaged in challenging offenders with their offending behaviour need to have the best information available to assist with this work. This calls for greater trust between the different parts of the criminal justice system and disclosure of vital information held by the prosecuting services.

- A first step might be the agreement to pass witness statements and precognitions to those working with sexual offenders within prisons where the offender is convicted of an offence listed under Schedule One of the Criminal Procedure (Scotland) Act 1975.

CHAPTER 10

Bridging the Gap I
Throughcare, the Multi-Agency Approach

A STRATEGIC VIEW OF MULTI-AGENCY CO-OPERATION

The *raison d'être* for any work with sexual offenders is the desire to protect the public. This can be tackled in two ways: first, by working with the victim to ameliorate the effects of the abuse and put into place those protective measures required to prevent further victimisation; and, second, by working with the offender to reduce the risk of reoffending and thus harming further victims.

> The focus of work on cases of sexual abuse is quite properly on the child and his or her protection, or the adult victim and thus on the investigation and management of the abuse. But there remains the problem of the source of the abuse. If sexual abuse is to be tackled effectively in the longer term, then attention must be directed to the abusers and the prevention of abuse. (Inter-Departmental Group on Child Abuse 1992, p.2)

However, the impact of the work undertaken in prison is severely diminished unless there is good follow-up, with support, supervision and further offence-specific work continued into the community on release. This co-operation is not always as readily forthcoming as it should be, for a variety of reasons. These may include lack of trust, professional preciousness, uncertainty as to what other agencies have done, differences in approach, lack of common or shared value systems, shortages in resources, different priorities or just poor communications. In the end it is only the offender who gains, by more easily manipulating the staff of one agency against those of another until he slips through the net. A strong call for closer co-operation was made in the introduction to a recent draft government paper on the subject:

> The impact of sex offending on victims and within the community and the high risk of re-offending on release makes it imperative that work done with sex offenders, whilst in custody and during supervision following release, is undertaken within the context of close co-operation between all the agencies responsible for the supervision of offenders and the protection of potential

victims, whether adults or children. This necessitates development of a high level of trust between agencies and a willingness to share confidential information as a normal part of the work. (Inter-Departmental Group on Sex Offending 1994, p.1)

The paper goes on to argue: 'Effective multi-agency communication and co-operation will be a key factor in seeking to reduce the risk of re-offending on release'. These areas of co-operation include exchanging information and agreeing upon philosophies and consistent programmes that work to the same theoretical and value base.

The earlier (1992) paper on working with abusers indicates that at a national level the strategic objectives in seeking to achieve the aim of reducing the seriousness and incidence of sexual abuse should be:

- to formulate a coherent policy for the management and treatment of abusers, and to evaluate and review policy at regular intervals

- to build up a better understanding of the characteristics of abusers and the context in which abuse takes place

- to view sexual abuse as a problem which requires assessment and treatment for the abuser as well as the abused and to help abusers learn ways of minimising the risk of reoffending

- to promote an inter-disciplinary and inter-agency approach to the planning, delivery and review of programmes for managing and treating abusers and others involved

- to encourage the development of local and national resource networks for staff working with abusers, in recognition of the high demands of their work

- to educate the public and professional staff about the nature and approach to sexual abuse.

The 1992 group (at Annex II) suggested six further objectives which could be achieved by inter-agency co-operation and identified the various contributions to the objectives which could be made by the social work child care and offender services, reporters and children's hearings, and the health and prison services. The six objectives are:

1. To seek to prevent known or suspected abusers from harming potential victims or further harming abused children.

2. Having identified abuse, to provide protection to children and support for them and their families, and to ensure that intervention with abusers enhances this protection and support.

3. To plan to provide services and programmes, and where appropriate training, in collaboration with voluntary and other organisations, aimed at

modifying the behaviour of abusers who are living in the community, in residential or health establishments or in penal establishments.

4. To monitor and assess the effectiveness of the services and programmes for abusers as a positive contribution to the protection of children.

5. To provide public education and information aimed at reducing the incidence and seriousness of abusive behaviour.

6. To provide staff development programmes to assist workers to discharge their functions effectively and efficiently. (1992, pp.2–3)

Indeed, the above objectives, especially 1 and 2, are also shared by the other players in the criminal justice system. What is critical to the success of dealing with the problems of sex offending, victims and offenders is that all agencies understand the need for the fullest co-operation and sharing of information. Without them, the offenders continue and the victims suffer.

Summary of key points

- Multi-agency co-operation is essential if protection for victims and the work undertaken with sexual offenders are to have any lasting effect. A clear strategy has to be put in place to make this happen.

THE CONCEPT OF THROUGHCARE

It is a well-established principle that there should be continuity of care from the community, through the stage of imprisonment and on return to the community:

> The main reason put forward for transferring responsibility for the provision of social work services in penal establishments was
>
> '...to give effect to the philosophy that the task of caring for people [is] a continuous process which need[s] to keep in perspective whole family and community ties'. (The Manning of Social Work Services in Penal Establishments in Scotland 1972)

> Underpinning this philosophy is a recognition that many prisoners face problems in the community which they will bring with them to the penal setting and which will again confront them on their eventual return to their family and community. For many prisoners and their families the experience of imprisonment will of itself generate or exacerbate practical, financial and emotional problems. (SPS and Social Work Services Group 1990, para. 2.2.1)

Therefore, work with sexual offenders and consideration of the problems arising on release should not be left to just before release. The concept of throughcare implies involvement with the offender from the pre-trial stages. Clearly, when the case involves offences against children, especially in the family home, there is a statutory requirement to identify the proposed location of the offender on release and a duty to protect identified children who might be at risk. In terms of the duties of prison authorities, the involvement commences on the reception of such a prisoner on remand. Although there is no 'proven offence', the nature of the charges often indicates that close co-operation with the relevant social work department is required in order to facilitate the preparation of reports.

On conviction, it should be the case that the prisoner is transferred to the proposed National Induction Centre for Sex Offenders as soon as practicable (see p.46). From there, the initial throughcare arrangements should be made, the appropriate involved agencies identified and notified, and contact established at an early date. Often, parameters will have to be set as to arrangements for contact with the family of the offender.

While the prisoner is serving his sentence, contact should be maintained with his social worker to ensure that realistic plans can be made for his release and reintegration into the community.

It is to be hoped that if the prisoner participates in offence-specific programmes, a relapse prevention strategy will be worked out between him and the group workers in prison. Such plans will need to be reviewed by the 'outside' social worker who may also have an important role in the implementation of the relapse prevention strategy itself. The prison Social Work Unit and 'core' staff will have to make direct contact with the proposed supervising officer prior to release. In any event, there should have been continuing contact between prison-based staff and those working in the community and with the victim to ensure ongoing exchange of information. A recent innovation in this area has been the work undertaken by prison-based social workers with short-term prisoners in Barlinnie Prison, Glasgow. These sexual offenders might be spending only six to twelve weeks in prison before being released. Their Creating Control Programme has links with groups in the community which continue its work, which may have only begun to look at denial, responsibility and victim awareness issues.

> ...we had devised a programme which was based on the principles of throughcare, in that a man serving a sentence no matter how short, could be introduced into the programme in Barlinnie and hopefully would want to continue with the same programme in the community. (Dempsey 1995, p.2)

In order for programmes to be effective, they have to be sustained and reinforced across agency settings. A brief programme of intervention carried out in a single setting is unlikely to be effective and may well become counter-productive, with the offender learning how to 'talk the talk', and being seductive in trying to convince others that he has changed when in reality he has not.

It is, therefore, important that the programmes in prison and in the community are consistent and work to the same theoretical and value base. (Inter-Departmental Group on Sex Offending 1994, para 3.5)

I hope this reflects some of the recurring themes of this book – that:

- working with sexual offenders is a long-term business
- the work begun in prison has to be continued in the community
- information, trust and values must be shared by professionals across agency settings.

In addition, it would be of benefit to both prison staff and community-based workers for there to be secondments and meetings arranged which allowed for a free exchange of ideas, values and experiences between staff from both institutional and community settings.

Information and contacts

Throughcare can only really be effective if those working in prisons and social work are aware of the range of programmes currently being operated in the other's domain. Information should be supplied to both prison service staff and social work/probation staff on what programmes are available within the prison service and in the community. This information will have to be collected locally and collated through the agencies' respective central offices. The prison service should provide up-to-date information on:

- the types of programmes being run, including brief description, length and target group
- locations
- expected outcomes or the next stage
- the staff involved (e.g. prison officers, social workers, psychologists, etc.) and their roles
- the contact names for the programmes (usually the manager), with details of address, telephone, etc.

The social work/probation services should provide for use in prisons (and other social work departments) up-to-date information on:

- any support services available for sex offenders, including hostel accommodation for men
- locations of such services
- the range of programmes being run in different areas, brief description, length and target group
- other complementary specialist services available

- the staff involved and their roles
- the contact names for the programmes and various services, with details of address, telephone, etc.

Summary of key points

- Throughcare begins before the prisoner is received into prison and continues throughout the sentence and on release. The ongoing exchange of information is central to this process. Prisons must work with social work and other agencies to ensure best practice.
- Prisons and social work departments should exchange information on the range of services available for sexual offenders within their own organisations.
- Secondments between prison staff and those based in the community will aid understanding of the throughcare process and enhance the commonality of values.

CHAPTER 11

Bridging the Gap II
From Prison to Home and the Community

BALANCING NEEDS

> A practice that deals only with victims cannot be a credible child protection policy, since the children are not protected unless we try to find ways of stopping abusers from further abusing. (ADSW Report of the Working Group on Sexual Abusers of Children 1991)

In working with sexual offenders and their victims, those involved must constantly remind themselves of the priorities to be faced and the requirement to get the balance right. There is no clearer example to be found than the tensions and conflicts produced by the desire of an abusive parent to return to the home where his victim daughter still resides. What are the wishes of the victim and abuser, and what about the other members of the family? Whose needs should be taken into account? Does the father still have a parental and developmental role in the child's upbringing? Does the fact that the daughter misses her father really matter? Can we assume his love for her is genuine? Does it now matter whether he misses his daughter and the rest of his family and longs to return home? Does the local community have any view about the proposed return of the offender?

There are a number of international conventions on rights and much subsidiary state legislation with apparently conflicting messages. There are obligations to ensure contact between family members, principally between parents and their children, and there are also duties of care for the protection of children from abuse. Getting the balance right is never going to be easy. When decisions have to be made, then considerations as to what is *in the best interests of the child* are usually paramount. But who decides what is in the child's best interest? Should it always be left to the court or a social work agency? If the solution is not obvious, then maybe the best judge is the child herself. We should never forget the most important voice to be heard – the voice of the victim.

Parental abusers in custody should find attempting to organise a return home a difficult and slow process. There should be no quick fixes and no short cuts. It will have to be established that the abuser has undertaken sufficient offence-specific work to minimise the risk of his relapsing and that the victim has received consistent support before the process of family reunification can be allowed to begin. At that point meaningful discussions between those group workers and social workers responsible for the offender within prison and community- or family-based staff working with the victim can commence. Tied into the process will be the release plans of the prisoner – whether by early release on parole or supervised release at the end of the sentence. In neither case should the fact that he is being released be the determining factor as to whether it is appropriate for him to return home. The primary consideration must be the safety of the victim and other members of the family.

PLANNING THE RETURN

A number of strands have to begin to come together if effective and safe integration back into the family and community is being planned. Where the victim has been a child, this could involve many or all of the following players:

- the offender/prisoner
- group work staff (prison)
- the personal officer (prison officer)
- prison-based social work staff
- the child's social worker (victim counselling and support)
- the family social worker
- the proposed supervising social worker for the offender[1]
- the child/victim
- the family (of the offender)
- the social work management of the area in which the victim and family live, or to which the offender will return
- the local authority child protection team
- the local police force[2]
- the court or Children's Hearing system
- the Parole Board
- prison management.

Although this appears to be a somewhat daunting prospect, it does reflect the real need to involve all those who may have a legitimate part to play in ensuring that

---

1   Under the arrangements for 'Extended Sentences' (Crime and Disorder Act 1998), throughcare or proposed supervising officers must regularly visit sexual offenders in prison prior to release.

2   The Sex Offenders Act 1997 made the notification of information to the police by persons who have committed certain sexual offences a statutory requirement. The information includes date of birth, name(s) and address of residence.

all factors are taken into account in planning for the release of the offender. It is this very complexity (and consequential cost) which demonstrates why it makes good sense to get offenders to address their offending behaviour and try to prevent further offending.

The information required to enable decisions to be made includes:

- an up-to-date assessment of risk
- a progress report of the work undertaken to address offending behaviour
- the offender's attitude to this work
- the offender's current view of his offending behaviour and his stance on victims
- the offender's current relationship with his victim and family
- the state of any existing or ongoing contact between the victim, family and offender
- the present stage of any relapse prevention work and how that meshes into the family reunification process
- a report on how the work with the child victim is going and her ability to cope with contact
- the view of the victim about contact with the abusive parent
- the opinion of the child's social worker
- the opinion of the rest of the family, the relationship between the offender and his partner and other children, and the risk he may pose to them
- the existing arrangements for, or restrictions, on contact as laid down by the court or the Children's Hearing
- the likely impact on the community of the release or planned visit to the home
- the address/location of the meeting or residence while on temporary release
- details of any special conditions or rules which are thought necessary to impose
- names of nominated social workers, or other caseworkers, who will supervise such a meeting
- the proposed duration of such a meeting or visit and the protocols or ground rules to be established
- the suggested date(s) and time(s) of the meeting.

In addition, where final release is being planned, arrangements will have to be made to ensure there are full details of:

- proposed accommodation and any conditions imposed about residence

- precise arrangements for family contact

- plans for employment and/or further education

- financial arrangements such as social security and welfare benefits

- proposals for supervision and support of the offender, the implementation of the relapse prevention strategy, the development of further offence-specific work and other issues concerning rehabilitation into the community

- arrangements for the support of the family, the child victim and protection measures.

The process of involving the full range of players and discussion of the wide variety of information required can only be achieved through good communication and networking. This is ideally implemented through a number of multi-agency case conferences or meetings involving the relevant parties at any one time. The objective is to ensure that the plans for the management of the release of the offender, his relapse prevention strategy and his supervision complement the work being undertaken with the victim and the family, and maximise the protection of the children who were his victims and those other children who might otherwise be in danger. This necessitates a high level of what this author terms the *six Cs* of the multi-agency approach – *care, caution, consideration, communication, co-operation* and *coordination.*

- *Care:* ensure that the interest of the victim is paramount, support her and the family, and ensure protection.

- *Caution:* remember that offenders can be selfish, manipulative and subtle, and that often the continuation of abuse will not be obvious to the onlooker.

- *Consideration:* take time to evaluate what is being said, particularly when the offender's wishes are being discussed, try to understand his real attitudes and motivations, and examine, realistically, the assessment of risk and the coping and protection mechanisms to be put in place.

- *Communication:* ensure that all relevant information is passed from one agency to the next without professional restrictiveness, remembering that the offender gains and the victim and other potential victims are put in greater danger if those who should know are not made fully aware of all the facts.

- *Co-operation:* the need for all parties to work actively together, meet and discuss matters of concern, and reach a common plan acceptable to all parties.

- *Coordination:* ensure that the details which have been worked out and agreed are implemented by informing others and through liaison and checking, and ensure that systems are put in place to support this process.

THE VICTIM AND FAMILY REUNIFICATION: A BRIEF PRIMER

This book is about the management of sexual offenders in general. It is not the intention to focus on one particular category of offender. Neither should it be inferred that by examining the issues surrounding family reconciliation I am suggesting that an aim of the offence-specific programme might be to help with family reunification. The object of working with sexual offenders is to reduce the risk of their reoffending and, as a consequence, minimise the harm done to others. All sexual offenders, be they members of paedophile rings, rapists of adult women, exhibitionists or perpetrators of incest, present problems when their return home is being contemplated. Many sexual offenders will not return home: they are no longer welcome, the family has split up, or their partner has left them or instituted divorce proceedings. Others may face legal prohibitions against making contact with members of their families. In some cases, however, family reunification might be contemplated. What follows is *a brief primer* on the issues, concerns and arrangements for such reunification. Many of the points mentioned are as relevant for adult victims, non-familial child victims or potential victims as they are in the example below of the process involved in the prospective return of a sexual offending father to the home where his victim child resides.

There is no greater need for communication between, and coming together of, the various players involved in offence-specific work with offenders, the criminal justice system, and community-based and victim support agencies than that required to deal with the range of difficult and interrelated problems which arise when the sexually abusive member of a family wishes to return to a family in which other members may also desire his return. There may be a whole host of conflicting interests which have to be resolved, and there are no simple or ready solutions. There are issues concerning what is in the *best interests of the child victim* and who is best placed to decide upon that: the child, other siblings, the mother, social workers or the courts. The offender's return might affect other children, adversely interfere with the healing process already begun with the victim or destroy the work already begun by restoring the family's need for security. Indeed, the abuser may believe that in being allowed to return he has had the 'slate wiped clean' and may lose the motivation to continue to look at his attitudes and offending behaviour and decide that there is no need to sustain maintenance work on his relapse prevention strategies.

It is because of the inherent dangers of contact with the offender, that we start with the premise that no contact should be made between the abuser and his victim. This is reinforced by the offender leaving the family home. Berliner (1982) outlined some reasons why this is the preferred course of action:

1. It is fairer to make the person causing the problem leave the home rather than the victim who suffered the problem, otherwise the child is likely to feel further 'punished'.

2. It is a statement that adult offenders are responsible for their own behaviour.

3. Victims should be allowed to continue to live as normal a life as possible in their own family environment.

4. It may help the family to focus on the victim's needs rather than on the needs of the offender.

5. The general level of tension in the home may be reduced when the offender is removed.

6. Children have the right to be safe in their own homes.

7. Losing the right to live in their own homes can help offenders learn that there are consequences to their behaviour.

8. Removal from the home provides the offender with a strong incentive to change, if making those changes is a condition of his returning to the family.

9. The mother, who usually sees herself as less competent and more dependent, may come to realise her strengths.

To understand the problems created by an abuser returning home, workers need to go back a step and look at some of the reasons why his removal was advantageous. Clearly, the removal of an offender is the prerogative of the court, whether by an order preventing his return to a particular address or through a custodial sentence of imprisonment. Occasionally, the abusive offender is simply 'thrown out' of the home. In any event, the outcome is the same. The result is the temporary physical safety of the child and the prevention of further abuse and additional emotional deterioration. The victim can feel abused, violated, degraded and, very possibly, physically hurt. The trust that she had in the adult can have been irreversibly damaged, and often she will feel guilty for reporting the abuse, and further guilt and responsibility for the removal and imprisonment of the adult, and the upheaval and distress all this has caused in the family. What a tremendous burden for any child. She may have been told or think that if only she had kept quiet about the abuse then none of this might have happened. Now, with all this out in the open, she begins to feel guilty for her part in the abusive events: maybe she really *is* a bad girl (confirming the abuser's stance) and there really *is* something wrong with her. Therefore, what she needs is support and reassurance that she was right not to keep the secret and that she is a good and valued member of the family. Is it not bad enough that she was abused by someone who broke her trust, someone who she had some affection for? The last thing the victim wants is the offender to blame her for the situation that he finds himself in, and the emotional blackmail presented by this sad, self-pitying adult who has lost everything and needs her forgiveness to survive. The pressure to forgive or excuse some of his responsibility (and thus allow him to deny the act) is a continuation of the abuse and a further application of victimisation. Therefore, the first golden rule of reunification is that there should be none – unless, that is, it can be shown that the offender has genuinely begun to understand the problems, taken responsibility for his actions, and understood and internalised the damage he has done to the victim. Without this first condition having been met, no contact should be made. Otherwise, the victim may well be revictimised and the abuse continued. This abuse does not have to be physical: it can take the form of the offender again imposing his will over hers or using verbal and non-verbal cues or triggers only known by the victim and her abuser but doing great damage, unbeknown to those others around.

Before any meeting or visit takes place, the victim needs to have made progress and know she is believed and supported, that it was not her fault (both the abuse and the consequences of its discovery) and that she will now be protected. The non-offending mother also requires support. She may still find it hard to accept that the person she trusted (her partner) committed such offences. She must come to accept that the abuse was neither her fault nor indeed that of her child. Any information that can be passed from the offender's worker to that of the family as to how he manipulated and gained access will be of help.

> It is also crucial for the non offending parent to hear how manipulative and devious her partner has been to gain access to her children, as many are crippled by the guilt of having not been able to protect their children, and therefore usually end up blaming themselves. (Dempsey 1995, p.1)

Should she decide to continue with the relationship, the decision should be made without pressure from the abuser. If she does try to rebuild the partnership, she will need to understand the process of sexual offending, cognitive distortions, grooming, and so on. The cycle of offending is important for her if she is to learn how to survive her partner's manipulations and protect her children in the future.

Thus, before any reunification process is begun, all three sets of players – the victim, the family and the offender – should have made progress in their respective healing, therapeutic and offence-specific work. As we have seen, the victim needs to work through a whole series of issues to the point at which she feels confident of the next step. She must feel vindicated in what she has done – that is, believed, accepted and valued. The mother and other members of the family should also be coming to terms with what has happened and the new responsibilities and relationships within the home. Finally, the offender needs to have made sufficient progress in addressing his offending behaviour. He needs to be open and not defensive about discussing his offending activities, and understand that by projecting blame he would only continue to hurt his victim. He should be able to see the abuse for what it was, a manipulation by him of someone who trusted in him, a breaking of that trust and a violation of her rights and expectations, inflicting hurt on his victim and exercising power and control over her for the purpose of giving himself pleasure and satisfying his fantasies. Attempting to bring members of the family back together again too soon, without sufficient progress having been made, can lead to a whole host of problems:

1. The offender may attempt to project the blame back on to the victim and others, and the victim, non-offending mother and other family members may begin to take responsibility for the problem and feel guilty for something which only the offender created.

2. The mother may be distracted from her task of protecting, supporting and believing the victim by attempting to reach a compromise which reassures the offender and to some extent allows him to reassert his former position in the family.

3. The mother and other members of the family may become uncertain about what and whose needs should take priority when the offender makes demands and asks for their attention.

4. Finally, the offender himself will then be 'off the hook'. He will have re-established himself in the way he wanted, and have less reason to continue addressing his offending behaviour. It is more likely that reoffending will occur and that the family environment will continue to be tense and fraught with difficulties.

The first step – the letter

If it is felt that it may be positive to attempt some degree of contact, this should be carefully discussed by all the relevant parties and agencies. It has been suggested by O'Connell *et al.* (1990) that the best way to proceed is to get the offender to write a letter to the child. However, there is a need to ensure that a letter from the offender should only be sent when the victim indicates that she wants this sort of contact. The letter should include the offender telling the child that he accepts full responsibility for what has happened and that she was not to blame for the abuse. He should express remorse and acknowledge that the abuse has caused her harm and hurt. He should recognise that what *he* has done has damaged the family, and that she was right to disclose and report him in order to get the abuse stopped. He is using his time in prison to get himself sorted out and is receiving help with his problems, and hopes that she is also getting some help to repair the damage he has done to her. The letter should avoid asking for forgiveness, and it should avoid exerting pressure or manipulating the victim's thoughts. Forgiveness (letting go of the feelings of betrayal and anger) should be something which may come as a result of the healing of her emotional wounds – not something the offender should ask for or demand. In addition, the offender should avoid writing things which might make the victim feel sorry for him or tell her how to think. She has enough work to do in healing her own wounds without the added burden of being told to be sorry for him or how she should feel about him. Both of these are facets of continuing abuse, of the offender continuing to assert control over her emotions and thoughts. The victim needs to feel sure that the offender will not try to manipulate or control her as he did in the past.

The writing of this type of letter is also part of the more generalised offence-specific programme in which the offender engages. As we have seen before, ordinarily, such letters are *not* sent. They are written as part of a process of making the offender aware of victim distress. The process will contribute to the programme and provide additional learning opportunities which can focus on his thinking errors. He will have to tackle victim empathy and demonstrate that he understands the hurt and damage he has inflicted. He will have to show how he has taken full responsibility for his actions, and any signs of self-pity can be used to show how offenders focus on their own needs at the cost of others. Finally, the therapist will be able to point out where he begins to try to manipulate the receiver of the letter and give examples of the subtle ways in which he may still be trying to exert control. If, as in this case, it is agreed that he should actually write a letter 'for real', he will, no doubt, have to write a number of drafts before the letter is suitable for sending, and it is likely that such a process might take place some time after completion of the STOP Programme. When it is felt that the letter is positive and no longer abusive, it may, after consultation between the offender's group worker and the victim's social worker, be sent.

The letter should not be sent direct, but sent between workers involved in the case so that the situation in which the letter is read by the victim can be managed in order to protect and support her. It is, therefore, best read by the victim with her social worker or counsellor and possibly her mother present. This enables the child to use the support that is available to her while she reads the letter and tries to understand what is being said. She may then decide what she wants to do, and the victim's reaction should be respected. If the letter is rejected, it is a clear indication (at the very least) that she is not yet ready for the next step. She might not believe the abuser or want to have anything more to do with him. She might not know what to do, or she might want to write a reply. Whatever her view, she will need support and reassurance. If she is ready to reply, she may need help to express what she feels and guidance over the choice of language.

Preparation for the first meeting

When both parties are ready for some movement towards reconciliation then a number of matters have to be resolved before a meeting can take place. The natural development is for a meeting between the victim and the offender, and some preparation is required before such a meeting can actually take place. There will have to be consultation between the victim and her therapist to check that she is really ready for the meeting and find out what issues she wants to discuss, as well as particular areas she might want to avoid. In discussions with the offender, his social worker will want to check that what is said at the first meeting is largely limited to a repeat of the statements made earlier in his letter or letters. The meeting should not discuss matters relating to the offending behaviour but should establish beyond doubt the offender's responsibility for his actions and the correctness of the child's actions. The final topic could be to look at the possibility of further meetings. Also to be worked out is the location of the first meeting. If possible, it should be on neutral ground and in a controlled environment. It may not be appropriate to bring the child to a prison with its austere setting, although such a location might aid the view that it is the adult offender who committed the offence, was bad and is being punished, and if so should take place in the Social Work Unit or a similar venue. Whether the prisoner is allowed to leave the prison may also be dependent on other factors such as his security category status. Meetings held outside prisons should probably take place in a social work office or the office of the child's therapist.

Planning for visits

The first meeting and any subsequent ones held in the social work or therapist's office will be well planned, controlled and supervised. If it is decided to allow further development by organising *visits,* then a clear set of guidelines or rules have to be established so that the offender understands the boundaries within which he operates. In many ways the rules should be complementary to the work undertaken on his relapse prevention strategy and manual. These rules will have to be talked through with the offender until he accepts them as his own; he will then be asked to present them as his own rules at a supervised meeting with his family before any visit is arranged. O'Connell *et al.* (1990) have detailed some of the rules which need to be applied to offenders when they visit any children and also victims. By integrating their lists, a composite set of guidelines can be established as a framework for meetings between victims and their abusers:

1. The offender will never be alone with the victim (or other children).
2. There will be designated adult chaperone(s) for the offender when he is with the victim. This should be someone with whom the victim is comfortable and is able to talk with about the abuse. The chaperone may

often be the non-offending parent, but this person may not be appropriate at the earlier sessions.

3. The offender will be in no way responsible for the supervision or disciplining of the victim. He will not administer any punishment or rewards. Any gifts for the victim will be given via the chaperone following prior discussion and the approval of both therapists (the victim's and the offender's).

4. The offender will not initiate any physical or affectionate contact with the victim. If the child wants to, for example, offer a hug or kiss of greeting or parting, she can do so.

5. The offender will need to minimise physical contact, even if it is initiated by the victim. The offender's response to affectionate gestures (as discussed above) should be modest and brief. The offender will refrain from other kinds of physical contact, such as tickling, horseplay, having her sit on his lap, walking hand in hand, and so on.

6. The offender should not present himself as wanting or needing care or special affection from the victim.

7. The offender will have no secrets with the victim.

8. The offender will not engage in discussions of sexuality, dating, boyfriends, and so on with the child.

9. Any further discussions about the abuse will take place in a 'treatment' setting with counsellors present.

10. Other special rules which are necessary to allow the child to feel comfortable may be established depending on the particular circumstances of each case.

In this way, all parties will understand the rules and there will be no excuse for the offender to deviate. To do so could, perhaps, be a sign of the offender beginning to lapse.

Once the rules have been agreed and satisfactory supervised meetings have taken place, the family can think about having fairly short visits, say of about two hours, with the offender. These can either be taken as part of an 'open prison' programme or when the offender has been released and is housed separately. They can take place without the child's social worker or therapist present, providing the chaperone (usually the non-offending mother) is present at all times. The visits are a way of developing relationships, and each new experience should be coped with and worked through before further developments occur. It is important at this stage that the visits take place in some public setting because the family home is used as the place of refuge for the child. In addition, the child may associate the adult in the home with part of the abusive cycle, the place where the offences took place being private and away from the watchful and caring eyes of others. Going out for a meal or some joint activity like going to the zoo or doing the family shopping provides an opportunity for interaction in a comfortable setting.

The family visits are opportunities to test out and develop relationships. If anyone, particularly the child victim, feels uncomfortable with what is happening, then the contact should be terminated and the matter discussed later with the appropriate social workers. The victim should not have to put up with discomfort and any additional suffering as a result of the contact. That is what happened when she was abused and should not be replicated during a visit. In addition, if the process appears to be working, then sometimes the rest of the family are keen to make progress. The tempo should be dictated by caution and the voice of the victim.

Longer visits and outings

After a number of short visits have proved successful, the next step is to lengthen the time spent together and vary the venues of the visits and the activities undertaken. This increase should be gradual and perhaps include visits to the homes of relatives. In addition, longer visits might be planned for special occasions such as birthdays and Christmas, always remembering the ground rules and the need for constant visual supervision by the chaperone. Again, in between visits, both the child and the offender should be seeing their social workers and discussing any problem areas that emerge. These visits provide a good test bed for the relapse prevention plan, the offender being able to use examples of what has happened on the visits to develop his coping mechanisms and test out his original strategies. Providing he sees the identification of lapse situations as a positive way forward, visits can be put to developmental advantage.

Planning the visit home

Providing that the visits and outings have gone well, the next stage is for the offender to visit the family home. As before, such visits should begin by being brief, and the offender must accept the role of visitor rather than someone returning to his own home. He should not make any assumptions about 'becoming the boss' once he steps over the threshold into the home. It should also be remembered that the family home has become the safe refuge of the victim and that she will lose this feeling while he is present. At the very least, then, her own bedroom must become the safe haven to which she can withdraw. Again, like previous visits and outings, the activity should be planned, and sharing a meal with the family is a useful activity for this purpose. In addition to the guidelines set out above, O'Connell et al. (1990) suggest six rules for visiting home:

1. The offender should never enter the victim's bedroom. The child, who has relinquished the sanctuary of her home, thus still retains the bedroom as a safe haven.

2. The offender should not be in any bedroom or bathroom with any children, even with a chaperone present.

3. The practice of locking the bathroom door should be practised by all members of the family (except for toddlers who may require the assistance of the non-offending parent).

4. Whenever possible, the offender should use separate bathroom facilities from those used by children, especially the victim. This again extends the safe haven concept.

5. The offender should never be left at the home when children are there, even if they are not in his immediate presence, unless a chaperone is also there.

6. The offender should be fully and appropriately dressed at all times. The non-offending parent is responsible for other members of the family being properly attired. (p.116)

Providing these visits to the home go well, the next step would be to have longer visits which are less formalised in structure. All the (16) rules still apply, but the activities can vary with meals, outings, helping around the house with cleaning chores, DIY, and so on. The activities and interactions of the family begin to take on an appearance of normality and the children might 'pop out' to play with friends. If other children are to make more than unplanned and momentary contact with the offender, then their parents will have to be informed about the offender and the 'rules' framework in which he operates. As these visits progress, the time spent will be longer and the offender will learn how he can fit into the home and family life without becoming too intrusive. Eventually, he may be spending most of the weekend, but not nights, in the home, and providing the visits and his presence still feel comfortable, and that he has been able to resolve problems that have arisen in a positive and constructive way, then discussions may inevitably lead to consideration of his staying overnight.

The overnight visit

This is a natural development as visits relax and lengthen. A further four rules for overnight visits are suggested by O'Connell *et al.* (1990) to add to the existing ones, in order to avoid problems and so that everyone knows what to expect:

7. Locks should be placed on bedroom doors and used at night so as to reinforce the principle of privacy.

8. The offender should be fully dressed at all times when he is outside his bedroom. This includes all trips to and from a bathroom (except en suite).

9. The offender should not roam about the house when his wife is asleep in bed. This requires that he retire at the same time as or before his spouse and arise at the same time as or after she does.

10. If he should have reason to get out of his bed during the night, he should fully awaken his spouse and inform her of what he is doing. (p.117)

Throughout the lengthy process described above, there should have been regular debriefing sessions between the social worker or therapist involved with the victim and likewise with the offender. This will have provided opportunities to discuss anxieties, fears and frustrations, and time for both the child and the adult to reflect on how the experience of them being together has felt. During this process, the two social workers or therapists should also have maintained contact and discussed points of mutual concern or fears expressed by the victim. As the process of staying overnight itself becomes more frequent, and after all the groundwork has been undertaken, it may be time for the final stage, the return home, to take place.

The return home

The move home should, like all the other developments which have gone before, be carefully planned. The object is to try to make the return home a success rather than a failure, and it may be that the offender should retain his former accommodation for just a bit longer, so that he can briefly move back out if things appear to be heading in the wrong direction. Nevertheless, it is to be hoped that by this stage, his reintegration into the family will be successful. Much of the credit for achieving this positive result will have been due to the systems in place – the ground rules laid down from the first planned visit and extended as the reunification process advanced. The temptation will be to shelve the rules as soon as practicable, but without them as the basis for the conduct of the offender in the home with his family there is a strong possibility he will begin to lapse. The rules (and there were 20 in all) are all designed to reduce the chance of relapse and are aligned to the type of guidelines the offender would, in any case, be creating for himself as part of his RPP (relapse prevention plan). This plan is known to his supervising officer and other support mechanisms, such as his partner. Any infringement of the rules should be challenged by his partner as the first step towards reoffending. A well-motivated offender will accept such comments as positive criticism to work on and discuss with his partner and supervisor or counsellor, and devise or adapt strategies to cope with the new developments. In this way he can view such occurrences as confirmation that he is improving his self-management skills.

The whole process of family reunification is a lengthy and challenging one and involves a lot of work and support for both the victim and the offender. The child's social worker and family workers will have to ensure the pace is not too fast, that all members of the family are comfortable with what is happening and that there are no undue pressures. The offender's supervisor will need to ensure that he is providing regular feedback from the visits and meetings, that he is being open about problems which arise and feelings that he may be having, and so on. The offender should also try to remain on some maintenance group to continue addressing his offending behaviour, and to critically examine and update his RPP. Most importantly, all professionals working in this area should never forget the first priority, which is the protection of the child victim from being reoffended against. To achieve this, all professionals should remember the six Cs: *care, caution, consideration, communication, co-operation* and *coordination.*

CHILD PROTECTION ISSUES

> The object of captors in this period (and all through the centuries up to the abolition of transportation in 1867) was to get rid of the offender with the least trouble and delay, to have him 'clenzit or conviktt' – freed or hanged; out of sight into the grave, the pit, or the next parish. (p.5)

Thus wrote Joy Cameron (1983) about punishments in medieval Scotland. To some extent, we still face the same problem today with sexual offenders, particularly child abusers and molesters. There is a debate which seems to have no resolution. Nobody wants a sexual offender in their backyard. They would rather he moved off to some other area – to the next parish! But here is the problem. It is better for everyone concerned to know who the sexual offender is, and to work with him to ensure that he does not relapse. Parents can only protect their children if they know from where the potential danger may come. And as we have seen from above, useful work can be undertaken with offenders to reintegrate them gradually into the family and the community. The alternative is that they are, at best, shunned and possibly physically intimidated or attacked, so that they leave the area and start afresh somewhere else, unbeknown to anyone. The dangers, then, are that:

- the offender will become 'lost' and disappear
- child protection measures cannot be invoked
- support mechanisms for the offender cannot be put in place
- there is a likelihood that the offender may seek out the company of other such offenders
- he will be lonely, confused, begin to fantasise and recommence his cycle of offending behaviour.

In England, some probation hostels will house sexual offenders and can therefore continue to monitor them. In Scotland, there are very few single-sex hostels which do this. There is some provision in Edinburgh and one in Glasgow which at times takes such offenders. However, a problem exists for those offenders who do not come from the city:

> If we are serious about trying to protect our young, we need to know where these men go once they are released from prison ... For obvious reasons most cannot return to the family home yet there is no safe alternative provided for most of these men ... men who live outwith the Glasgow boundary have usually no alternative but to move into bed and breakfast accommodation where they will usually be surrounded by vulnerable lone parents with children. (Dempsey 1995, p.1)

Much of the work of child protection involves the identification and 'treatment' of abusers. Rates of recidivism are high and are not reflected in the reported rates of offending. Evidence from research indicates that punishment (imprisonment or other penalties imposed by the court) without the offender addressing his offending behaviour is not a deterrent. In fact, it seems that the greater the risk of detection and punishment, the greater will be the effort of the offender to prevent disclosure and detection.

> The starting point must be an acceptance that abusers need to be managed through the Criminal Justice System. Prosecuting perpetrators of sexual abuse not only validates the child's disclosure but is a powerful and public message about the unacceptability of their behaviour. (Aitken 1992, p.2)

In addition, those responsible for the management of such offenders have a parallel responsibility to support child protection issues through their work and through communication of information to other agencies. The effectiveness of this is dependent on co-operation between those working in the criminal justice system and those in the child protection system. According to Aitken (1992), it is essential that a close relationship exists between practitioners servicing these two systems to ensure consistency, management of perpetrators and greater protection of children. She argues that lack of knowledge and information about such offenders and the addictive nature of their abuse has led practitioners and courts to underestimate the level of risk presented by abusers and resulted in some inappropriate decisions being made. Multi-disciplinary co-operation should not just exist when release or family reunification is being contemplated. It should start at the outset. However, the compartmentalised approach is sustained by the demands of the court:

> At present separate Court requests are often made to Social Work, Psychiatric and Psychological Services to provide an assessment on the abuser for the Court. Ideally a multi-disciplinary assessment should be made, at least a greater degree of collaboration between all agencies involved and a greater consensus of what information is required to provide an informed assessment needed to facilitate appropriate management and sentencing of the abusers. (Aitken 1992, p.4)

The Children's Hearing system

The child's perspective is an important issue for child protection. Children should be able to understand when they have been wronged and hope that when people in authority are trying to help them it feels good. There should be relief rather than further anxiety when the abuse is exposed. Yet even Scotland's Children's Hearing system, recognised as being one of the most enlightened pieces of Children's juvenile justice, retains problems. The philosophy and ethos of the Hearing system lays emphasis on the fact that a decision by a Reporter to refer a child to a hearing as being 'in need of compulsory measures of care' is regarded not as a punishment but more as a protective move. The 'Reporter' occupies a unique position among justice systems. Like the Procurator Fiscal, the Reporter can decide whether a case goes forward for consideration by the hearing for compulsory measures of care. However, he or she is independent, is not required to be legally qualified and is appointed by the local authority, and the Reporter's decision on individual cases cannot be challenged or overturned. The Reporter deals with all referrals (or complaints), has discretion in deciding whether to bring a case to a hearing and is the legal adviser and clerk during the hearing. If, at the hearing, when the child is present, either of the parents do not accept the grounds of referral, the case will be sent to the Sheriff for proof; the Reporter will then present the evidence and argue the case before the Sheriff. Also, at present, if the child is too young to understand, the case will be sent to the Sheriff for proof. As part of the government's current Review of Scottish Child Care Law it is likely this provision will be deleted. In addition, the panel may discharge the case. In cases where the child understands, what the child sees is the parent denying publicly what has happened, and for the child this continues the abuse of power and subsequent victimisation.

If the case is returned to the panel to proceed, the parents and child all have a right to be present. This means that if the child is asked to explain what has been happening or how she feels about the abusing parent, that parent may be in the same room. This is not a comfortable or sensitive process and even though the parent can be asked to leave the room, the panel have a duty to inform him of what has been said on his return.

There is also a difference in the levels of proof required. A hearing can act providing the grounds of referral are accepted. The Sheriff will refer the matter back to the hearing to proceed providing he finds the facts in the grounds for referral established. These may be different from what is required to pursue a criminal conviction successfully. It is therefore possible for an abusive parent, at least in the short term, to remain in the home. A home supervision order, which returns the child home with social work supervision, would not be appropriate. The Children's Hearing Panel, at any point from the first hearing onwards, would then have little option but to seek a place of safety order, taking the child away from home and placing her, probably, in a foster home or an assessment centre. Again, the child, who should be supported and made to feel safe in the family home, is taken away and could well feel that she is being further punished for disclosing and speaking out against the abuser.

From all that has been said above, and from the issues raised in Chapter 10, we can see that for child protection to have meaning there must be a broad strategy in place. An effective *child protection strategy* should have the following aims:

1. To educate children, the public and professional staff about the nature of sexual abuse so that children will not keep secrets but disclose and know that adults will listen and believe them.

2. To build up a better understanding of how abuse occurs and its effects so that parents and adults working with children will be aware of the signs (such as dysfunctional behaviour, aggression, withdrawal, or use of inappropriate language and behaviour), and those dealing with offenders can make appropriate decisions.

3. To provide protection and support for those children identified as victims and for other members of the family likely to be at risk in the future.

4. To provide assessment and programmes for offenders to help them address their offending behaviour and learn ways of minimising the risk of reoffending, recognising that their management and supervision is a long-term problem.

5. To promote an inter-agency and multi-disciplinary approach to all aspects of child protection, including the sharing of information and a common understanding of purpose.

6. To maintain full records on offenders, including previous criminal and sexual offending history, and last known details of location, to be made available for child protection purposes.

7. To integrate information on child abusers and sexual offenders with information held by the police on paedophiles and their networks and the traffic in pornography.

8. To retain information about victims and vulnerable children and ensure that child protection measures remain in place as appropriate.

9. To provide comprehensive training and development programmes for staff engaged in supporting victims or working with offenders, and to enhance resources and networking for such staff because of the high demands of this work.

10. To monitor and assess the effectiveness of programmes for offenders and the services provided for victims and families so as to identify improvements in the delivery of child protection.

And finally, a child protection reminder

One of the issues all agencies have to be aware of is the risk that children who have been abused within the family continue to run. Anna Salter uses the phrase 'just because the touching stops – the abuse doesn't'. When the victim is brought together with the abuser, even where other people such as the child's social worker is present, it is easy for verbal and non-verbal cues known only by the offender and his victim to be given, thus perpetuating the abuse. It is the generation of fear by the adult which can create or recreate a no less serious form of abuse and rekindle all the fear and emotional trauma of the past. So we have to be careful and think of the interests of the child before we consider the emotive appeal of the abusive parent.

When planning for contact with former victims, it is important that none of the players make the following assumptions:

- That offence-specific work has been undertaken by the offender, and even where such work has taken place, that the offender is now transformed into a different person. We still have to ensure that it is safe for the offender to make contact with the victim, and those contacts have to be closely monitored by someone who knows how sexual offenders operate.

- That sufficient work has been undertaken with the victim. Especially with children, it is necessary to ensure that they have reached the stage where they feel comfortable with, and not threatened by, a proposed meeting, and that they are not being pressurised by other members of the family.

Lastly, agencies have to remember that when in doubt the child, the victim, has priority. Offenders may make emotional pleas about their continued separation and the suffering they are experiencing, and the deprivation experienced by the child of a male or father figure. Agencies must always remember who is responsible for the problem (the offender) and who subsequently deserves the prior consideration (the child). That is why it is essential to have good co-operation between agencies, and for a proper process of 'throughcare' which does not begin just before the offender is released. Sexual offenders are experienced manipulators. They will use gaps caused by poor communications to their own ends.

Summary of key points

- Child protection must be based on putting the needs of the child first.
- Protection is enhanced by providing the offender with supervision and support in the community.
- A strategy should be developed which supports child protection.

SOCIAL WORK, TRAINING, RESOURCES AND RESPONSIBILITIES

Social workers are expected to play an important part in the identification of abuse and the assessment of risk, provide counselling and casework support to victims, and contribute to the delivery of intervention programmes for offenders who are prepared to address their offending behaviour. These are not easy tasks and require professionalism, objectivity and training. In addition, much of this type of work is stressful and emotionally demanding. Social work staff working with victims and abusers require support and networking. All of these elements require resources and, consequently, funding.

In Scotland, social workers have statutory duties in relation to child protection matters and are also expected to become involved with offender services. Recently the Scottish Prison Service indicated the nature of social work involvement expected in prisons:

> Prison-based social work units are increasingly involved in the development and delivery of intervention programmes designed to address particular forms of offending behaviour, and have a key role to play in assisting Governors to provide these opportunities for prisoners ... The development, consolidation and maintenance of intervention programmes for offenders convicted of child abuse should be a feature of regime plans and social work unit management plans in all establishments holding such prisoners ... In view of the highly complex and skilled nature of the work required of prison-based social workers in this area, Governors should liase with the relevant local authority to ensure continuity of service in this crucial area of work. (SPS 1994)

It is therefore imperative that social workers receive a high level of training in this area. Such training includes formalised courses, attending lectures, reading, attending workshops, seminars and conferences, and importantly, experiencing at first hand the delivery of these specialised skills through observation and participation at interviews, groups and counselling sessions. All agencies, be they local authority social work departments, voluntary sector child protection agencies or the prison system, have a duty to provide relevant training to their staff and those social workers based with them.

With the focus throughout the public sector on providing value for money, and tight budgetary constraints, the ability of organisations to provide anything but basic support is limited. Yet all workers in this area require a range of support mechanisms to allow them to cope when what is being said to them by victims and/or by abusers creates upset, conflict and turmoil within them. Social workers and specialists provide support to others, but who provides them with the support they need? That is why the resources have to be put in place to encourage networking and 'days away' when they can attend a conference, or meet others at in-service training days.

The whole area of working with sexual offenders is itself comparatively new, and as the subject develops and knowledge and practice improves, those involved in the delivery of such programmes need time to look at the developments elsewhere, evaluate the findings of research and examine how they can evolve the delivery of their own programmes. In fact, it is amazing to reread some of the criminological literature from the sixties and the early seventies. Sex offending is principally discussed in relation to homosexual offences and the Wolfenden Committee Report (1957), issues relating to prostitution, the difference between art, pornography and obscene publications in the *Lady Chatterley's Lover* trial, and discussion on sexual norms and myths about rape. It is Professor Marshall's own work, and that of a handful of others, from the start of the seventies, on treatment methods for sexual offenders which has moved this whole subject forward.

Work with abusers requires a different approach from that of traditional social work casework principles. For a variety of reasons, not all social workers may be able or willing to become involved in this area of work. This should be recognised and practitioners allowed to make the choice. Social workers do not require 'special' skills to undertake this work. Skills which form part of the basic training, such as communication, engagement, gathering information and assessment, are used. However, these skills do need to be enhanced by theoretical material, training in models and methods of intervention, clear guidelines on the purpose of intervention and effective supervision and support. According to Aitken (1992), the main points are:

- The practitioner operates from a basis of scepticism rather than trust.
- The practitioner controls the agenda.
- There can be no guarantee of confidentiality for the abuser (for example, if the abuser gives information indicating that a child is at risk, then this must be passed on appropriately).
- Court sanctions and those imposed by supervision requirements are used as an aid, rather than as an alternative, to therapy.
- Demands are placed on the client to discuss and explore intimate areas of sexual history and functioning.
- The practitioner uses assumptions drawn from research. These assumptions are:
  - The abuser's actions were premeditated.
  - The abuser's role was active and conscious.
  - The abuser rehearsed the offence(s) in fantasy.
  - The abuser perceived the victim as a sex object.
  - The abuser targeted the victim.
  - The abuser groomed the victim/family/environment.

- The abuser made the victim available, and made the victim avoid disclosing.
- The abuser's offending is repetitive.
- The abuser's motivation to adhere to a programme of work will fluctuate.
- The abuser will be at risk of reoffending for a long time.

Finally, social work departments need to provide community-based intervention programmes for sexual offenders. Their clients may be those who have been released from prison with or without a supervision requirement, those who have or who have not already undertaken intensive programmes, and those offenders who have been placed on probation and given a condition of attending an offence-specific programme or those who are attending in the community on a voluntary basis. Whatever the route, social work departments cannot afford to miss the opportunity of providing these programmes – which will have a resource cost in trained personnel and facilities in which to undertake the programme.

There will be an increasing requirement to continue the work already begun in prison. The new Creating Control Programme in Barlinnie Prison has its extension in the Strathclyde Social Work Department in Glasgow, and the Tay Project in Dundee takes sexual offenders on release to their area and provides a continuation of offence-specific work.

Responsibilities

Additionally, recent legislation (i.e. the Prisoners and Criminal Proceedings (Scotland) Act 1993, the Crime and Punishment (Scotland) Act 1997, the Sex Offenders Act 1997 and the Crime and Disorder Act 1998) has had a huge impact on the responsibilities placed on social workers in prisons and in the community. These primarily concern supervision in the community and from prison on release. However, the tasks spread over a wide range: pre-sentence reports and assessments; notification of registration requirements; notification of supervision requirements and arrangements; counselling work with offenders; supervision of caseload through prison sentence to release with regular visits to prisoners; exchange of information; risk assessments; close supervision; arrangements and conditions for life in the community; and liaison with the police and other agencies.

The most recent guidelines (SWSG 1998) indicate the tasks associated with the introduction of extended sentences, though many of these duties already existed under the range of previous legislation and the National Standards for Social Work. Such tasks for community and prison-based social workers now include:

- Preparation for the court of a social enquiry report prior to sentencing, including risk assessment (looking at a whole range of factors) where an extended sentence is being considered to assist the court to reach a view about future risks and the role which supervision might play.

- Assisting the court and later the Parole Board in assessing the need for, and value of, any additional requirements during supervision.

- Notifying the prison, the prison Social Work Unit and the prisoner, and visiting the family within agreed time scales.

- Working closely with the prisoner, family, prison officers and specialist staff, social work staff in prisons, and other specialist agencies or staff towards effective pre-release planning, including notifying and advising the prisoner of the various obligations under Sex Offender Registration, extended sentence supervision and any Schedule One child protection matters.

- Regular visits to the prisoner on a six- or twelve-monthly basis.

- Providing a home background report for parole (or home visit) purposes, to be informed by an assessment visit.

- Increased contact with the offender's family.

- Supervision over a long period (perhaps up to ten years) combining elements of risk assessment and management, overseeing of the offender's activities and circumstances, the provision of practical assistance (with, for example, accommodation, employment, training opportunities or financial matters), monitoring compliance with licence conditions, and assistance with resettlement and reintegration.

- The provision of personal change programmes while in the community, and contributing to such work while in prison.

- Reviewing and updating the supervision plan on a regular basis, arranging meetings and frequency and nature of supervision.

- Holding at least eight supervision meetings in the first three months for those on extended sentences, of which three must be in the form of a home visit.

- Seeking to add, delete or vary conditions of supervision or, in some cases, recommending revocation and recall to the Secretary of State.

- To provide, as appropriate, progress and completion reports and updated assessments to the Secretary of State (i.e. Parole Board).

- Exchange of assessment and other information between social workers in prisons and the community, personal officers, psychologists, and the police in relation to risk assessment under Sex Offender Registration.

Social workers can expect to be busy!

Summary of key points

- Training and support of social work staff in dealing with the wide range of problems presented by sexual offenders is a high priority.

- Recent legislation has resulted in social workers undertaking a wide range of duties in relation to sexual offenders.

SUPERVISION AND SUPPORT ON RELEASE

To be effective the treatment team must build in ... monitoring, support and guidance through the services available to the offender on his release. This will require a large additional work load in co-ordinating the service to prisoners on their release. (Cooke 1994, p.138)

Sexual offenders require support from those around them if they are not to relapse. Ideally, they should have their own relapse prevention strategy, which can be discussed with their social worker and/or family, to provide methods of controlling or intervening in the offending cycle of behaviour. Offence-specific therapy groups should be available on release and participation in such groups would provide added support. The National Objectives and Standards for Social Work Services states:

Action to address the problems of the offender – by helping the offender to understand the reasons underlying his/her offending; helping him/her to face up to his/her offence and its consequences for the victim, the victim's family, the offender and his/her family and for the community; helping motivate the offender to change; helping the offender to find ways of avoiding such behaviour in the future. (SWSG 1991, at 3(5), 3.1.2)

Providing the resources are in place, social workers would be involved in helping to address such behaviour and motivating offenders to change.

In Scotland, the changes brought about by the Kincraig Report (SHHD 1989), enacted in the Prisoners and Criminal Proceedings (Scotland) Act 1993, which provided for all long-term prisoners to complete their full sentence on parole, to some extent began this process. With the introduction of Sex Offender Registration (1997) and extended sentences (1998), all recently convicted long-term sexual offenders should be on post-release supervision, which can last up to ten years in determinate cases. Such prisoners will now clearly require supervision, but it is also probable that if the disposal of the court is a short-term sentence, the judge may take the opportunity, provided by the 1993 Act and the more recent Crime and Punishment (Scotland) Act 1997, of additionally imposing a supervised release order, which will cause the offender to serve the second part of his sentence under supervision in the community. There is, therefore, a need to establish a resource of appropriately trained social work staff.

They will need to understand what work has been undertaken in prison and how they are to facilitate the relapse prevention strategies prepared by offenders.

In addition to some of the social work tasks outlined above (see pp.161–163), the Skinner Report, *A Commitment to Protect, Supervising Sex Offenders: Proposals for More Effective Practice* (SWSI 1997), also suggested a whole range of practical steps which could be taken to strengthen supervision. If a high-risk offender resides in specialist or approved accommodation, participates in programmes and has constructive activities, the task of supervision is made easier. However, for many this will not be the case. The report suggests a range of practical approaches which are not in general use but could be applied, to a greater or lesser degree, preferably with, but not necessarily dependent upon, the agreement of the offender. The report lists 19 practical steps (pp. 28–29) which are summarised below:

- requiring the offender to keep a daily diary of activities – with checks
- a frequent schedule of home visits
- electronic monitoring of movements to check veracity of self-reports
- working with the police in surveillance activities
- checking house and car for warning signs, e.g. pornography and photographs
- telephoning offenders daily
- recruiting someone to act as a 'second report'
- conducting periodic 'intensive reviews' with in-depth monitoring
- agreeing 'family reports' with the offender and his family
- periodic 'intensive assessments'
- unannounced 'report veracity checks' – checking out with third parties
- organising 'spot checks' on offenders (out of office hours)
- whole-day report sessions, perhaps conducted by two staff
- observation of offenders in social settings
- second worker watching/videoing sessions to detect evasion/manipulation
- offenders requested to produce documentary evidence of activities
- more use of 'interrogative' supervision, probing answers and statements
- checking that offenders have positive activities in the community
- 'Turn about' intensive daily supervision for high-risk offenders.

This is an interesting and exciting list with plenty of practical measures to strengthen supervision. However, it is likely to be highly resource intensive in its application.

An additional problem might be that, at present, there are not many hostels or halfway houses providing supported accommodation for ex-prisoner sexual offenders. Without suitable accommodation, it becomes difficult to keep tabs on such men. The Scottish Association for the Care and Resettlement of Offenders (SACRO) provides resettlement hostels which help with this process, and the Hamish Allan Centre in Glasgow also assists local men. Support, however, is crucial. The offender needs somewhere to stay and he needs to know there is someone to whom he can turn to discuss problems. That, again, calls for trained staff and resources. This is an issue for social work departments, local authorities and their housing departments, the voluntary sector and government. Like many other issues relating to sexual offenders, a co-ordinated approach to support on release is long overdue. One consequence of the Sex Offenders Act 1997 has been that the Social Work Services Group of The Scottish Office has recommended the development of local forums where expertise on these matters can be shared (paragraph 23 of Circular 11/97). In addition to probation and statutory supervision on release, local authorities also have a statutory responsibility to provide advice, guidance and assistance to people who ask for it within twelve months of release from custody.

NOTIFICATION OF INFORMATION ON OFFENDERS
The Sex Offenders Act 1997

The Sex Offenders Act 1997, which came into force on 1 September 1997, requires persons convicted of specific sexual offences to notify the police of their name(s), date of birth and home address, and any subsequent changes. This also includes the requirement that the offender notify the police in his home area of any premises where he stays for a period of 14 days or more, or two or more periods, in any period of twelve months, which, taken together, amount to 14 days or more. If the offender has no fixed abode or is homeless, he must give the police details of a place which he visits regularly and where he may be contacted. Failure to notify the police with correct details is an offence punishable by a fine and/or imprisonment. However, the Act only applies to offenders who were currently within the criminal justice system (on 1 September 1997) and new cases. Those former sexual offenders who are no longer imprisoned or on compulsory supervision are not required to register.

Recent statistics from Edinburgh Prison show that 140 prisoners were affected by registration requirements in the 14-month period since its introduction.[3] About 60 prisoners were already serving sentences at the time of implementation, and a further 80 admitted since. In the same period about 50 were released at the expiry of their sentence.

3　　Figures supplied by the Social Work Unit, Edinburgh Prison, November 1998.

Parliament's intention was to ensure that information about sexual offenders held by the police would be kept fully up to date, so that the police and other agencies could effectively carry out their responsibilities to prevent crime and protect vulnerable members of the community and other members of the public. In order to achieve this, police forces would have to share information with local authority social work departments.

> *Local authorities should agree arrangements with their local police forces about when, and to whom in the social work service, the police should give information notified to them under this Act.* Such information will include personal and confidential details about the offender and the nominated officer in the authority who receives the information must keep it securely, and strictly confidential. (SWSG 1997, para. 9)

Once the local authority receives such information, it is up to them to collate available information and try to assess the likely risk that the offender may present to previous or potential victims

> and thereafter take appropriate steps to reduce risk to children, or other vulnerable people in the area. (SWSG 1997, para. 20)

What constitutes 'appropriate steps' is not clearly defined. It includes court action to protect the child through compulsory measures of supervision (of the child) and/or an exclusion order placing a restriction on the offender's behaviour or movements. It can also involve disclosure of information about the individual or discussion about his possible location of residence. Great care has to be exercised by local authorities if they are contemplating sharing information with any person outside their agency:

> *The local authority should not normally disclose personal information about offenders to staff outside the social work service unless they believe serious harm might result from not sharing information about the risk the offender poses. In such cases information may be shared with specified staff on a 'restricted' basis.* If the local authority decide that, in a particular case, it is necessary to share information with staff outside the social work service, the basis for this decision should be carefully recorded. Any disclosure should be limited to such information as is necessary to reduce the identified risk and may mean not divulging the person's full details including their name. Where the social work service, in consultation with the police, decide that the offender is likely to pose a serious risk to others in the area they may decide to hold an inter-departmental meeting to plan what action is necessary. The local authority should be aware that by attempting to reduce the risk an offender poses in one area they may put other people in another area at greater risk, and should consider the sum of the potential effects of any decisions they may take, before choosing a particular course of action. (SWSG 1997, para. 21)

The above paragraph constitutes two clear warnings: first, on disclosure of information and, second, about the consequences of decisions which might make the offender move on to another area. If sexual offenders are to be encouraged to seek support in the community, then actions which lead to them being hounded out of an area (such as the case from Stirling in 1997) will be counter-productive. Clearly, a high-risk offender will pose a threat to any community. If the issue does not concern the offender's potential to continue the perpetration of abuse on previous victims, then every community has as much, and an equal, right to be safe from such offenders. But all communities also have a duty to try to make such offenders less of a risk by providing guidance and support. The concept of getting rid of the offender by moving him out of sight into the next parish is both short-sighted and restrictive. The 'not in my backyard' approach assumes an insular and predominantly selfish attitude, lacking in real care for the wider community in which we all live.

In exceptional circumstances, the police might decide to make notification available to others. Before considering disclosure to a third party, the police would have to consider alternative courses of action. These might include:

- discussion with the offender
- warning him about avoiding high-risk situations or areas, such as when he is seen loitering near a school
- discussing his case with a supervising officer (if he is on supervision) and possibly considering the use of breach proceedings or recommending revocation of licence
- the exercise of statutory responsibilities by social work services for the support and protection of vulnerable individuals.

However, after fully assessing the potential risk in consultation with social work services and any other relevant statutory authorities, exceptionally, the police may decide

> that an offender presents so great a risk that they should make notification information available to other agencies and specified persons, in addition to the social work service, preserving confidentiality as far as is reasonably possible. (SWSG 1997, para. 24)

They should take into account the following factors:

- the nature and pattern of the offender's previous offending;
- his compliance with previous sentences or court orders;
- any predatory behaviour which may indicate a likelihood that he will re-offend;
- the probability that a further offence will be committed;

- the likely harm such behaviour would cause;
- the extent to which potential victims, such as children, are vulnerable;
- the potential consequences of disclosure to the offender and their family; and
- the potential consequences of the disclosure for other aspects of law and order. (SWSG 1997, para. 24)

Care has to be exercised about to whom, and in what manner, such information is divulged. The police must keep a record of the grounds for such a decision. They should also be prepared to offer advice and guidance on how the recipient of the information should respond.

> The police will provide notification information only to an identified individual, or individuals directly affected by the risk of harm such as a previous victim or victim's family or an offender's new partner, or with responsibilities towards others for the prevention of harm, such as a headteacher or playgroup leader. A police officer will disclose information in person and such information should be limited to that necessary to minimise perceived risk. The disclosure will be confirmed in writing and the police officer will ensure that the individual is aware that the information should not be disclosed further. (SWSG 1997, para. 26)

Notification of 'third parties' is envisaged as the exception. There is no intention, under the Act, to move to automatic *public notification,* as occurs in a significant number of states in the USA. Indeed, the police are liable through the civil courts if they do not exercise their judgement and discretion in a reasonable way.

Public notification of sexual offenders: 'Megan's Law' – the issues[4]

1. Setting the scene

The issue of 'public notification' of sex offenders is one which, especially for communities, is charged with emotion. However, we have to try to lay to one side the feelings which this subject can arouse and focus on what we want to achieve and how that can be best met. It can be argued that *the fundamental objective of the criminal justice system should be to prevent crime rather than to deal with its consequences.* Therefore, what we do with sexual offenders on release should be to ensure that, where possible, they do not offend again or, if that seems a tall order, then to delay and minimise the harm they might perpetrate. The totality of our objective should be focused on harm reduction as that is the best way to prevent further victims. The proponents of public notification would claim they have this objective firmly in mind. Those of us who believe in the importance of providing interventions for

---

4   Some of the issues surrounding public notification of sexual offender release were aired in an interesting debate in articles by Robert E. Freeman-Longo 'Prevention or problem?' and Lucy Berliner (April 1996) 'Community notification: Neither a panacea nor a calamity' in *Sexual Abuse: A Journal of Research and Treatment 8, 2,* 91–104.

sexual offenders to enable them to address their offending behaviour and modify their belief systems would argue that these courses of action (and not public notification) seem to be the best guarantee of harm reduction. Anything that drives a wedge between programme delivery and support of the offender must give rise to concern. However, whether the two systems can, to some extent, coexist is a matter which deserves further consideration.

2. The public response in the USA: Megan's Law

On 29 July 1994, Jesse Timmendequas sexually assaulted and murdered seven-year-old Megan Kanka in Hamilton, New Jersey. Megan's death outraged community members, especially upon discovering that Jesse Timmendequas was a twice-convicted sexual offender (child molester) living anonymously as a neighbour within their community. The circumstances surrounding Megan Kanka's death, and similar incidents, prompted New Jersey citizens to launch a campaign for legislation that would require authorities to notify community members when a convicted sexual offender moved into their community. In memory of Megan, her family and friends coined the legislation 'Megan's Law'.

The public is naturally outraged at such crimes, and that outrage is often reflected in the sensational way such cases are reported in the media. The sense of anger and shock that such cases generate creates a response which can be often more emotional than logical. In the USA, the result of this reaction has been a wave of law-making to stiffen penalties, increase sentence lengths, and introduce supervision requirements and public notification of sexual offenders released into the community. In fact, the federal government and most US states have now passed such legislation.

The question which needs to be asked is whether this response will, in fact, reduce the prevalence of such crimes and whether these changes are based on research or on an assumption, a 'feel-good' factor, which may in the long run result in unwelcomed consequences.

Laws about public notification of sexual offender release have been developed in the USA to alert the public, specifically members of the local community, that they are living in the presence of a dangerous offender. By increasing community awareness through these laws, it is believed that (1) parents will be able to inform their children about who is dangerous and whom to avoid, and (2) public notification will reduce the likelihood that a sexual offender will reoffend because everyone will know that he is a sexual offender and it will be more difficult for him to lure a potential victim.

3. The system in the USA

A system of notification has been adopted by many US states. The scheme works as follows. Every sexual offender ready for release from prison is screened by the state according to risk and placed into one of three categories based on the seriousness of the crime, use of force, history of criminal behaviour and number of victims. This information is then placed in a centralised database maintained by the state department (c f public safety) and made available to all law enforcement and probation agencies in the state. Indeed, nowadays, such information is widely available on the internet from State websites.

Once an offender is released from prison and moves to an area, he must register with the local police. The law requires law enforcement agencies to notify the public of certain offenders who move into their jurisdictions.

There are three levels of classification for sexual offenders, with Level 3 being the most serious risk:

Level 1	Verify offender's address through a personal visit; notify other residents in the home; and verify that the offender has registered with the local police. This information might extend to victims and witnesses.
Level 2	Perform all Level 1 procedures; review offender's history; provide information that would include the name, description, vicinity of address, and general history of the offender to schools, community organisations, religious groups, youth clubs and neighbours as appropriate.
Level 3	Perform all Level 1 and 2 procedures; notify immediate neighbours and schools in person; forward information that includes the name, description, specific address, photograph and history of the offender to community groups, print and electronic media. In addition, community notification meetings can be held.

There clearly is some concern about the consequences of notification and most information about such procedures also contain statements such as:

> *It is important to note that acts of harassment, intimidation and / or retaliation toward an offender based on the public notification information is prohibited by law.*

4. Advantages of public notification

Public notification seems logical to its supporters. It gives the impression of being a workable solution to the problem of child sexual abuse that makes people feel safer.

1. *Knowledge:* It alerts the public and specifically local communities that they are living in the presence of a dangerous offender.

2. *Informing children:* Parents will be able to inform children about who is dangerous and to avoid. The greater the risk the offender presents, the more information will be available, including photographs of the offender.

Informing children might also be extended to schools giving out information in class, having notices on walls, and also to youth groups undertaking similar duties.

3. *Identification:* Public notification may reduce the likelihood of reoffending as everybody knows who the sexual offender(s) is/are. It takes away the anonymity of the offender. He may, therefore, be less able to get into higher-risk situations such as hanging around school playgrounds or parks, babysitting or becoming involved in working with youth groups.

4. *Feeling safer:* It makes people *feel* safer. With the knowledge, people are better in control of their lives and can plan and take preventative steps as appropriate. They also know that others share this information and may also be 'looking out' for one another.

5. *Promoting understanding:* It promotes interest and education in a subject which is worthy of discussion. Community notification meetings bring together various professionals who help to disseminate information on how families can talk to and protect children and begin to understand the nature of sexual offending.

6. *Harnesses support:* Community notification creates an informed group of relatives, friends and neighbours who could support the offender and thereby prevent reoffending. They might be positively motivated to become involved and provide necessary support and involvement.

5. Disadvantages of public notification

A number of issues can be identified which give rise to concern that public notification systems are not as simple or straightforward as their proponents would wish us to believe, and raise a series of questions (Freeman-Longo 1996).

1. *Origins:* Public notification was created as a response to horrific sexual crimes and murders. Most sexual crimes are less horrendous and public notification may tend to brand all sexual offenders alike. The public may not be able to distinguish between types of crime and offender.

2. *Risk determination:* Notification procedures tend to be mechanistic and are based on historical data including past convictions. It may not be easy to sort out those past offenders who pose little or no future threat to their communities. It could be argued that individuals who do not pose any further threat, either because they have been through programmes and are rehabilitated, or because their offence was minor or isolated should not be subjected to the same treatment as those who may still pose a threat. Some systems are based on risk assessment on release, others on conviction data and some are determined by prosecutors at the time of sentence.

3. *Legislative questions (rights and punishments):* Community notification also creates a new punishment for persons who have already served their sentence. Since this law would apply to individuals for (say) ten years after their conviction or release (usually whichever is the later), it effectively changes the rules for persons who have already served their sentence by subjecting them to a new penalty of public disclosure and humiliation. Such a system can be especially damaging for those who have been rehabilitated and have reintegrated themselves into their families and communities. This new system is likely to be in violation of the European Convention on Human Rights and, perhaps, would constitute a cruel and unusual punishment. Retrospective, or *ex post facto*, legislation is always difficult to impose, but would be necessary to ensure a complete listing – otherwise all past or existing convicted offenders would be excluded, rendering such a system of little value. There may be additional issues about the right to personal privacy. In the USA, a number of constitutional challenges have been made to this legislation.

4. *Plea bargaining:* Cases of sexual offending are often difficult to prove and prosecutors sometimes accept plea bargains to lesser offences. Offenders who use plea bargaining to downgrade their charges may be dangerous, but the lesser offence may not be subject to public notification. The presence of additional punitive elements may encourage plea bargaining to the long-term detriment of public safety.

5. *Decrease in reporting:* Evidence is emerging from the USA that there may be a decrease in the reporting of juvenile sexual offences and incest offences by family members and victims who do not want to deal with the impact of public notification on their family. 'As of Fall 1995, New Jersey reports experiencing a decrease in the number of juvenile sexual offenses being reported by parents who do not want their child subjected to public notification laws.' (Freeman-Longo 1996, p.97). Further, many child molesters are incest offenders, and have only offended within the family. Although their offense is odious, they are unlikely to attack strangers, they generally respond well to 'treatment' programmes and recidivism rates for this group are low. Their dangerousness to the community at large may be minimal. Public notification for this type of offender might therefore be counter-productive.

6. *Effect on families of offender:* The families which share the same accommodation are also identified, stigmatised and victimised. If names and addresses are put on computers (e.g. by postcode and house number), then there may be future adverse effects (such as job opportunities or credit rating). Members of such families become objects of comment and this may negatively affect their rights.

7. *Violence:* Public notification sometimes creates violent responses in the community. Examples already exist of houses being burnt down (in the USA), beatings, vigilantism, and pickets and protests outside the houses of the offenders. Sexual offenders (and their families) are driven out of their homes. In Scotland, we have already faced disturbances in Stirling and Aberdeen.

8. *Mistakes:* Sometimes innocent individuals are mistakenly identified as 'that man' by the public and are beaten up. Offenders may give false information about themselves, their address, etc., resulting in innocent people suffering; computer errors could also result in similar problems.

9. *Impact on victims:* Public notification affects more than just the offender. When the case is public and the community knows the identity of a sexual offender, they may also know the identity of his victims, especially if that victim is local or, indeed, a member of his family. How should the community help such a child victim to respond to the possibility of taunts or being shunned at school?

10. *Age of offender:* From what age should a sexual offender be liable to notification? Will it be 21 years old, 18 or 16, or juveniles from the age of 13 or younger? Serious offending does not begin merely after the age of 21. So any cut-off point has to be arbitrary and will exclude some dangerous individuals. Also, the younger the age of inclusion, the more likely will it be to have an adverse impact on the development of the young person. Public notification might become an obstacle to developing friends and normal relationships, reduce self-esteem and inhibit the individual from receiving therapy.

11. *Effectiveness:* Can public notification be effectively administered? How many offenders' faces can children memorise? And what about offenders from the next town and neighbouring towns and villages? Should they also be memorised? And what if an offender travels for the day? One report in a newspaper indicated that Megan Kanka was warned by her mother to stay away from the house – but this did not save her life. Sexual offenders are notoriously manipulative and they plan offending and groom and target their victims.

12. *Costs and resources:* What do we do if a child abuser fails to register? Do we have the resources to 'hunt down' the offender wherever he may be? Public notification is likely to reduce the likelihood of offenders registering and will require continuous monitoring by police and social workers to ensure offender compliance. These same individuals will have to validate addresses and changes, and notify schools, clubs and residents about new offenders.

13. *Discrimination against offender:* Public notification may entail difficulties in finding a job (or even loss of existing employment) and lead to discrimination in areas where such information is not relevant.

14. *False sense of security:* Registration gives a false sense of security. First, not all offenders register. In the USA, about one in four sexual offenders fail to register. The person who registers is the offender who complies and may therefore not be the most deviant. It is the other offenders, who have not registered, that may be more dangerous. Second, because convicted sexual offenders are only the 'tip of the iceberg' and there are many more people offending who are not known about. Often, children are molested by men who have befriended their mothers. These women tend to be vulnerable and poor and are less likely to go to the local police station, library, council office (or wherever) to search the Sex Offender Register and, since many sexual offenders have never been caught, they are not always in the register! Finally, public notification may soothe local community fears but it will not prevent known sexual offenders from going to an unsuspecting community and selecting a victim. The public therefore have a sense of security which is not realistic. Just because the man they see is not on their local list, it does not, therefore, make him or them safe. One Civil Liberties critic in USA commented: 'Megan's Law is a slogan, not a solution.'[5]

15. *Communities living in fear:* Indeed, the opposite of the above can result – namely, not feeling safe. As public notification laws begin to identify increasing numbers of offenders in an area, this will result in communities feeling terrorised and at risk. What will happen when a particular community discovers that it has a number of known child sexual abusers living in its area? Will people feel safer? How will this fear affect the children when their parents think it is no longer safe for them to go out and play? How will children feel if lists of names and photographs are shown of people that are dangerous and must be avoided? In the end they might feel terrorised and frightened. Children have the right to a secure and 'innocent' childhood. We have not assessed what living in fear of offenders for many years may do to the development of ordinary children.

16. *Effect on mobility:* Public notification is likely to create future problems for our communities. With the publication of lists, or the disclosure of the fact to potential residents that a neighbour is a known sexual offender, it is likely that this information will have an adverse effect on the attractiveness (and even the value) of housing in a particular street or area. Communities might then be faced with the option of either seeing the desirability and

5   'The American people need to demand more from their legislators than easy, quick-fix approaches, Megan's Law is a slogan, not a solution.' Mark Kappelhoff of the American Civil Liberties Union, quoted in the Fort Worth Star-Telegram, 1996 (internet).

willingness of people to settle in their area diminish or somehow effecting the removal of the offender.

17. *Offenders' responses:* The fear of being targeted in the community (or followed) may cause offenders to break off contact with their supervisors or offender groups. The sexual offender needs to be part of a proper social network, not to be banished. He also needs to learn appropriate skills to survive and function in the community. Ostracism may result in offenders despairing of ever living a normal life or being accepted in the community. Such hopelessness produces an apathetic response to attempts to inculcate conformity with community morals and values. Ultimately, if offenders are driven away from their support mechanisms, they will become alienated and angry and give up on any 'compact' they may have made with society.

18. *Misplaced responsibility:* Public notification places responsibility for community safety and appropriate individual conduct on the community instead of on the offender. Programmes are most effective when offenders are required to take full responsibility for their own behaviour. Comprehensive intervention programmes using relapse-prevention and cognitive–behavioural techniques emphasise the offender's responsibility to notify persons in his support systems of his offending behaviour, patterns and risk factors which contribute to reoffending. Unlike public notification, each person in the offender's support system assists the supervisor (therapist or case social worker) in monitoring the offender's behaviour by reporting any problems. This system places the responsibility on the offender to ensure supportive monitoring whereas statutory public notification imposes responsibility on the community itself.

19. *Confidentiality and ethics:* A small number of sexual offenders commit such acts as a consequence of suffering from mental illness. Would individuals also be subject to public notification if their offending has a 'medical' or psychiatric cause? Generally, medical diagnosis is confidential, even where risk might attach, such as in the cases of HIV or other contagious diseases. Of greater significance may be the problem of obtaining proper assessment by professionals. Offenders and abusers who are in need of help may go for assessment and therapy. If such professionals are then required to submit the information they have gained for public disclosure, there is likely to be a conflict of interest from an ethical point of view.

20. *What works?:* There is, currently, no known evidence available to support the suggestion that public notification works. However, what we do know is that properly constituted programmes, both in prison and the community, have a significant effect on reoffending.

6. Is there a balance?

Community notification does not necessarily have to be a substitute for preventative efforts. The problem is that we do not fully know how to prevent sexual offending. Community notification could, perhaps, be seen as one component of a community's response to convicted sexual offenders. The principle would be that law enforcement agencies are granted the legal authority to be able to inform certain members of the public of the presence of a dangerous sexual offender in the community. This would be a discretionary power and the authorities would not need to notify the public of offenders who are considered low-risk and those who have successfully undertaken programmes. However, those offenders who refuse to admit to their offences, take responsibility or become involved with intervention programmes require the imposition of external controls because they are unwilling to exercise personal responsibility for reducing the risk of reoffence.

Those against community notification might argue that sexual offenders are being unfairly singled out. However, this is inconsistent with the general premise that sexual offenders require specialised 'treatment' regimes. If the public desires to protect itself from known offenders, is that not a reasonable and rational response to the presence of danger? Community notification offers the opportunity to promote an educated and concerned public. In the USA, it is often accompanied by a community meeting that brings together individuals in law enforcement, corrections, education, the church, and victim treatment and prevention specialists as well as other social agencies. Families are provided with information, and confidence in government and social agencies as sources of support is enhanced. It has even been argued that notification can be made a vehicle to help community members take responsibility for reaching out to offenders and providing the jobs and support systems they need.

Under the Sexual Offenders Act 1997, notification to specified third parties is considered exceptional and only where the offender presents a great risk. If a more generalised system were to go ahead, some safeguards could be built in – including judicial review of the offender's record prior to any release of information. On the other hand, there is no easy resolution to the problem of communities taking action by themselves. When driven out, where do the convicted sexual offenders go? If they are given new accommodation in another town by the authorities, do you tell the residents of the new local community or not? If you do notify them, why should they tolerate the offender in their community if the previous one was not prepared to do so, and if they don't, then where does the offender go next? If you do not tell the residents of the next community, then why not? Do they not have an equal right to know about sexual offenders in their midst? In the end, the offender may move without telling anyone, and without support systems there is a much greater chance of reoffending. We know that as support diminishes and feelings of loss of power and low self-esteem develop, so does the urge to combat these deficits through fantasies and then abusive acts.

7. Conclusion

Whether public notification is an appropriate component of a comprehensive community response to convicted sexual offenders requires further debate. This debate should be informed by the facts available and the known results. All social policies have costs and benefits, and the issues they raise are complex and not amenable to simple solutions. The critical issue is whether such systems will reduce the totality of harm perpetrated by such offenders. If the public feel that knowledge about dangerous sexual offenders in their area will help them better protect their families, then such systems must be examined closely. There must be very good cause for a position of 'knowing better' than the public.

From an 'informed' viewpoint, wholesale community notification is not the answer. It does not provide a solution for two reasons. First, we only know about a small number of offenders and identifying known individuals gives a false sense of security to communities about the rest of the people within them. It is also useless if known offenders choose to travel somewhere else for the day. Second, sexual offenders are best managed with appropriate support systems. Where they are hounded out, they will go underground. They are then driven to the very conditions we know are more rather than less likely to support offending. The better solution is to attempt to maintain systems of registration in which police and social work departments are made aware of those offenders in their areas and can monitor and support them while respecting their rights as private citizens.

AND AFTERWARDS...

The prison sentence is over. The offender has undertaken offence-specific intervention programmes while in prison. He has been released on supervision and joined in further work. He even attended voluntary supervision for a while after the requirement to do so ceased.

Even if this is the ideal case, how are we to be sure that when the interest in him lessens, as other more recent offenders make demands on our finite resources, that he is not going to relapse? The answer is, of course, that we cannot be certain.

By now, we should have learned that the offender has to take responsibility for his own actions. After all, we have been trying to get him to see that for himself through all the work on denial. Haven't we got him to understand all the damage and harm he has caused to his victims? Surely, he would not want to do that again? Well, what happens when he starts getting those feelings which make him aroused and a little flushed, and then later he starts fantasising? He has not done anything yet, but the relapse prevention strategy that we both worked on for so long and in so much detail – will that not advise him on what to do next? Anyway, all the time spent on looking at his cycle of offending behaviour means that he knows what is going to happen next if…

So he is out there alone. All the work done with him means that he has a chance. All the support mechanisms, the relapse prevention manual, the telephone numbers, the friends that know about his offending and whom he can call upon – that surely counts for something. In fact, he has got my phone number too, and he said he would ring if he needed to. Although I have not heard from him, no news might be good news. He has not been arrested. Maybe all the work done was useful. At least he has not offended for a while and that is something. What job did he say he was…?

Have you ever had that sort of conversation with yourself? All we can ever do is to try our best. However, there is a real world out there and it will be an uphill struggle, not only because for him there might always be a propensity to offend, but because the culture of our society implicitly condones the very attitudes which support offending.

> …just listening to the way schoolboys talk about girls or considering how certain newspapers and comedians continue to confuse sex, soft pornography and rape makes it apparent how endemic such attitudes are in our culture… Rapists and child abusers do not have to invent justifications for their actions; they simply share attitudes prevalent in society. (Wyre and Swift 1990, p.73)

CHAPTER 12

Other Multi-Agency Issues

PAROLE AND RELATED MATTERS

The Parole Board are rightly concerned about the potential risk to the public of the release of persons convicted of sexual offences. Yet unless the prisoner is serving an indeterminate life sentence, released he must be by the end of his (determinate) sentence. It is therefore possible for a sexual offender to go through his sentence untouched by the experience, and potentially as dangerous to the public as before. In fact, as we know, some prisoners will claim it is the experience of being imprisoned that has made them decide not to come back (whether that is a resolution to stop offending or not to be caught!). However, if they have not attempted to come to terms with their offending behaviour and undertaken work to address these issues, it is likely that they will have used the time to network with other sexual offenders and feed on their own distorted value systems and fantasies. This serves no one's best interest.

With the development of structured intervention programmes in many countries, it is pleasing to note that parole boards are increasingly making it a condition for sexual offenders to have undertaken some sort of programme before being considered for early release on licence. At least this carrot provides some incentive for those so motivated. But experiencing the programme is by itself not enough. There has to have been some assessable change which leads the staff involved to believe that the offender presents a reduced risk.

The concept of throughcare must be central to the whole process of planning for release. If applicable, there should be a facility for the Parole Board to be brought into early discussions on how it is envisaged that the offender will be reintegrated into the family or the community, and what additional conditions it would be appropriate to include in the licence. If an offender is to be granted early release on parole, the supervising social worker or probation officer must have been involved in the preparatory case conferences and be fully aware of the family situation and the work already undertaken with the victim and the offender.

Earlier, it was suggested that videotaped material could perhaps be included as part of the parole dossier and submitted for use by the Parole Board. The Board have a difficult task in assessing which prisoners may have made some progress in addressing their offending behaviour and, as a consequence, may pose less of a risk to the public. One of the ways such 'changes' might be observed is to videotape a developing series of *snapshots* of how the offender views his offence and the effects of his actions, and how he now identifies responsibility, i.e. who does he blame. Coupled with a look at how he perceives his cycles of offending behaviour and the strategies he would intend to use in breaking them, these snapshots would help the Board by providing greater information and a 'feel' for the prisoner. Such recordings could be made at roughly two- to three-monthly intervals, the first being made after assessment and before the offender enters the group programme.

These recordings could then form part of the dossier (which under open reporting procedures the offender also can see), and provide a supporting illustration of the evaluation and observations made by the core workers in the parole report.

In Scotland, with the introduction of the 'relevant part' for discretionary life sentences, judges can now fix the minimum (or mandatory) custodial part according to the seriousness of the offence and the previous record of the offender. This can be done with the knowledge that only *after* that part has been served will consideration be given for release by the Secretary of State, if satisfied that the prisoner no longer requires confinement for the protection of the public. That being the case, it might be that discretionary life sentences will be given where perhaps shorter 'relevant parts' are warranted, but where serious concern might exist about the risk of reoffending on release should the accused be given a determinate sentence. In other words, in Scotland, the legislation is now in place to enable judges to consider giving discretionary life sentences to some dangerous sexual offenders where the offence, in the past, would have more usually warranted a fixed sentence, on the basis that once the 'punishment' element had been served, the Secretary of State could only continue to detain the prisoner if it was considered that he still posed a very real threat to public safety. This would provide an added incentive for sexual offenders, so sentenced, to try to demonstrate that some change had begun to take place. (In fact, Peterhead Prison already accommodated twelve such individuals sentenced before the 'relevant part' legislation came into force.) Judges have already taken the view that some types of sexual offenders and sex offences fall into this category.

An increase in discretionary life sentence prisoners would place an additional burden on both the prison service and social work agencies. In prison, the offender would demand as professional an approach to the assessment of risk and perceived changes in attitude as we can develop. On release, the lifer is subject to supervision. Although this will be a further demand on resources, the advantage would be that such sentences attract a life licence. The offender is therefore bound to accept statutory supervision for the rest of his life, at whatever level is determined appropriate at that time, by his supervising social worker.

There remains a further problem – those sexual offenders not caught up in the parole scheme. Before the law changed in Scotland, it was possible for a long-term prisoner to complete his sentence and to be released without the requirement for supervision (under the Prisoners and Criminal Proceedings (Scotland) Act 1993). What then resulted was a dilemma for the Parole Board. If the offender was considered dangerous, early release could not be justified. Yet the Board might take a risk and give a token period of parole on licence, say one month, in order to link the offender to the supervisory and support services of the local social work department. The statutory requirement for him to be supervised would end at the end of the month (the point at which he would otherwise have been released), but it was hoped that the contacts already made would continue beyond that period.

Non-parole supervision: Supervised release orders

Under current Scottish legislation, long-term prisoners (those serving four years and over, including life) are subject to statutory supervision, for the remainder of their sentence served in the community from the time of their release, and for those convicted after September 1998 and serving determinate sentences to lengthy periods of supervision on extended sentences. However, for those offenders subject to sentences of under four years the picture is different. For those sexual offenders sentenced to terms of between twelve months and four years (of which they are only required to serve 50 per cent in custody) there was no requirement to be placed on licence and, consequently, supervision, unless at the time of sentence the judge also passed the additional sentence of a 'supervised release order' (under the 1993 Act and the Criminal Procedure (Scotland) Act 1995 (Section 209)). Indeed, in Scotland in 1995, 70 sexual offenders were sentenced to less than a year in custody and released without supervision into the community (SWSI 1997). But with the implementation of Section 4 of the Crime and Punishment (Scotland) Act 1997, courts must now normally impose a supervised release order on any offender sentenced, for the relevant offences, to imprisonment for any determinate term or, on indictment, an extended sentence as provided for in the Crime and Disorder Act 1998. Only in exceptional circumstances may the court decline to make a supervised release order. The order, which can also be made for those on indictment with sentences of less than twelve months, is for a minimum period of three months, and depending on the length of prison sentence and category of offence could be imposed for up to ten years. This is a significant change and particularly welcome for short-term offenders who, until recently, were often not subject to any supervision at all. In fact, in the first two years following the introduction of supervised release orders (October 1993–September 1995), only 112 such orders were imposed in Scotland, and only a mere 19 were for sexual offenders. It is estimated that during the same period about 170 sexual offenders were sentenced to imprisonment for between twelve months and four years, so only about one out of every nine was made subject to supervision on release. (SWSI 1997) In addition, as previously mentioned, those offenders who receive short sentences after being tried on indictment may be subject to the provisions of extended sentences or, in exceptional circumstances, receive a supervised release order where the sentence imposed is less than twelve months.

A 'snapshot' survey in Barlinnie Prison of Schedule One Offenders (those men convicted of offences against children) showed that of the 51 held, seven were serving under twelve months, 25 were serving twelve months to under four years, and 19 were serving four years and over, including life (Barlinnie Social Work Unit, 1995). These figures are indicative of the number of individuals in each category. In particular, the short-term prisoners were nearly all serving sentences of three months or six months, and since the time spent in prison was between 6 to 13 weeks, it is likely that for this one prison alone there could be a throughput of up to 40 such short-term offenders in a year. Unless they were also subject to a separate probation order, there would have been no supervision for them on release prior to the 1997 Act.

In Edinburgh Prison, a similar picture emerges. These figures are not a 'snapshot' as above. They give total new admissions of prisoners convicted of sexual offences against children. The annual admissions were therefore 61 and 65 respectively (Social Work Unit, Edinburgh Prison, November 1998):

	serving under 12 months	serving 12 months to under 4 years	serving 4 years and over, including life
1996/97	11	26	24
1997/98	14	28	23

Summary of key points

- The Parole Board have an important part to play in supporting the process of working with sexual offenders and in ensuring that realistic plans are proposed and achieved for reintegration into the community.

- The use of videotaped material showing 'snapshots' of the offender's progress during the intervention programme can illustrate comments made in the parole dossier.

- Short-term-sentenced sexual offenders also require supervision and support on release. Recent legislative changes which have resulted in virtually all sexual offenders being given post-release supervision are to be welcomed.

LIAISON WITH OTHER AGENCIES
Other players and interested parties

The police

The police are involved in protection of the public, crime prevention, investigation and apprehension of suspects. As in most jurisdictions, there is existing liaison with the prison services for planning of joint incident management and ongoing intelligence matters. In Scotland, the prison service could become more closely involved through networking the computerised Scottish Prison Service Information Network (SPIN) with the police Criminal Records Office to provide data on the past offending of prisoners. This would also provide the police with data on the identities of those in custody, their locations and expected release dates. Both parties could benefit from improved intelligence networking. In addition, the police have a role to play in child protection by keeping an eye on known ex-offenders and coordinating the intelligence on child abuse, the activities of paedophiles and the trade in various forms of pornography. In this context, informal links with the social services can sometimes be fruitful. Since 1 September 1997, the police have also been required to maintain a list of sexual offenders who have notified them of their presence within the force area and assess the risk posed.

The Crown Office

There is currently little contact between prosecutors and prison and social work services. To some extent this is understandable, as their functions are completely different. In the case of child abuse, whether a criminal prosecution is successful or not, measures have to be put in place for the protection of the child. Informal contact is maintained at a local level with prosecutors, and they are involved with any allegation of crime within prisons and sudden deaths. However, crucially, the prosecution service holds victim and witness statements relating to alleged and proved sexual offending which would be of great use to those involved in delivering intervention programmes.

The administration of courts

Those in prisons responsible for the administration of warrants, receptions, transfers and releases have contact with clerks of courts in arranging for the presence in court of accused persons and witnesses held in prisons. Clerks of courts are expected to comply with the relevant circulars on annotation of warrants, and queries about warrants are addressed to them. Fines paid at prison are passed to the courts. There remains a degree of separation between prisons and the courts and an aloofness on the part of the latter, despite the fact that prisons are the courts' next 'customer' in the chain. In terms of information, courts and prisons should already be linked by computer so that offence and conviction details are common to both. Regrettably this is still not the case in many countries, including Scotland.

The judiciary

Except for cases arising out of incidents in prison, judges only deal with prisoners as defendants and witnesses. Yet there must be some expectation that prisons will fulfil a particular function or range of functions when a judge passes a sentence of imprisonment. Is it a symbolic act of public reprobation? An exemplary sentence passed to deter others? Is the sentence imposed as a punishment, a deterrent from future wrongdoing or a period during which the public are protected from the dangers presented by the offender? Is he to be 'treated', educated, reformed, trained, rehabilitated or what? Of course, these are unfair issues to raise as they question the very basis of our criminal justice and penal systems. In fact, judges do occasionally visit prisons and know what goes on inside them. They are also expected to provide notes of circumstance about long-term custodial or life sentence cases. It is accepted that, when background reports indicate a non-custodial disposal, judges will be advised what the period of probation or community service is designed to achieve. But in sentencing, what do judges expect from prisons?

Social work services (central government)

The prison service and the coordinators of social work services are required to meet formally, at least once a year, to consider policy, service development and review implementation (SPS and Social Work Services Group 1990). In Scotland, the SWSG are responsible for overseeing social work offender services both in the community and in prisons, and for Inspectorate provisions and the Children's Hearing System. Those responsible for the development of social work services must be ready to facilitate and resource further initiatives to develop services for sexual offenders on release. Such developments might include the provision of social work supervision and support linked through hostel accommodation for male offenders and a range of intervention programmes (both closed and open groups) to enable sexual offenders to address (or continue to address) their offending behaviour.

Social work departments

Local authority social work departments provide offender services within the community and on contract to prisons within their area. They provide a vital link for those offenders returning to their home. They are expected to provide services to families where children are victims, but only offender services are ring-fenced with 100 per cent funding from central government. (Peart and Asquith (1992) argue for 100 per cent funding for family services, which would allow for better throughcare strategies and greater coordination (recommendation 12).) Directors of social work already meet with the governors of prisons located in their own area. Good liaison with social work departments is crucial for the development of a cohesive and effective policy for sexual offenders released into the community.

Voluntary agencies

There are a range of organisations concerned with providing support to ex-prisoners, offenders' families and victims, and child protection bodies. In Scotland, for example, Barony Housing, SACRO and the Salvation Army offer a range of such services to ex-offenders and are involved in a number of initiatives. The Apex Trust provides assistance with training and employment prospects. The Scottish Forum on Prisons and Families provides a network of contact between prisons and groups involved with family contact issues and family support groups. Charities such as Save the Children, The National Children's Homes (NCH), Action for Children, the Royal Scottish Society for the Prevention of Cruelty to Children (RSSPCC) and Children First have a primary concern for the child through protection, support and rights. There are also victim support groups. And the list goes on. These organisations, and there are many of them, provide valuable services, some of them partly funded through grants from government, and they can bring alternative perspectives to discussions which need to be taken into account. They too have a valuable role in policy formation and their voice needs to be heard.

Research and criminal statistics

There is a lack of information on the prevalence of sexual offenders within the criminal justice system. There is a need to establish a database on such offenders which will advise prison management and social work agencies about the scale of the service provision required. There is also a need to evaluate the various intervention programmes currently on offer and provide 'follow-up' studies. This work necessitates keeping good information on not only the statistical numbers involved but also the actual individuals as they progress through the custodial, social work and voluntary sector agencies to provide linear case studies. This work too cannot be effectively undertaken without good inter-agency co-operation.

Prison services

Prison services have a crucial role in undertaking important work in the area of addressing the offending behaviour of sexual offenders. To be effective, such work has to be begun within prison and continued in an integrated way on release into the community. Clearly, therefore, the work of prison services has to be coordinated with other agencies and services. Within prisons, this work also requires coordination of a range of inputs: prison officers, social workers, psychologists, and to some extent education staff and psychiatrists may become involved in supporting such programmes.

The Parole Board

The work of the Parole Board can have a significant impact on the way in which prisoners approach their sentences and the extent to which external agencies are involved in release programmes. It is only to be expected that others will look at their decisions to see the various 'signals' that their policy gives to prisoners, the way they view the use of parole, their position on issues about offenders engaging in programmes, the attitudes they expect prisoners to hold, the risks which might be taken, the conditions which are written into licences, and even how they exercise their powers of recall in certain cases. In the exercise of their functions, the Board create policy. However, to some extent, their desire for the best outcome will be constrained by what is actually available within the community. It would be no use, for example, to stipulate as a condition of a release licence that the offender should be housed in a hostel where support can be given for addressing his offending behaviour if no such facility exists in the area to which he intends to go on release.

Bringing these groups together

In most jurisdictions, the management of the process of dealing with sexual offending is spread across a number of departments and agencies. In Scotland, arrangements are no different. Separate bodies are involved in providing care for victims and the investigating of alleged crimes. There is the requirement for special attention to be paid to offenders by social work departments and other child protection agencies. Courts and the judiciary will take their own views of such offences. Statements by witnesses made to the police or prosecutors can be useful to the therapist; sexual offenders usually require protection as 'vulnerable types' in prison; and the prison system itself is developing special offence-specific intervention programmes for this type of offender. Difficult judgements have to be made by the Parole Board and ministers (elected politicians) about risk and dangerousness on release. Provision for supervision of such offenders is diverse and in places scant. But there is little in the way of coordination.

A tentative step has been taken in the suggestion that local forums might be established (in Circular SWSG 11/97, paragraph 23, on the Implementation of the Sex Offenders Act 1997). Government and its departments have a leading role to play in order to change this uncoordinated state of affairs into a workable process. Although in Scotland the Scottish Association for the Study of Delinquency (SASD) performs a significant role in bringing most of the criminal justice players together in an informal and social setting, such 'ad hoc' arrangements are not the answer. In each jurisdiction, there is a need to bring all the key players together to develop a cohesive approach. Scotland is a small enough country in which to bring together all the players. The Skinner Report commented as follows:

> Scotland is well placed to develop effective collaborative services because of its size, the establishment of unitary authorities with a strong corporate function across social work, housing and education services, and the opportunities to bring together at strategic and operational levels the work of these authorities with the police, the Prison Service, Children's Hearings and the health services. The fact that at the level of Government policy these responsibilities are held in one department, The Scottish Office, is another advantage. We must ensure we capitalise on these opportunities. (SWSI 1997, p.13)

Summary of key points

- There is a need to bring together all agencies and departments involved to improve co-ordination and inter-agency cooperation in the management of sexual offenders.

CHAPTER 13

The Prisoner's Tale

The following article appeared in the Easter 1995 issue of *The Grapevine*. The magazine, produced in the education unit at Peterhead, is written by prisoners for prisoners.

'STOP' the Myth (N. 1995)

I am in prison for Indecent Assault to, and injury against a 32 year old woman, and am doing a 6 year sentence. I am currently in 'C' hall.

I've decided as a member of the 'STOP' programme to write about how I felt before going into 'STOP', going through it, and how I think life after it will be. I hope this may dispel any fears anyone may have.

When I first came into prison in March 1992 I didn't care about anyone but myself. I thought I had been hard done by and why should I be punished this way. The selfishness and contempt I showed towards prisoners, warders, my family and most importantly my victim was way out of line. For years before and after I offended I portrayed myself as a hardman and unhurtable. To put it mildly, I was the best thing since sliced bread. I couldn't have been more wrong.

I came to Peterhead in May 1992 and moved into 'A' hall. I carried on as usual. I thought I was better than the next person. I also thought my crime wasn't as bad as the rest. From May until September 92 I went around this prison with blinkers on, hiding the full extent of my offence from myself and the others around me. I felt something had to be done. Shortly after September 92 it was explained to me and the rest of the prison population that there were plans for therapy group work programmes to take place in 'C' hall. I saw my chance to do something. We moved into 'C' hall in January 1993 and contemplated the start of group work. At this time 2 groups of 10 men were picked to start the groups off. I wasn't successful and, to be honest, I was relieved because I was scared of telling other prisoners about my offence. I was afraid of what they would tell the rest of 'C' hall about me. I had my image to protect and would they shatter it by telling my story. For most of 1993 I saw these twenty men going into their respective groups, then watch again as one or sometimes two or three came out, drained and red eyed. God was I scared.

Then the stories started of how they make fun of you and your offence, plus all the 'HOT SEAT' stories. We've all heard them. I felt at this time that I couldn't go through with it. I had to get out of 'C' hall. The thing that stopped me was that I had run long enough and that too many people had been hurt through my actions. In September 93 I was accepted for group work with nine other men. I was very apprehensive but got down to work. I won't kid anyone on, the group work is hard, it has to be, it wouldn't be worthwhile doing otherwise. You're pulling your life apart and looking at where you went wrong, where you learned habits and why you see yourself as you do. It's not easy. I went through the first six month stage of group work, pulling myself apart and looking at all aspects of my life. The shock I got when I realised I wasn't perfect frightened me, but I had to accept it, because no matter how hard I try, I'll never and could never cut the bad bits out of my life. I don't want to anyway. I wouldn't be the person I am today without my bad bits. I also went through the first stage, waiting on the 'HOT SEAT' etc. to happen. I can remember saying to myself, where's this 'HOT SEAT', this isn't what I'd expected. But the most important thing for me was that I was still in one piece. I had learned new things about myself from looking at parts of my life I would never ever have looked at and I felt a lot better for doing so. I felt this way from being honest about ME. I had got rid of all the burdens I had carried and felt released from the image I had set myself. I was now looking forward to the second stage of group work to continue my learning.

When I started stage 2, I almost slipped back into the old me. We were now dealing with the hardest part for offenders and that is VICTIMS. We all have them. We're not in prison for nothing. I now have a greater awareness of victims, of what they go through and what they have to live with for the rest of their lives. It was hard for me to accept that ME, the hardman! has affected an Innocent woman for the rest of her life. But I have and I now must live with that.

I am now almost finished the 'STOP' programme and have just learned that I've been given 11 months parole for the work I've put in, the rewards are there. I didn't go into the 'STOP' programme thinking of parole (I REFUSED MY FIRST CHANCE) or, that by just being there, that I'd be cured. I'm sure we all know of someone who's been through 'STOP' and has re-offended. I am the only cure for my offending behaviour. I am the only one who can stop ME from offending again and from coming back into prison. This won't be easy, as people outside will be expecting me to still be the same person, him who would do anything for a laugh and it will be easy for me to fall into the trap.

I go out of prison in April and cannot guarantee that I won't be back. No-one can. What I can guarantee is that I will live my life the way I want to and not to bow to the pressure of others. They must accept me for who I am and not what I used to be or could be. I don't want the weight of any more victims on my conscience again.

I've also heard the stories of how the social workers are only in it to get info on you (RUBBISH). I have a social worker and an officer in my group and the help they have given me is priceless. You may say that because I work in the social work offices that I would say this, that is also rubbish, as I was saying this long before I started work up the road.[1] Anyway, if I thought they were only in it for themselves I would say so, and both of these people know this. How many more excuses can we find to stop us from looking at our behaviour? I say excuses because that's all they are.

The 'STOP' programme for me has been the best thing I have ever done and all we have to fear from 'STOP' is change. If our change means less victims it has to be worth it. You only get out of 'STOP' what you put into it. So give it a chance, I did and I lost nothing.

WHAT DO 'YOU' HAVE TO LOSE.

SHUGGIE, 'C' hall.

---

[1] It should be noted that this prisoner worked as a 'passman' or 'trusty' in the prison's Social Work Unit, keeping the place clean, and making tea and coffee. He was not involved in 'social work' matters and did not have access to information on prisoners.

CHAPTER 14

Postscript

AND WHY DO WE UNDERTAKE THIS WORK?

> ...unlike property offences, sexual assaults strike at a range of vulnerable emotional capacities which can damage for the future the individual's self respect and perception of worth, her ability to trust, respect, love, care, give and receive. In fact, as we know, victims who survive can be all but destroyed. (From 'Governor takes the zero option', *The Scotsman* 15 June 1995, p.15. This article was abstracted from an unpublished article by Alec Spencer, 'Zero tolerance: The real issues.')

All the evidence available suggests that by undertaking such work we *can* reduce the number of victims. As indicated before, staff are keen to do exactly that, by at least *delaying some offenders* from reoffending and by providing offenders with the skills, insights and social and interpersonal norms to *help them prevent relapsing* into offending patterns.

> Last, and perhaps more importantly, even very small reductions in recidivism rates occasioned by treatment result in significant savings, given the great expense of legal/correctional intervention. In the end, [however,] treatment must be seen as the prevention of further sexual victimization. (Quinsey 1990, p.2)

As quoted earlier in this book:

> ...an often neglected aspect of offering treatment to offenders is the real reduction in suffering that occurs when even a few of these men are prevented from reoffending... Whenever treatment, no matter how unsophisticated, reduces reoffending by *any* degree, it saves innocent victims much suffering. (Marshall *et al.* 1990, p.6)

No one will ever know who the victims might have been. The victims of sexual offenders have a particularly harrowing time, and for children the impact is wide-ranging. It is the adult who defines the 'experience' and directs the child. The child will not understand the long-term consequences of being used as an object for sex and how it will affect their sexuality in the future. The child's trust in the adult or adults is destroyed, and they will feel betrayed, let down and abandoned. Victims feel guilt and they often feel responsible for the abuse, having kept secrets to protect the offender. They feel worthless and think they are *different* from other people. As a result of the abuse and violation of their bodies, victims begin to feel powerless. This only fuels a cycle of despair which leads to suicide attempts, running away from home and turning to alcohol or drugs, and leaves them at high risk of further victimisation. It is not surprising, then, that US studies have shown a close link between incest and running away, and running away and prostitution. In one study (Silbert and Pines 1981), 96 per cent of the sample of prostitutes were runaways.

The staff at Peterhead have only been engaged in this work for a relatively short period. However, it has led me to believe that not only *can* we do something, but that we have a *duty* to try. All of us engaged in this work have to develop an integrated strategy, within prison systems, on how to take these issues forward, and in the wider context of the criminal justice system, particularly with social work services and other agencies working in the community, so as to develop proper throughcare and effective measures for the support of such offenders. The public has a right to demand that their criminal justice system does everything possible to protect them, not only by keeping the offender in prison, but also in a dynamic and proactive way by attempting to break patterns of offending behaviour.

What motivates staff in prisons, and drives them forward with such enthusiasm, is the hope that outside, in the community, are people whose lives can in future be saved from being wrecked through prison staff working with those who come within our walls and who must one day be released. Put very simply, in relation to sexual offenders, prison staff are now *working for safer communities.*

CHAPTER 15

A Model for Multi-Agency Casework, Cooperation and Management of Information about Imprisoned Offenders who are Subsequently Released to the Community[1]

This chapter is intended to draw on information provided throughout the book and suggest a model framework (or checklist) for a multi-agency approach. It follows the sexual offender from his admission into prison to the point at which he is released and looks at the types of information and processes involved in his casework management. In drawing together the various strands, it is possible to prescribe a model or blueprint of a workable process for the management of sexual offenders – an ideal for which to aim!

1. RECEPTION INTO PRISON AND ASSESSMENT

On reception into prison of a sexual offender, the prison should receive all relevant information required for the assessment of risk and to facilitate subsequent offence-specific programmes; it should establish links between prison-based and community-based services; and it should begin to develop a prisoner's sentence plan.

1. Courts should ensure that documentation (including accompanying warrants and indictments) clearly indicates that the offence is a sexual one, and where the offence is against children, that the age of the victim is

---

1 The terms social worker and probation officer, and social work department and probation service used below are interchangeable.

included on the complaint or indictment. The information will also need to annotate any requirements imposed for Sex Offender Registration or compulsory supervision on extended sentences.

2. The prison administration should ensure that prison-based social workers are immediately informed of such an admission and that the relevant processes are set in place by prison-based social workers for prisoners identified by the court as having been convicted of a sexual offence against a child. This includes advising the prisoner of the statutory duties of the social worker in relation to child protection and the various administrative arrangements which will need to be made. The social worker should also advise the prisoner of his rights and obligations, including the voluntary nature of his engaging in offence-specific work, the parole process and the requirements for statutory notification of the police and supervision on release.

3. As soon as possible after reception, the prison should receive copies of all reports made available to the court: pre-sentence social work (enquiry) report; offender assessments; psychiatric and psychological reports; and any reports undertaken after sentencing. In addition, copies of the trial judge's report outlining the circumstances surrounding the offence for which the sentence was imposed should be made available to the prison.

4. Notification should be received by the prison of the name and address of the supervising or contact social worker (throughcare process).

5. Details should be passed to the prison Social Work Unit of any initial problems known to have arisen as a result of the imprisonment – both for the family/victim and in relation to the offender himself.

6. Along with other agencies, such as the prosecution service, the social work department should provide as much additional information as is possible to help with risk assessment and effective delivery of the intervention programme.

7. An assessment of the extent and seriousness of risk the offender is likely to constitute on release should be undertaken by prison officers, psychologists and social work staff. Particular attention will have to be paid to the future risk to children, including any risk which might arise during the period of imprisonment. In addition, an assessment should be made of the offender's readiness to address his offending behaviour.

8. Prison and social work staff should establish a dialogue with the relevant social work department to agree on a basis for future co-operation in order to enhance the programme for the offender and the work done with the victim.

9. Prison and social work staff should agree the initial sentence plan with the prisoner. This should include involvement in the offence-specific

intervention programme and other offence-specific or lifestyle issues, and also include issues relating to family contact.

10. Prison-based social workers should be responsive to the needs of the child when working with offenders, particularly where there is the possibility of ongoing contact between the prisoner and the victim(s). It should be the duty of the child's social worker to explore the child's wishes with regard to ongoing contact between the offender and the child, and to help arrive at the best course of action, taking into account what might be in the child's best interests. Where there is to be contact between the prisoner and his child, the child's social worker must seek to ensure that such contact, particularly if it is to be through an access visit, is consistent with the child protection plan and does not jeopardise the child's welfare. Where necessary, the local authority responsible for implementation of the child protection measures may seek to limit or control access, using the appropriate legal channels. If the child is already subject to a supervision requirement from a court or Children's Hearing, any alteration to access arrangements should be sought through that body (SWSG 1994).

2. DURING SENTENCE

It is to be hoped that the offender will undertake offence-specific work to reduce his propensity to reoffend; that together with staff he will update and develop his sentence plan; that prison-based social workers maintain good liaison with external agencies; and that all parties progress plans for a realistic release strategy.

1. Prisons should ensure the delivery of intervention programmes by prison officers and prison-based social work staff to offenders and assist with the formulation of relapse prevention plans. In addition, the object should be to try to maximise the impact of the intervention programme and influence behaviour following release. For example, the offender should be encouraged to continue to maintain contact with the local social work department on a voluntary basis after release, even when the statutory obligations no longer exist.

2. Prison staff should ensure the continued development of sentence plans with the offender throughout his sentence, coordinating a range of interventions, group programmes and educational and vocational opportunities, but, in particular, those designed to modify, contain or control offending behaviour.

3. Prison and external social work staff should be involved in periodic reviews of the progress of the offender while in prison. This should involve attending meetings or case conferences and may include discussion of the sentence plan. The reviews should include information on:

- the progress being made by the offender in offence-specific work
- issues concerning the victim and family and their attitude to the offender
- how the community may view or react to the offender
- how the family can, if appropriate, begin to be involved in family reunification issues.

4. Where home leave or home visits are being considered there should be the fullest discussion between the prison- and family-based social workers to ensure that such contact is acceptable and can be managed. Sufficient information about the offender's case and notice of any proposed visit or home leave should be given to enable decisions to be taken about any action required to protect children. Details to be arranged and specified include:

- the address of meeting or residence while on temporary release
- any special conditions or rules which will apply
- the names of social workers who will supervise a meeting
- notification to police and local social work department of the proposed visit or home leave
- the dates and times of the proposed visit or home leave.

5. Social workers and personal officers should be involved in the offender's programmes of preparation for release. In addition, the designated supervising officer should maintain regular contact with the prisoner through visits.

6. Prison-based social work staff should be invited to contribute, either in writing or in person, to all child protection case conferences or other statutory reviews concerning offenders for whom they have casework responsibility while in prison.

3. RELEASE AND SUPERVISION IN THE COMMUNITY

The aim should be to create a coordinated and collaborative approach to the release of sexual offenders, particularly those convicted of offences against children, through the sharing of information. There are requirements to conclude arrangements for release through multi-agency meetings; review the progress made by the offender and, if family contact is to be re-established, the progress of victim(s) and family; closely manage and monitor the family reunification process; and arrange for adequate social work supervision in the community, with support through additional offence-specific work and/or implementation of the offender's relapse prevention strategy.

1. For cases which are being considered by the Parole Board, there should be information about the home background (prepared by the appropriate social work department), including any implications for victims or for the protection of children; details of the work undertaken with the offender and his response; an indication of the further work required; and an assessment of the risk and viability of any relapse prevention strategy. If further (or a continuation of) offence-specific work is to be included as a condition in a release licence, some assessment of the offender's suitability to undertake this work should be made and provisional arrangements agreed in good time.

2. Arrangements for release should include:

   - details of proposed accommodation and any conditions imposed on residence; social security and welfare benefits

   - precise arrangements for family contact

   - plans for employment and/or further education

   - implementation of relapse prevention strategy, further offence-specific work and other issues concerning rehabilitation into the community.

   Where the release is the consequence of a discretionary decision, the reasons for release, together with a copy of the notification of release and any conditions imposed, should also be conveyed to all relevant parties, together with any other information considered pertinent by the decision-making body.

3. There should be a multi-agency approach to planning for release, with enhanced levels of contact through case conferences or meetings involving prison group work and social work staff, and community-based social work and family support staff. In addition, effective liaison at social worker and management levels should take place between local authority and child protection staff. The local police from the proposed area should be involved and invited to attend meetings.

4. The initial proposals or plans for release – such as accommodation and supervision arrangements – should be circulated before the case conference and any special arrangements noted. In particular, issues relating to child protection matters should be specified. Where possible, every effort should be made to ensure that plans to protect the child(ren) and intervention and management plans for known abusers are complementary. Depending on the circumstances of the case, the appropriate social work department(s) might be one or more of the following areas:

- the area in which the offender's own children are living
- the area or areas in which the child or children who were previously offended against now live
- the area to which the offender is proposing to be released and where there are children in the household (or hostel)
- the area to which the offender is proposing to be released even when there are apparently no children involved. (Points summarised from Social Work Services Group Circular, SW/11/1994 (6 October 1994), *Child Protection: The Imprisonment and Preparation for Release of Prisoners Convicted of Offences against Children*.)

5. The meeting(s) or case conference(s) should particularly focus on detailed planning for the prisoner's release; there should also be a meeting between the prison-based social worker, the proposed supervising social worker, any other relevant staff and the prisoner himself to examine and further refine his release plans and relapse prevention strategy.

6. Social work departments should be advised immediately of any changes to the information or plans already supplied and agreed, particularly any change in the address or area in which the offender intends to reside on his release. In addition, if it becomes known that the children previously offended against have moved or are intending to move to the area of another local authority, then full information must be passed to the new local authority to enable proper child protection measures to be put in place.

7. On release, the local social work department and police force should be notified that the offender has completed the custodial part of his sentence and is transferring to their area (in compliance with the Sex Offenders Act 1997).

8. As part of the monitoring and evaluation process of the offence-specific intervention programmes, dialogue should be maintained between the supervising social worker and the prison-based social worker.

9. A six-monthly report should be prepared by the supervising social worker on the response of the offender to his release and the impact, relevance and effectiveness of the programmes undertaken while in prison. In addition, the report should include comment on his attitude to further offence-specific work, where appropriate, and an evaluation of the relapse prevention strategy to date. A copy of this report should be forwarded to the prison.

Summary of key points

- The 25 points in the model for multi-agency co-operation (which follow the offender from reception into prison and assessment through to planning for release and supervision in the community) provide a comprehensive system for the flow of information about the sexual offender.

The Sex Offender Treatment Programme (SOTP), England and Wales

In 1991 a cognitive–behavioural group work programme for sexual offenders was established by HM Prison Service, England and Wales. The principles of the SOTP are, in broad terms, the same as those of the STOP Programme.

The structure of the component parts is broadly similar, but there are differences in how the programme is delivered in providing additional interventions and risk assessment. The programme is as follows (Mann 1998):

Stage 1: Assessment

It is intended that all imprisoned sex offenders who have at least a year to serve in prison should be offered the opportunity to engage in the SOTP. Prisoners who express an interest in participating in the SOTP have to undertake a range of assessments designed to (1) identify the level of risk and treatment priority, (2) exclude those for whom the SOTP would not be effective, and (3) provide baseline measures of clinical variables against which progress in treatment can be gauged (Mann 1998). The assessment includes:

- four semi-structured interviews looking at social and personal history, offence issues, and victims
- the Hare Psychopathy Checklist Revised
- psychometric testing across a number of areas, e.g. personality, offence-related attitudes, empathy, social functioning and loneliness
- penile plethysmographic assessment of sexual preference (available in seven prisons)
- medical assessment to check suitability for the SOTP.

The psychologist will then decide if the prisoner is appropriate for the SOTP; usually only those in total denial would be sifted out.

Stage 2: The core programme

This is the central element of the programme and consists of a 180-hour group work course that covers similar ground to that of the STOP Programme, viz.: reducing denial and minimisation of behaviour, promoting recognition of the harm caused to victims and developing relapse prevention skills. The core programme utilises a variety of treatment methods:

- cognitive therapy techniques and the Socratic method of questioning
- psycho-educational methods, e.g. viewing videos for developing empathy
- role-play techniques, scenarios, 'hot seats' and role reversals
- relapse prevention using a board game.

The adapted programme

A modified version of the core programme, known as the 'adapted programme', has been developed for prisoners with educational, intellectual or communication difficulties. The programme has adjusted treatment goals slightly to suit the capabilities of the client group, uses more active communications, e.g. through drawing and symbols, and there is a heavier emphasis on role-play.

Supplementary: The thinking skills programme

The core programme can be supplemented with a 'thinking skills' programme, lasting about 50 hours, which is a cognitive-based skills training package designed to improve decision making, perspective taking and some interpersonal skills. It can contribute to the effectiveness of relapse prevention strategies.

Stage 3: The extended programme

This stage was introduced in March 1998 for high-deviance sexual offenders whose intervention needs extended beyond the goals of the core programme, and focuses more on issues of interpersonal, social and sexual functioning. It adopts a slightly more complex cognitive–behavioural model which incorporates the notion of cognitive schema, with group members identifying their own schemas and drawing out 'life maps'. It also involves an element of individual therapy conducted by a forensic psychologist.

Stage 4: The booster programme

The booster programme is the shortest of the SOTP courses, consisting of about 50 hours of group work. It is designed for all sexual offenders who have completed at least the core programme, and runs in lower security prisons where sex offenders would be most likely to spend the latter part of their sentence. It is designed to act as 'revision' of the core programme and to provide further opportunities to practise relapse prevention strategies before release into the community.

Stage 5: The post-treatment risk assessment

There has been growing pressure to conduct accurate risk assessments on every sexual offender released from prison. As a consequence, the Structured Anchored Clinical Judgement system (Thornton 1997) has been adopted. Based on actuarial risk assessment, the SACJ also allows for 'dynamic' modifications to the level of assessed risk by performance in therapy (see also pp.78–88). Post-programme assessment is undertaken following completion of the core programme and is repeated on completion of subsequent programmes. This risk assessment provides the basis for further planning of interventions.

Stage 6: Throughcare to community treatment

A variety of arrangements exist to provide support and, as appropriate, supervision on the release of sexual offenders. This is arranged on an individual basis, and can vary depending on the prison and local authority or probation area.

Multi-site

It is of particular interest that the SOTP has been developed on a multi-site basis. The programme currently runs in 25 prison establishments and has a throughput of about 670 sexual offender prisoners per year. It is the largest of its kind in the world. To ensure standards, consistency and integrity of programme delivery, the central coordination is handled from the Programme Development Section at prison service headquarters in London. The programme is managed on each site by a tripartite team: the treatment manager, usually a forensic psychologist, who is responsible for programme integrity; the programme manager, usually a governor, who is responsible for the practical aspects of programme delivery; and a senior probation officer who is responsible for throughcare arrangements.

Use of lay personnel

Like its counterpart in Scotland, the SOTP was designed so that it could be delivered by lay personnel (for similar reasons to those already outlined on pp.52–53) who would be trained in the theory and skills required. Mann and Thornton (1998) believe that lay therapists, or paraprofessionals, 'can be used effectively to carry out therapeutic work with sexual offenders provided they are carefully selected, trained, and supervised' (p.56).

Commitment to programme evolution

Mann and Thornton believe that sexual offender treatment must be an evolutionary process. That is, as providers of such programmes they should continually monitor and research their practice in order to identify issues and learn from experience. They have appointed an international panel of experts in the field of work with sexual offenders to provide advice and guidance, and support the accreditation process. The team conduct their own research and take onboard the research findings from elsewhere. Using feedback and research are important for developing and maintaining excellence of standards. The Programme Development Section are making a number of changes to the programme, e.g. in victim empathy and relapse prevention, in response to research findings. The STEP 3 Report (Beech *et al.* 1998) confirms the improvements made in the SOTP and indicates some outcome data. Their conclusion is that this large-scale programme is proving to be effective, the longer-term programmes demonstrating particularly good results for highly deviant offenders.

Case Studies from the STOP Programme

EXPLANATION

The STOP Programme adopts a group work approach to addressing sexual offending and the core programme runs over a period of approximately twelve months. Following assessment, there are two phases to the programme:

- Phase 1 focuses on such issues as denial, cognitive restructuring, victim empathy and cycles of offending.
- Phase 2 emphasises issues surrounding relapse prevention.

Each group comprises eight to ten offenders who have been convicted of offences against children and/or adults. Groups meet twice weekly for two and a half hour sessions and are led by prison officers and social workers. Priority is given to those men considered to be at high risk of reoffending. In total, the programme lasts for 80 sessions or about 200 hours.

AIMS OF THE PROGRAMME

1. To engender the acceptance of personal responsibility.
2. To address the consequences of the offending behaviour for both self and victim(s) (including secondary victims, e.g. family, friends).
3. To develop personal strategies that will assist the exercising of self-control and the avoidance of situations likely to lead to offending.

CONTENT OF THE CASE STUDIES

The case studies are reports on a variety of offenders (rapists, incest cases and paedophiles) who have participated in the STOP Programme with varying degrees of success. The responses are generally presented under five headings and comment on how the offender has addressed the issues. Some cases, however, have been reported in a slightly different way, reflecting the individual nature of the process and the particular issues raised by individual offenders.

Cognitive distortions

This section focuses upon the issues of denial and minimisation in respect of responsibility for sexual offending and challenges the tendency of offenders to cast blame elsewhere for their behaviour.

Cycles of offending

This section aims to help participants understand and identify the components and patterns of their cycles of offending behaviour. Attention is given to sexual arousal issues such as identifying behaviour and thinking sequences, and the role of fantasy in sexual offending.

Victim awareness/empathy

The victim is considered to be a central feature of the programme. Therefore, this element of the programme is aimed at assisting participants to gain an understanding of the emotional, social, psychological and physical impact of the offences upon the victim. Additionally, it examines the 'ripple' effect of offending.

Social functioning

The purpose of this aspect of the programme is to enable participants to see that behaviour does not occur spontaneously but that it can be triggered by events and is informed by beliefs, thoughts and feelings. There is considerable input into the 'thoughts–feelings–actions' chain to encourage the identification and expression of thoughts and feelings.

Relapse prevention

The programme will not and cannot 'cure' sexual offenders. However, the programme aims to provide participants with the means to exert greater control over their behaviour. This element of the programme aims to assist the participants in identifying those internal and external factors that might place them at risk of reoffending and enable them to take appropriate action.

Conclusion

This section provides a brief summary report of the response of the offender to the programme and a revised assessment of risk.

Note

The names and, where appropriate, details have been altered to protect the identity of the individual offenders and references to other persons contained within the case studies.

ALLAN: INCEST OFFENDER MAKING A GOOD RESPONSE

Allan was convicted of a number of charges of lewd, indecent and libidinous practices and offences under the Sexual Offences Acts. He was sentenced to six years' imprisonment. Allan's victims were his two daughters, Gail and Jenny, and this was his first conviction.

Cognitive distortions

At the onset of the programme, Allan's levels of distorted thinking were fairly extensive and wide-ranging; the most fundamental was the belief that meeting his needs through ambition and drive would also meet the needs of those around him. This extended to his inability or unwillingness to recognise any victim and, consequently, to acknowledge any level of grooming, manipulation or planning of the abusive behaviour. Allan also failed to recognise the seriousness of the offence, which for a substantial part of the programme he considered as horseplay, denying any level of sexual motivation in his behaviour.

Throughout the programme, Allan made very many useful connections for other people in the group; however, his defences remained such that for a substantial part of the programme he did not appear to see any correlation between his distorted thinking and that which he was identifying in others.

Significant points during the programme appeared to impact on Allan, namely his acknowledgement of his manipulation of Gail; his reaction to the group's perception that they felt manipulated by his refusal to attend some sessions (Allan withdrew from a few sessions while he was in dispute with prison management); the realisation of the emotional impact of the abuse on one of his daughters, despite her outward appearance of well-being; and his reaction to those sessions of videos which highlighted the profound lifelong effect of abuse on victims.

During the later stages of Phase 2, there appeared a marked change in Allan's attitude and thinking, in particular concerning the inequality of his relationship with Gail. A significant shift was also seen in his previously held views on the need to achieve at any cost; he began to see how this drive for success had adversely affected the whole structure of his life. This recognition is in itself very positive, but he will need extensive and sustained changes in his relationship with Gail and other members of the family in order to prevent a regressive return to previous values.

Cycles of offending

Whilst Allan recognised the existence of sexual fantasy in offending he did not relate this to himself. However, he did acknowledge that as a male, he indulged in what he considered 'normal' male sexual thinking – trophy hunting. This was a starting point for Allan; he came to realise that he would require more awareness of self and of the needs which he might be meeting should he pursue inappropriate thinking.

Allan's acknowledged lack of awareness of his emotions and apparent inability to recognise how he was feeling was a cause for concern. However, his extensive use of an emotion diary during Phase 2 appeared to act as a catalyst, and he started to break through the barrier to his emotions.

Allan's ability to read and exploit the needs of others was a character trait which he honed and developed in his choice of career, and is a skill of which he will need to maintain keen awareness given its potential influence on his future life.

On the surface, Allan displayed a high level of self-esteem. However, had this been a true reflection, one could question his need to continually reinforce his self-image through material possession, 'ownership' of his family and high achievement. Perhaps a re-examination of his position within his family or origin will help produce a more balanced view of his self-worth and allow for more positive self-development.

Victim awareness / empathy

Constant referral to one victim and minimisation of the level of the abuse along with the long-time denial of any impact on his daughters served to reinforce Allan's perception that his behaviour was not abusive and that no real damage had been done. Only in later stages, when one of his daughters stated she was receiving counselling, was there a recognition of the possible impact of his behaviour.

Relapse prevention

Allan recognises that in order to change his lifestyle and avoid reoffending, he needs to recognise and acknowledge the thoughts and feelings which precipitate his behaviour. One particular area of risk is his use of manipulative behaviour, either through coercion or anger, in order to meet his own needs.

Allan's past perception of his relationship with Gail, which he now acknowledges was based on inequality, is an area he will need to address continually. The control he exercised over his wife was a reflection of his abusive relationship with his daughters. There is a primary need for Allan to reprioritise his life so that the needs of others come before his own and his desire for success at any cost. Central to all must be sustained contact with his own emotions.

Conclusion

Throughout the programme, Allan was an able group member, challenging others and enabling them to perceive how their distorted thinking had underpinned their offending. However, it was only in later stages that he began to recognise his own.

Originally, Allan wrote copious notes, giving rise to concern that by externalising the words into writing rather than internalising the thoughts and feelings he could remain distanced, thereby depersonalising the work of the group; this is an area central to the success or failure of any relapse prevention strategy that he may gain as a result of his work in group.

BOB: INCEST OFFENDER MAKING A POOR RESPONSE

Bob was convicted of assault: assault; assault with intent to rape, to her severe injury and permanent impairment; and assault to injury. These offences against his eleven-year-old daughter resulted in Bob being sentenced to six years' imprisonment. Bob has a number of previous convictions for burglary, attempted burglary and actual bodily harm.

Cognitive distortions

From the outset, Bob carefully stated he acknowledged responsibility for his offending. However, we would say that there was a consistent theme of shared responsibility with his former partner. Bob's expressed understanding that his children had the capacity to make informed choices over a whole range of largely adult concerns proved disquieting.

Throughout the programme, Bob referred to the fact that there had been significant social work intervention in his family. While on the one hand he said he welcomed this, in group discussion it became obvious that he strongly resented it. In fact, he seemed to be blaming the social work department for being either too interventionist or adopting the minimum of intervention; either way social work services were in a 'no win' situation. Bob made it clear from the beginning that he wished for help with his offending behaviour but spent a large proportion of the programme avoiding the issue. Bob appeared to be looking for the programme to say that he was 'cured', which was never the aim.

During the programme, there were occasions during which Bob appeared to demonstrate more trust in group workers and members. However, this did not appear to last very long.

Bob admits that he finds it very difficult to trust others; this, however, relates to an apparent view of the world in which people are either for him or against him. It is unfortunate that Bob found it difficult to focus his considerable energy on developing trust in others during the programme as he may well have derived significant benefit.

Cycles of offending

Bob acknowledged from the outset the importance of fantasy, the beginning of which he attributes to his partner. He also recognises how his failure to deal appropriately with the unacceptable content of the fantasy, i.e. sexual relations with his victim, was instrumental in his escalating pattern of behaviour.

Bob maintains that his genital examination of his daughter had no sexual connotation. Additionally, he maintains that at the time of committing the offences there was also no sexual connotation. This suggests that there is some considerable denial and that Bob has difficulty in accepting the degree to which the offences are irredeemable.

In terms of the thinking and behaviour patterns prior to the offences, Bob relates that nothing significant occurred to trigger the offences. In fact, Bob's whole life seems to be one in which he spends his time reacting to situations created by others, e.g. his wife, family, work, etc.

Bob's attempts to clarify the events leading up to and including the offences unfortunately served no purpose other than to confuse. Although his fellow group members showed considerable patience in this area of work, they felt strongly that Bob was 'weaving webs'.

Victim awareness/empathy

Bob appears to attribute greater levels of understanding and interpretation of his behaviour to his victim than we are sure is realistic.

Bob's work in group indicates that he does have the capacity to understand some of the effects of his behaviour on his victim and others. In his search to make amends, he has tended to adopt a blinkered approach to the wider effects of his offending. For example, the effects on his family have been traumatic because he has been sent to prison.

Bob maintains that he was abused himself; however, he does not appear to be able to link what has happened to him with his own victim's experiences, except at a concrete level. Throughout the programme, Bob often sought to place himself in the role of the scapegoat: he often spoke about his inability/refusal to trust others, e.g. group workers and members, and adult family members and social workers, all of whom he saw as threatening. As a result of this failure to place trust in others, which Bob acknowledges he has found very difficult, he has found it very difficult to develop a more internalised form of victim awareness/empathy.

Bob is a man of some ability whose capacity to develop in this area is recognised; however, it would be to his benefit were he to realise that other adults need not necessarily pose a threat to him.

Social functioning

Although Bob understood the concept of the thought–feeling–action chain, he appeared to struggle in trying to apply this to his own experiences. This was reflected in the conflicting themes of Bob as a victim of circumstances and of Bob as a successful performer in a variety of roles, e.g. worker and parent. This dichotomy served to confuse the attempt to provide an accurate picture of Bob.

Bob admits that his level of self-esteem has been a major contributing factor in his inability to develop trusting relationships with other adults. His presentation, which often manifests a self-deprecating style, appears to be a defence against other adults getting to know the real Bob.

Bob's account of events in the family prior to the offences is confusing and at times contradictory; for example, from rigid boundaries to an absence of boundaries.

Bob appeared to demonstrate an ability to develop a certain rapport with other group members. He needs to develop his ability to challenge and be challenged in order to enable him to examine his beliefs. Whilst on occasion Bob demonstrated a certain warmth, he seemed reluctant to sustain this position. Overall, we felt that Bob did have measurable social skills which he is aware of how to use appropriately. We would encourage him to use these skills in order to develop more healthy, functioning relationships.

Relapse prevention

Bob's relapse prevention plan is somewhat confusing, however; this is, in part, due to Bob being both honest and anxious to cover every eventuality. Bob's plans for the future are overshadowed by his reactions to people and events which leave him as the victim of circumstances.

Bob's expectations for the future are extremely optimistic. We wonder how he can develop more satisfactory relationships with other adults in view of his acknowledged problems trusting other people.

Nowhere in Bob's relapse prevention plan does he mention the possibility of him reoffending. Instead, he has chosen to focus on employment, developing a new relationship with a woman, access to his children (including his victim), his relationship with his ex-partner and relationships between a new partner and his first family. Although this is consistent with Bob's stated view that he will not reoffend, it is Bob's inability to acknowledge the possibility that he might reoffend which is disappointing. This is likely to remain a source of friction between him and those with responsibility for child protection.

There are many positive and important elements in Bob's relapse prevention plan, but we would urge him to keep his plan more simple in order to allow other people to assist him.

Conclusion

Bob sees himself as having changed during the programme and believes he has learned a lot about himself and the reasons for his offending. At the same time, he maintains that he does not feel he has been believed by others and cannot understand why people do not believe him.

Although there were periods when he showed an ability to develop close relationships with fellow group members, this was not sustained due to his tendency to withdraw when people were getting close to him.

From the outset, Bob made it very clear that his main reason for participating was in order to return to his family. Despite his former partner's remarriage, we are not convinced that Bob has worked through all the issues of loss involved with this relationship. Bob needs to resolve a number of key areas regarding his relationships with his former partner and his children. Concentration on some of these matters may well have hindered Bob's progress in the group.

Although Bob admits total responsibility for the offences, there has been a persistent theme of Bob being unable to accept the sexual nature of his convictions. This denial of the significance of the offences, linked to his refusal to consider the possibility of reoffending, is a cause for concern. In view of the fact that his relapse prevention plan places considerable emphasis on his former partner and access to his children, we would consider him to pose a similar level of risk of reoffending as at the outset of the programme. Equally, should this plan fail, it would seem possible that he might find or form another family. We are not convinced that he has developed sufficient strategies to cope with the stresses that this would involve. In the light of this, we would consider him to pose a continuing risk.

Bob has still not reconciled his self-image as family man/provider with that of a convicted sex offender. Until there is a shift in this position, Bob is going to experience marked difficulty in living a pro-social life.

Whilst Bob found the programme very difficult at times, we were encouraged by the fact that he did complete it. It is with some regret that we feel that Bob's lack of trust in others prevented him from gaining more benefit.

CLIVE: RAPIST MAKING GOOD PROGRESS

Clive was convicted of rape and sentenced to life imprisonment. Clive had committed this offence whilst on parole licence for a previous offence of rape, for which he had received a lengthy prison sentence.

Cognitive distortions

From the outset of the programme, it was clear that Clive had begun to look seriously at his attitudes towards women. An example of this was how he made a considerable effort to use a more acceptable form of language, e.g. 'women' instead of 'birds'.

It was evident from the beginning that Clive was very anxious to engage in the change process and this resulted in him almost rushing ahead without fully internalising the new material.

In terms of altered perceptions, Clive made significant progress in developing the ability to accept that his offences against adults were no different than those against children. He accepted the seriousness of his offences from the outset. However, as the programme developed, he began to show a deeper understanding of the effects of his behaviour upon others. Clive worked hard at acknowledging the pro-offending lifestyle he has lived throughout a significant part of his life.

It was noticeable between Phases 1 and 2 that there was some 'slippage'. However, this is not unusual and it was encouraging that Clive himself recognised that this area needed to be addressed. A major shift in Clive's thinking has been that a group work programme alone is not enough to consolidate and develop his efforts to develop pro-social attitudes. Additionally, he has taken responsibility to maintain the gains, e.g. he is more honest in his relationships with family and friends.

With regard to casting blame for the situation he has found himself in, Clive is to be congratulated for never once placing responsibility on either his victim or others for his current position.

Cycles of offending

Clive provided a detailed account of the events leading up to his current conviction. Clive admits that very soon after being released on parole he was living a lifestyle which he referred to as 'living a lie'. This manifested itself in heavy drinking and using both family and girlfriend exclusively for his own wants. In terms of the actual offence, Clive was very honest in stating that he was not going to take no for an answer. Equally, he was honest about his decision that he was going to have sex with the victim.

Clive was able to identify the thought–feeling–action chain quite specifically and admitted that he had allowed himself to commit the offence by 'distancing' himself from the victim. This allowed him to see her as nothing more than an object. Clive spoke about his victim making repeated requests that he discontinue his sexual advances. He recognises that he strongly resented women telling him what to do. This inevitably resulted in him using physical force in order to get his own way.

Clive recognises that his lifestyle prior to this offence resulted in a set of attitudes and behaviours which would promote pro-offending thinking.

It has been encouraging that Clive has shown such honesty in disclosing details of his offence, and that he has been brave enough to internalise the seriousness of his actions.

Victim awareness / empathy

From the beginning of the programme, it was clear that Clive had a sound understanding of the physical consequences for his victim. However, as the programme developed, he began to show an awareness of the emotional and psychological impact of his offending. There was evidence of a realisation on his part that he could not seek absolution for his offences from his victim. Equally, Clive began to become increasingly aware of the implications this offending had for relationships with his family. Although Clive showed an awareness and empathy for his victim at a verbal level from the outset, it was evident during the life of the group that he had internalised issues concerning victim empathy. Evidence for this can be found in the level of frustration and anger Clive felt towards other group members who at times showed little capacity to understand, or indeed concern for, the impact upon the victims. This was not a self-righteous reaction but rather one of bewilderment.

It has been very encouraging to witness the degree to which Clive has shown a heightened awareness of victim empathy issues. However, he recognises, and we would agree, that this is an area in which he needs to be continually vigilant in order to prevent 'slippage'.

Social functioning

Clive came to the programme with a prison-wide reputation for being 'jail-wise' and as someone who knew how to manipulate the system. However, within the programme, we have been impressed by his level of honesty in respect of himself. He also proved to be a very valuable group member in the manner in which he both supported and challenged other members. Throughout the programme, Clive made great efforts and expected the same of others.

From early on in the programme, Clive tried hard and achieved some success in this area. However, as the programme progressed, he began to develop a more reflective approach, which was an indication of his personal development. In terms of his social functioning, Clive identifies the loss of his macho image and need to be in command as important. However, he sees the gains as being an overall improvement in his relationships with others and an improved capacity to alter his perceptions of both men and women. His unquestioning acceptance of his own belief system was something that genuinely had a strong impact on him during the programme. For example, he never realised how different he was from non-offending males.

There was a certain 'richness' to Clive's involvement in the programme and this enabled him to demonstrate a greater degree of trust in both group members and group leaders than he had intended.

Clive is a man who possesses considerable charm, which to date he has chosen to use to his own advantage. There is a recognition, by him, that his considerable personal strengths need to be employed more appropriately if he is to lead a pro-social lifestyle.

Importantly, he is beginning to show signs that he knows what he needs to do. For example, he is taking part in various positive activities within the prison, studying for a degree course and developing more mature relationships with family members.

Relapse prevention

Because of the nature of Clive's sentence (a discretionary life sentence) it would be unrealistic to expect a fully formed relapse prevention plan at this stage. However, Clive has recognised the need to engage in more pro-social activities. Not only does he believe that he needs to undertake some form of maintenance programme in order to maintain the gains he has already made, but he has already started to implement an action plan for pro-social activities within the prison. For example, he is studying for a social science degree. It has been encouraging to see Clive beginning to adopt a more mature and responsible approach in his relationship with his wife. There is a recognition of the equality and trust required to maintain a healthy relationship. Clive has shown an alteration in his thought processes which is reflected in a heightened awareness of other people and an expectation of mutual respect.

Clive admits that he came on the programme with a very clear idea that he would participate in a limited manner. However, he soon realised that he was participating at a much broader and deeper level than originally envisaged. Clive consistently showed that he worked hard, both within group sessions and at homework, and supported other group members. He has shown the ability to relate the content of the programme to wider issues both in the prison and outside. Clive's approach has been marked by his level of honesty, not only towards other group members, but in relation to himself. His questioning of his own thoughts and feelings indicates an understanding that the process of change, in his case, is neither quick or easy. Clive, originally, identified his attitudes as needing to change and felt that there was a simple solution to this. It is evidence of his increased maturity that he began to appreciate the complexity of the attitudes which inform offending behaviour.

Conclusion

As a result of Clive's past record and the nature of his current conviction, it must be said that we felt Clive to be at high risk of reoffending at the beginning of the programme. We feel, at present, that this risk has been reduced as a result of his performance on the programme. However, it is of paramount importance that Clive is given the opportunity to consolidate the obvious gains he has made.

Overall, we have been impressed by the level of warmth and trust Clive has shown towards others in the group. Equally, we feel that Clive has the capacity to continue to develop his personal qualities in order to achieve a more acceptable and satisfying life.

DAVID: RAPIST MAKING A POOR RESPONSE

David is presently serving an eight-year prison sentence following a conviction for rape. David has recently undertaken his second review for parole purposes, in which he was unsuccessful. However, he intends to reapply for parole licence later this year. During his time in Peterhead, David has involved himself in educational and social activities as well as undertaking an alcohol awareness course.

Cognitive distortions

David made a very encouraging start to the programme, particularly in respect to general victim issues. This was illustrated by a change of his description of the offence from 'adultery' to 'rape'. However, exploration of relationship issues demonstrated that David held entrenched views on traditional male and female roles, and his role as head of the household. While initially David placed a lot of responsibility on the failure of the relationship between his partner and himself, he later began to show a more realistic perception of the quality of that relationship.

David also showed a marked tendency to look on his own past childhood experiences as the reason why his adult life has been blighted. It might be helpful for David to develop a more realistic perspective on his experiences if he is to move forward; he appeared to be trying to do this towards the end of Phase 1.

During Phase 1 of the programme, David's ability to challenge and be challenged developed considerably, and he appeared to display, at times, considerable insight. Unfortunately, we became concerned during Phase 2 of the programme as David increasingly sought refuge in his Christian faith in which, apparently, there appeared to be no consideration of the concept of free will. During Phase 2, the progress David had made was eroded somewhat; he attributed this to the break between Phases 1 and 2. David maintained that it was the reality of his arrest, conviction and imprisonment that told him he had 'done wrong'. While this is not an uncommon position, David never really moved on from a place defined by others to one which he could define for himself.

Cycles of offending

David devoted considerable time to outlining events prior to the night of the actual offence. His account reflected his feelings of increasing isolation, frustration, anger and hopelessness. However, he admits that on the night of the offence he and his estranged partner were enjoying a social occasion with friends. This does not seem to support David's view of himself as isolated. In addition, David's description of sexual thoughts about other women does not suggest that reunification with his partner was of paramount importance.

Although, initially, he underplayed his role in the offence, which was carried out with another man, he did, following challenges from group members, indicate that his role had been more proactive. For example, it was he who suggested that all three take a short cut through the park. He also admitted that it was his intention to have sex with the victim.

David's initial account of the offences reflected a brave attempt on his part to take on responsibility for his part of the offence. However, later in the programme, when his offence was referred to, he seemed to be distancing himself from it. Although David began to make some progress in identifying those internal and external factors leading up to the offence, this is an area on which he needs to refocus.

Victim awareness/empathy

In relation to David's level of victim awareness and empathy, we found his response very encouraging. His early work in this area reflected an honest attempt to understand the victim experience. However, David's consistent tendency to provide reasons for his behaviour and seek forgiveness, whilst understandable, resulted in him not gaining as much as he might have. Similarly, David made frequent references to his own victim experiences but did not appear to be able to link these to the experiences of others.

It was evident throughout the programme that David has a range of unresolved issues in his own life; a difficult area would appear to be relationships with women. If David is to move on, he perhaps needs to gain a better understanding of his range of emotions so that he is better equipped to understand the feelings of others.

Social functioning

In both exercises and group discussion, David did show the capacity, although he struggled, to express his thoughts and feelings. What became apparent was a theme in his thinking that placed him in the position of victim, for example, in reference to partner's behaviour: 'How can she do this to me?' This thinking was linked in turn to a range of feelings – anger, bitterness and rejection – which he seemed to think gave him permission to behave in unacceptable ways, e.g. domestic violence. It was also apparent that there had been a theme of reactive and negative feelings for many years.

Relapse prevention

At present, David's relapse prevention plan is almost exclusively devoted to reliance on divine intervention. While we have no intention of criticising his Christian beliefs, we feel strongly, however, that he is unable to recognise the importance of the concept of free will.

There appear to be a number of similarities between David's relapse prevention plan and his lifestyle prior to his offence. We understand from David that his life was focused on religious activities, and when he failed to maintain this he ended up developing a pro-offending pattern of behaviour.

We were disappointed by David's apparent failure to appreciate the importance of other group members' perspectives on what was a simple and realistic strategy for reoffending. It was unfortunate that David was unable to build into his relapse prevention plan some of the gains he had made in Phase 1.

Conclusion

Despite a promising start, David failed to live up to his true potential. Throughout the life of the group, David had tried hard to challenge other group members in a helpful, non-abusive way. However, he did not always respond positively to the challenges of others.

A consistent theme throughout the programme was David's low level of self-esteem, and although many of the group members attempted to improve his level of self-worth he seemed to have genuine difficulty acknowledging this, whilst accepting that it was well intentioned. Consequently, we were forced to conclude that the level of risk of reoffending does not appear to have been reduced.

Because of his inability to build on the gains of Phase 1 (he, in fact, lost ground during Phase 2), combined with an incomplete relapse prevention plan, we feel that David still continues to present a level of risk similar to that at which he started the programme, i.e. medium–high. We would strongly encourage David to use his obvious abilities and capacity for change in a more pragmatic way.

ED: PAEDOPHILE (GIRLS) MAKING GOOD PROGRESS

Ed was convicted of a number of charges of contravention of the Sexual Offences (Scotland) Act 1976, Section 5: offences of lewd, indecent and libidinous practices and behaviour, and offences of indecent assault. Ed was sentenced to nine years' imprisonment for these offences, which involved a number of girls between the ages of three and fifteen years. Ed had been convicted for a sexual offence involving a young girl some years previously.

Cognitive distortions

From the outset of the programme, Ed showed a considerable need to work in depth within this area – specifically, in respect of what is acceptable between adults and children. An example of this was Ed's assumption that children/girls fell into two categories: good, obedient children and bad, strong-spirited children. Ed also seemed to feel that a more relaxed and tolerant parenting style equated with children controlling the family.

Ed also appeared to believe that the underlying reasons for his offending were external, e.g. his partners were not sufficiently affectionate to meet his needs, or the children were sexually experienced.

Another particular issue was Ed's apparent inability to differentiate between the ages of the children he abused (3–15); this reflects his ability to objectify relationships.

During Phase 1 of the programme, Ed began to give serious thought to his thinking patterns and at a verbal level began to show some evidence of change. In Phase 2, however, he seemed to realise the benefit of consolidating this change, which gave him greater impetus. It was encouraging that Ed began to show a capacity to identify some of the unhelpful thinking errors that allowed him to abuse sexually, although he still needs to continue to develop this area.

It has been encouraging to see Ed shift from a position in which he saw himself as powerless and in the control of others; he now agrees that this is not always the case. In fact, he recognises that appearing to be a 'victim' enabled him to control the family situation.

Ed has always, at a verbal level, accepted responsibility for the offences. Throughout the programme, he has shown that this acceptance of responsibility has been incorporated into his revised thinking and feeling patterns.

Cycles of offending

Throughout the group, Ed had found it very difficult to speak, although less so during the second half of the programme. In fact, Ed agrees that he was afraid to disclose offence details, particularly in respect of the youngest child who was aged three years.

In identifying his pattern of offending, Ed accepts that children present little threat and are easy to manipulate. He saw their primary attraction as being non-threatening. Ed identified a pattern of spending a considerable amount of time in giving his undivided attention to children – more than he perceived the parents as being able to give. An example would be Ed's willingness to be used as a babysitter, which allowed him to create situations in which he could gain the trust of the children and their parents. It is, perhaps, an indication of his capacity to gain the trust of adults and children that he was able to abuse undetected for over ten years. Ed has been able to acknowledge that although he knew his behaviour was illegal he enjoyed it – an encouraging disclosure.

Although Ed admits to being surprised that he was not apprehended during or shortly after the abuse started, this does not fit in with the obvious precautions he took in maintaining the secrecy. This is an area in which Ed still needs to do further work.

Victim awareness / empathy

As mentioned earlier in this report, Ed did demonstrate the capacity to objectify his victims. From the early stages of the programme, it was evident that Ed's understanding of the effects of his behaviour upon the children was qualified by his capacity to objectify his relationships. However, as the programme progressed, it seemed to us that the enormity of what he had done began to impact on him at a more emotional level. This was evidenced to some degree by his participation in a range of exercises, particularly victim letters, in which he was able to identify his breach of trust and his using of the children for self-gratification, and recognise the lasting effects of sexual abuse.

Although Ed recognises that these offences affected a broad range of people, e.g. the parents of the children, a recognition of this alone is not enough to prevent reoffending. Therefore, he will have to continue to work through some of these issues.

The social and psychological effects is an area that Ed seems to have given some consideration, but again needs further work in.

Ed seems to have some considerable problems developing emotional intimacy with both adults and children, and although he feels more secure in his relationships with children the closeness he experiences does not appear to be long-lasting. However, in the course of the programme, he has begun to demonstrate an increasing ability to trust others and take risks. Although this is encouraging, he still needs to work at this.

To summarise, Ed has worked hard and the group experience itself has not made this any easier for him. Therefore, although the gains appear to be small at this point, this does not reflect his effort in group, which has been considerable.

Social functioning

At the beginning of the programme, Ed struggled to recognise and distinguish between thoughts, feelings and actions – particularly thoughts and feelings. However, as the programme progressed, he began to show that he was gaining a better understanding of this. Ed gives the impression of being a quiet, reserved, mild-mannered man who is inclined to take the 'path of least resistance' with other adults. However, when faced with challenges from fellow group members he appeared at times to see them as personal attacks and seemed to adopt entrenched positions. Nevertheless, there were occasions when he did show the ability to give serious consideration to what other group members were saying in respect of his own offending history. This is encouraging.

Ed identified the area of communicating with other adults as problematic. This would be evidenced by the difficulties he has experienced in his long-term relationships with adult women. Although Ed identifies his relationships with adults as being problematic, we are left wondering why he sustained relationships with his wife and subsequently with his cohabitee for a considerable length of time, even though he describes both as unhappy for substantial periods of time.

Although Ed appears to function at a socially acceptable level in many areas, his difficulty in coping with the emotional demands inherent in a reciprocal relationship results in him withdrawing or disengaging at an emotional level.

Ed agrees that he needs to continue working on his capacity to communicate effectively with other adults, particularly with those with whom he would wish to form meaningful relationships. Equally, he is aware of the need to improve the level of his self-esteem. This has been noticeable in his developing confidence within the group.

Relapse prevention

We are encouraged that Ed accepts that he will need to continue to adopt a proactive approach in terms of relapse prevention. He is aware that he will continue to present a risk to children and equally aware that he will need to take avoiding action.

Ed has begun to grasp the importance of the concept of internal and external factors relating to the offending. For example, he has gained an awareness of feelings such as 'I will never be happy' and the good feelings that he has when gaining the attention of children. Equally, he recognises external factors such as his failure to make emotional connections with other adults and his stubbornness, which results in mood swings as a means of controlling the responses of others.

In preparing his relapse prevention plan, Ed has identified crucial areas such as, for example, relationships with another woman, illegal fantasies and his perception of potential victims as 'not nice girls'. He is aware of the inherent dangers, for him, in all these areas. This is encouraging. In terms of leisure pursuits, he recognises the need to involve himself with other adults. He also recognises the need for other adults, in terms of support, on his return to the community. However, we feel that it is imperative that this is formalised and structured in order for Ed to gain the maximum benefit.

Conclusion

Having embarked on the programme, Ed progressed quite slowly through Phase 1, largely due to his fear of disclosure of both himself and his offending. This, in itself, is an indication of how serious he perceived his offending to be, and he is to be congratulated for taking this initial step in the process.

During Phase 2, Ed grew in confidence and his level of participation increased. He is aware that he will need to continue to practise his social skills. Although Ed has begun the process of considering the thoughts–feelings–action chain in relation to his offending, there is scope for further work in this area. Although it is encouraging that Ed has developed a good working relationship with the group workers, the time has arrived when he will need to take more risks on issues surrounding his offending. This will allow him to develop the confidence to engage more fully with a community-based supervision and support network.

In terms of risk of reoffending, at the outset of the programme, we assessed Ed as high risk due to his previous conviction for a sexual offence, the number of victims, the long period over which the offences took place, and the age range of the victims. Whilst we feel that the level of risk Ed presents at the moment has been reduced, there is a need for further work. We have been impressed by Ed's continuing involvement with the programme and should this level of commitment continue it bodes well for the future.

FRANK: PAEDOPHILE (BOYS) MAKING GOOD PROGRESS

Frank is currently serving a life sentence following conviction for offences of abduction and lewd, indecent and libidinous practices. His victim was a seven-year-old boy.

Frank has a large number of previous convictions, mainly of an acquisitive nature. He has one other similar conviction from 15 years before his current sentence, and a few years before that was convicted of abduction of an adult, which he acknowledges could have resulted in rape.

Frank was selected for inclusion in the STOP Programme and was keen to accept and participate in it, indications from him being that he had participated in extensive counselling over a considerable period, from which he had apparently developed a strong perception of his need for such work. This position was reflected by an open acknowledgement of his ability as a master games player.

From the outset of this programme, it was indeed apparent that he had considerable confidence in the group situation, although he was perhaps not quite as open and self-aware as he may have felt he seemed. This related to a number of events and life experiences to which we will refer at a later point in the report and which had undoubtedly become cornerstones of rationalisation and justification over an extended period.

Cognitive distortions

As stated, Frank is a capable communicator with good social skills and a broad outlook which provides a solid base for the future but which, at the same time and with inappropriate application, provides a wide avenue for a return to old ways. This will need to remain a focus of attention since no one change in life will prove in itself sufficient to prevent slippage over time.

He initially began the examination of the origins of values from a predominantly 'later life' standpoint, thus avoiding, to some extent, the pain of relating his childhood experiences and victimisation, although this inevitably impacted at some level. This, however, diminished with further work and examination of the more extended implications both in and out of group. In this, it must be recognised that this period is the source of many fundamentally negative experiences which may recur at times of emotional stress; it is important that the onset of such feelings be identified and addressed in accordance with his relapse prevention strategy.

A fundamental element of his system of justification has in the past been focusing blame and responsibility on others. It is felt, therefore, that he would do well to continue to review this, since for his own benefit, he needs to address as fully as possible those areas not yet addressed. Similarly, in relation to his unresolved feelings of conflict in relation to his close family, his own abusive activity within it and the inappropriate assumption of responsibility for the actions of others, continued work would be appropriate to maintain change. His ability to read and understand other people is high but this has been, out of habit, self-centred in purpose. His awareness of his ability to exert power over others is high both in and out of group. Whilst he verbalised his wish to give up this role, his efforts were somewhat disingenuous and his presentation of himself as insular and remote may in itself be the attraction to others which reinforces the levels of power he operates and perpetuates the cycle.

Cycles of offending

The initial examination of this element seemed to be divided into distinctly separate areas. These comprised the two detected sexual offences against male children for which Frank had received prison sentences (the current one included); acts of criminality to which there were definable links with interpersonal conflict, i.e. jealousy, anger, etc.; and other acts which, through his work he became aware were abusive in greater or lesser magnitude, perpetrated against both family members and those with whom he considered at the time he had functioning relationships at some level.

From this frequently harrowing process emerged commonalities of thought, feeling and behaviours, and the tools with which he could begin to examine the roles and responsibilities undertaken by him in these events in clearer perspective. These were applied with varying success but produced an overall picture on which to build and continue development.

Victim awareness/empathy

Frank has, in numerous ways, experienced victimisation, and whilst this provides at one level an access to the impact of his own abusive behaviour, it does not provide the full answer. There are, undoubtedly, areas in common here but, ultimately, each victim has their own experiences, and considerable painful work was necessary on his part to move from what he described as 'the wee boy' within himself who was in torment when images of abuse or suffering were present to a degree of empathic feeling which recognises the needs of others. In this area, he will need to pay close, continuing attention to the dividing lines between responsibilities and decisions taken from the very different perspectives of survivor and abuser. This would be particularly crucial to the development of appropriate feelings and actions in future relationships, whether social or more intimate, and the consequences of feelings and actions.

Relapse prevention

From available information, fully supported by his own input, Frank's life experiences to date have been of abusive, unstable relationships. We would, therefore, question whether, whilst he continues to misuse his social skills, he can successfully develop an intimate, non-abusive relationship. Having striven to identify key areas within the extensive information collated, we feel that considerable avenues of support will need to be available. An inescapable area for ongoing attention is therefore the maintenance and strengthening of his marriage, which it is fair to say has, in the past, been based on a range of unstated expectations and less than full honesty on the part of both partners. This, in the remaining period of sentence, would, therefore, be a crucial area for development.

Realistic consideration of the future relationship which is envisaged with both close and extended family members will require clarification within his own mind. Despite extensive work undertaken both in and out of group, we are still uncertain whether further consideration will need to be given to Frank's use of substances to avoid addressing emotional difficulties, including self-pity.

Conclusion

Throughout the programme, Frank maintained a high-profile role and was very able in expanding on appropriate issues, to the benefit of other group members. Whilst, initially, there was some concern that he was emotionally very self-controlled, over time this appeared to be less of a problem.

Despite his assurances to the contrary, we still, at times, had concerns that Frank continued at some level to exhibit his game-playing skills.

Frank has acknowledged a lifetime of distorted thinking patterns, and whilst he appears to have made significant progress, it is understood that, for him, this is only the beginning of the process of change required in order to maintain an offence-free lifestyle.

GEORGE: PAEDOPHILE (GIRLS) MAKING A POOR RESPONSE
Phase 1

George surprised us by the lack of work he has done in relation to his offending behaviour considering he has served eight years of a double life sentence. He continues to deny the severity of his crimes while seemingly being under the impression that he will be released within the next couple of years. From day one of the programme, George did not seem to want to get in touch with his thoughts or feelings, whether this was in an attitudinal exercise or linked directly to his offence. This was something that he had difficulty doing throughout the programme.

In an effort to help him catch up or keep up with the rest of the group, the leaders spent a lot of time working with George outside of the group in one-to-one situations. This was time George failed to make best use of and, in consequence, due to his inability or unwillingness to work, we did not regain any of the ground already lost by him in group.

It was only after much deliberation with programme supervisors and group leaders that George was allowed to continue on into Phase 2. It was felt that due to the modular approach used in Phase 2, George would find it easier to deal with his offending behaviour in small, more manageable pieces with him, hopefully, being able to link all these aspects together by the end of Phase 2, or at least to have a better understanding of his behaviour.

Phase 2

Fantasy

From day one in this module, George saw no harm in having legal or illegal fantasies. Throughout work done in Phase 2, we cannot see any significant changes in these attitudes. He continues to be unable to link fantasy with lapse, eventually leading to relapse.

Sexuality

George showed a very sparse or basic knowledge of sexuality and sex. However, when it came down to his offending against children, it became obvious that he had used a lot of the children's own natural inquisitiveness and innocence to continue to offend against them. This came to light more by the group asking him questions, relating it to ways they had offended themselves, than anything George willingly shared with the group.

Anger management

From what George has said, anger does seem to have played a major part in his offending. What does stand out, however, is his inability to deal appropriately with his anger. One example of this could be the anger he still displays over an incident relating to his removal from another prison at the beginning of his sentence. This is not an isolated case. There are three occasions on which he has harmed himself, i.e. punched doors or walls, rather than confront and deal with the reasons for his anger.

Cycles of offending

George appeared to be having difficulty developing a comprehensible pattern of behaviour in group. To clear some areas of doubt for others in the group, the leaders asked him to forget about a cycle at present, deciding that it would be more beneficial for all concerned, including himself, if he clarified his offences, not only relating to his present sentence but to past sentences. This he agreed to try to do, but again got bogged down by his denial of certain offences he had been charged with. To date, we still have no clear understanding of the depth of his offending or indeed of how many victims he has had.

Victim awareness / empathy

From the outset of the group, George could only see himself and his family as victims. To a certain extent, this is still true. At a verbal level, he can identify feelings victims may have, but when asked to explain the direct impact that his offending has on the victim he seems unable or unwilling to do so. Much of this difficulty could be related to some aspects of his offending about which he is still firmly in denial.

Relapse prevention

In some areas, George's relapse prevention plan was realistic and workable, e.g. his signs for others to notice, though he has identified some areas which, as far as we know, have not been a problem for him in the past. Other signs and areas which he has mentioned in group are totally unrealistic for someone with his record of offending.

George has not tried to write down a realistic support network beyond his immediate family. While, due to his length of sentence, this is undoubtedly a difficult area for him, we feel he could still have tried a bit harder and this is an area that will have to be picked up on in the future.

Conclusion

The group as a whole tried many different and varied approaches to encourage George to be open and honest about his offending behaviour. All have met with an astounding lack of success.

One of his major stumbling blocks is his total denial of the charge of full sexual intercourse with one of his victims.

One of the methods the group used was to ask George to look honestly at the offences for which he is willing to accept guilt. Yet again, we are not sure whether he was unable or unwilling to do this.

Our plan of forwarding George to Phase 2 may have helped him in some areas but overall was not a great success. On saying this, he may benefit more from the STOP Programme in the future if he does the cognitive reasoning group before going back through it. We also feel he should go through a course on anger management before his release.

HARRY: PAEDOPHILE (GIRLS) MAKING A VERY POOR RESPONSE (WITHDREW FROM STOP – CONSIDERED HIGH RISK)

Harry was sentenced to twelve years' imprisonment following conviction on charges of assault and lewd, indecent and libidinous practices and behaviour. The victims of these offences were two eight-year-old girls who lived in the vicinity of Harry's home, Wendy and Emily.

Harry's offending behaviour includes four earlier sexual offences, all of which involved young girls. It would appear that this pattern of behaviour emerged when Harry was a fourteen-year-old boy. At this time, he received a probation order following conviction on a charge of lewd and libidinous practices and behaviour. When 18 years old, Harry was convicted of assault with intent to ravish resulting in committal to a mental hospital, where he was to remain for ten years. A further conviction two years after being released from hospital for assault, and lewd, indecent and libidinous practices and behaviour, resulted in Harry being imprisoned for six months. Harry was further convicted of indecent assault four years later and spent a short period in custody. The remainder of Harry's offending history includes theft, fraud and breach of the peace. Clearly, Harry's sexual offending history would appear to be a well-established, entrenched pattern of behaviour.

In discussion of the sexual elements of his offending history, Harry is extremely vague and gives the impression that these events happened out of the blue. This position gives rise to some concern if this is, in fact, what he truly believes. An attitude such as this would, necessarily, make it more difficult for Harry to recognise any changes in his thinking and behaviour which would indicate an increased likelihood of offending.

Harry withdrew from the STOP Programme, designed to examine offending behaviour, at an early stage. It appears that Harry did not gain substantially from his involvement in this work, in that he still does not recognise either his continuing risk of reoffending or the seriousness of his offences to date. In contrast, Harry appears to feel that he did gain from his work in the programme.

When discussing the risk of reoffending with Harry, it became clear that he does not consider himself to present a risk to children in the community. This begs the question of the level of understanding he has of his own cycles of offending. When presented with the scenario of possible future risk, Harry becomes defensive and angry at the suggestion that he may offend again at some future date. He tells me he loves children, but not in a sexual way. He still maintains the position that his victims encouraged his actions by, as he puts it, 'cuddling up to him'. It is difficult to engender any further discussion around this area due to his position in respect of his thoughts about children, as stated above.

Harry will be homeless upon release, due to his inability to repay arrears on his former tenancy. He tells me he will be looking for accommodation in a bed and breakfast hotel in [a major Scottish city]. In the past, he has spoken of living in a particular district, and it is my feeling that he may return there after his release. Harry tells me that should he not be able to find accommodation in the area he may travel to England, where he believes his brother may be able to assist.

Harry realistically assesses his chances of securing employment on release as slim. This begs the question of how he will fill days of unstructured time when his financial resources and social network appear to be poor. One might conclude from this that the dangers inherent in such an impoverished lifestyle can only serve to heighten this man's risk of reoffending.

IAN: PAEDOPHILE (SOME CASE NOTES)

Progress record after ten sessions

Ian's level of participation in group has been of an unacceptable standard. He appeared only to be interested in the group process when the focus was on him. His recent disclosure work was of an acceptable standard and his honesty and candour were appreciated; however, when the spotlight turned from Ian to someone else, his participation dropped to an unacceptable standard. When Ian is prompted by other group members, his questions are relevant and helpful, but it is unhelpful to the group process that it is necessary to prompt him constantly.

It is felt that this behaviour is selfish, but it does reflect the way he behaves in relationships outside of the jail environment. Ian appeared unconcerned when challenged regarding his behaviour with his wife and could offer no reason for his behaviour other than 'that's the way it is'. When the group as a whole stated to Ian that his behaviour in his marriage was abusive, he refused to acknowledge this. We are concerned that Ian is unwilling to change and is quite happy to continue through life presenting the same level of dangerousness that he has in the past. This would lead us to question his motives for participating in the STOP Programme and his commitment.

Ian appears to become angry when the group members point out that there is a possibility of his reoffending. Is it possible that he is scared of reoffending? If this is the case, then Ian should begin to examine how to use his time in the programme more constructively.

Progress record after 40 sessions

It is encouraging to note that despite the recent turmoil in Ian's personal life he has managed to a greater degree to leave this outside of group. We do feel, however, that he needs to address his level of participation in group. Shortly after his ten-session review and our subsequent conversation, his contribution to group improved greatly. During this time, Ian took several risks and made statements that were both relevant and helpful. Recently, however, as the time drew nearer for his own disclosure, he contributed less and less to the group process and apparently appeared to be trying to hide within the group. This behaviour leads us to believe that Ian may be reaffirming old beliefs and attitudes with regard to blame and responsibility.

We appreciate the difficulty he has with the written assignments, but are encouraged by his levels of honesty and candour.

Background case notes[1]

Ian tells me that his mother and father divorced when he was approximately two years old. There were two children of that marriage, Ken and himself. His mother moved away and lost contact for some time. His father married the woman Ian regards as his mother when he was less than four years old. Recollection is naturally poor in these earlier years, apart from the abusive experiences which have been tentatively linked with those years as Ian cannot be accurate, understandably.

Ian spoke not only of sexual abuse but also of severe physical chastisement. He equates this with the fact that his father was in the army and expected similar levels of discipline in his family. Ian remembers the family being materially very well off when he was a young child.

His father and 'mother' had a daughter, Agnes, when Ian was aged ten. He apparently jumped on this baby so violently that she required hospitalisation. He tells me that he was terrified she would also be abused and that he knew from his own experiences of being in hospital for treatment that children were safe in hospital. It was also at this time that Ian began to manipulate periods in hospital by not managing his medicine properly. He says he always loved his sister and did not feel jealous at the new arrival.

Ian would appear to have begun to abuse children almost as soon as he became sexually aware himself, and appears to have developed a pattern which is deeply entrenched but which contains elements of escalation in terms of risk taking and sadistic tendencies. The following are remarks made by Ian, and paraphrased for recording purposes.

1. All the victims had dark hair – he preferred children who looked something like he did as a child. He says that because of this he would not have touched his son, Michael, as he was a blond child.

2. Many of the school-age victims were skipping school at the times of the assaults and were less likely to tell about offences because they should not have been there anyway.

3. Ian told all the victims not to tell anyone.

4. Ian thinks some of the victims had been victimised previously. He thought he could tell this by them seeming to know what to do. He thought this particularly with respect to his current victim and the previous one.

---

1   This piece of work is based solely on information supplied by Ian. At times it is far removed from histories obtained from other sources. Indeed, there is some confusion as to whether Ian's older brother Ken had abused him rather than Ian's father. Ian maintains that it was his father and 'Uncle', his brother Ken being in a hospital for the mentally handicapped.

5. His masturbatory fantasies are acknowledged as involving only five- to seven-year-old boys.

6. Ian chose this age range because he thought they would not tell, and if they did, no one would believe them.

7. Ian used previous victims and offences for the majority of his masturbatory fantasies. His preference was to use the most recent incidents.

8. Victims would be picked up, carried or dragged to locus, or he would spot a child, watch until he was sure the child was unaccompanied, and would then follow them about until they went into a public toilet. Ian enjoyed it when they cried, enjoyed the resistance. (He appears devoid of any feeling for the victim in the post-offence period. He fails to acknowledge the impact on the victim despite his own early experiences.)

9. Ian states he has been warned, by the police, on approximately twenty occasions about his behaviour towards little boys. He thinks charges have not been pressed because parents did not want children to go through a trial, because children could not piece together coherently what had happened to them and because there was probably not enough evidence.

Ian tells me he will never offend again because, if he does, he will lose his wife. When it was put to him that this had not stopped him in the past, he said that it was different this time. She had said she would leave him if he got into trouble again.

Ian's relationships would appear to be another confused area in his life. His relationship with his wife would appear to be from one angle very controlling but from another angle very dependent. Whilst both are considered to be of low intelligence, Ian is assessed as being the less able of the pair. Ruth, his wife, seems to be quite astute at managing money; Ian describes how she would provide him with a daily allowance. Reports would suggest that Ian manages the relationship with a view to meeting his own needs at any cost. He is said to be manipulative and controlling, using moods and violence. He, himself, denies that there was any physical violence within the marriage. However, having observed his behaviour in our work together, I would have to agree that he is extremely manipulative and would like to be controlling. He described a recent manipulation within the prison. He seems to have hall staff extremely concerned about his 'problem', which is the situation he wants.

Ian tells me that should he offend again he will commit suicide; he says that he wishes that one of his previous suicide attempts had succeeded. Whilst note must be taken of such statements, it could be argued that this is consistent with the level of manipulative behaviour Ian displays.

Ian maintains that when he leaves prison after this sentence he and Ruth will go on holiday, and then they plan to move away from their home town. Mention has been made of towns in England where they have friends, where his natural mother lives or even going to Belgium. It remains to be seen whether they possess sufficient material resources and emotional stamina to bring these plans to fruition.

The children of the marriage have been adopted out. The third child, Robert, is presently subject to a place of safety order and is also being considered for adoption. Ian is vehemently against plans to take the child away and feels that the community-based social workers are plotting against him. It is to be noted that Robert is not Ian's biological child but the result of a brief liaison Ruth had with someone else. However, Ian says that he intends to bring up this baby as his own and will fight in the courts to retain his parental rights. When we discussed a comment in an earlier report which suggested that Ian had been distant with Michael and had not participated in his care in the way he had with his daughter Hannah, he said that he was *afraid that something might happen*. This is despite his persistent denial that he would ever harm his own child. Community social workers have questioned whether he had, in fact, behaved inappropriately towards Michael but have never been able to substantiate their fears. Ian tells me that he would have no qualms about living in a household where there were children, whether they were his own children or not.

Ian tells me that he has almost always been able to find work of an unskilled nature. Latterly, this has been in bars, but he did spend some time working as a care assistant in a home for the elderly. *Also, he tells me that during the period immediately after leaving school he did voluntary work with handicapped children. This would seem to have involved taking them out unaccompanied, as well as on organised outings.*

Additionally, Ian tells me that at one time he and Ruth ran a small grocery business. This begs the question of how much unlimited access he had to vulnerable children. It also seems that they used to have a fair number of children visiting their home, and babysat for neighbours. Again, this begs the question of access to vulnerable children, since all their accommodation seems to have been in fairly deprived areas, which seem to contain a high proportion of single parent families.

References

Abel, G.G., Becker, J.V., Cunningham-Rathner, J., Mittelman, M.S. and Rouleau, J.-L. (1988) 'Multiple paraphilic diagnosis among sex offenders.' *Bulletin of the American Academy of Psychiatry and the Law 16*, 153–168. Reproduced with revisions by G.G. Abel and J.-L. Rouleau (1990) 'The nature and extent of sexual assault'. In W.L. Marshall, D.R. Laws and H.E. Barbaree (eds) *Handbook of Sexual Assault: Issues, Theories and Treatment of the Offender.* New York, NY: Plenum Press.

Abel, G.G., Becker, J.V., Mittelman, M.S., Cunningham-Rathner, J., Rouleau, J.-L. and Murphy, W.D. (1987) 'Self-reported sex crimes of nonincarcerated paraphiliacs.' *Journal of Interpersonal Violence 2*, 6, 3–25.

Adshead, G., Howett, M. and Mason, F. (1994) 'Women who sexually abuse children: The undiscovered country'. *The Journal of Sexual Aggression 1*, 1, 45–56

Aitken, D. (1992) *Assessment and Management of Perpetrators of Child Sexual Abuse.* Workshop paper given at ADSW Social Work Conference, Aviemore, October.

Andrews, D.A., Zinger, I., Hoge, R.D., Bonta, J., Gendreau, P. and Cullen, F.T. (1990) 'Does correctional treatment work? A clinically relevant and psychologically informed meta-analysis.' *Criminology 28*, 369–404.

ATSA (1997) *Ethical Standards and Principles for the Management of Sexual Abusers.* S.H. Jensen (ed) Beaverton, OR: Association for the Treatment of Sexual Abusers.

ATSA (1998a) *Phallometric Testing with a Group of Child Molesters: An Examination of Reliability and Validity Issues.* Research by Yolanda Fernandez. Vancouver.

ATSA (1998b) *Deception and Denial in Sex Offenders.* Address by Anna Salter. Vancouver.

Barbaree, H.E. (1990) 'Stimulus Control of Sexual Arousal: Its Role in Sexual Assault.' In W.L. Marshall, D.R. Laws and H.E. Barbaree (eds) *Handbook of Sexual Assault: Issues, Theories and Treatment of the Offender.* New York: Plenum Press.

Barbaree, H.E. and Marshall, W.L. (1989) 'Erectile responses amongst heterosexual child molesters, father-daughter incest offenders and matched non-offenders: Five distinct age preference profiles.' *Canadian Journal of Behavioral Science 21*, 70–83.

Barker, M. and Morgan, R. (1993) *Sex Offenders: A Framework for the Evaluation of Community Based Treatments.* London: HMSO.

Bass, E. and Davis, L. (1988) *The Courage to Heal: A Guide for Women Survivors of Child Sexual Abuse.* New York, NY: Harper and Row (paperback 1990) London: Cedar.

Beckett, R., Beech, A., Fisher, D. and Fordham, A.S. (1994) *Community-Based Treatment for Sex Offenders: An Evaluation of Seven Treatment Programmes.* A report for the Home Office by the STEP Team. London: Home Office.

Beech, A., Fisher, D., Beckett, R., and Fordham, A.S. (1998) *STEP 3: An Evaluation of the Prison Sex Offender Treatment Programme.* Research, Development and Statistics Occasional Paper. London: Home Office.

Berliner, L. (1982) 'Removing the offender in cases of family sexual assault.' *TSA News* 5, 3.

Berliner, L. (1996) 'Community notification: Neither a panacea nor a calamity'. In *Sexual Abuse: A Journal of Research and Treatment, 8,* 2, 101–104, New York: Plenum Press.

Blake, J. (1990) *Sentenced by Association: The Needs of Prisoners' Families.* London: Save the Children Fund.

Bowlby, J. (1988) *A Secure Base: Clinical Applications of Attachment Theory.* London: Routledge.

Brown, A. (1994) 'Sex offender programme: A suitable case for treatment.' *Prison Report No. 26, Spring 1994.* London: Prison Reform Trust.

Brownmiller, S. (1975) *Against Our Will: Men, Women and Rape.* New York, NY: Bantam.

Butwell, M. (1996) *Broadmoor Special Case Register.* Special Hospital Research Unit, Broadmoor Hospital.

Cameron, J. (1983) *Prisons and Punishment in Scotland from the Middle Ages to the Present.* Edinburgh: Canongate.

Chaney, E.F., O'Leary, M.R. and Marlatt, G.A. (1978) 'Skill training with alcoholics.' *Journal of Consulting and Clinical Psychology 46,* 1092–1104.

Chiswick, D. (1998) Correspondence with Author. October.

Colorado. (1998) *Standards and Guidelines for the Assessment, Evaluation, Treatment and Behavioral Monitoring of Adult Sex Offenders.* Colorado Sex Offender Management Board, revised September 1998. Denver, CO: Colorado Department of Public Safety.

Condy, S., Templer, D., Brown, R. and Veaco, L. (1987) 'Parameters of sexual contact of boys with women.' *Archives of Sexual Behaviour 16,* 571–585.

Cooke, D.J. (1994) *Psychological Disturbance in the Scottish Prison System: Prevalence, Precipitants and Policy.* Occasional Paper, No. 3. Edinburgh: Scottish Prison Service.

Cooklin, S. (1989) *From Arrest to Release.* London: Bedford Square Press.

Cooper, C.L., Murphy, W.D. and Haynes, M.R. (1996) 'Characteristics of abused and nonabused adolescent sexual offenders.' *Sexual Abuse: A Journal of Research and Treatment 8,* 2,105–119.

Council of Europe Committee on Crime Problems (1993) *Report on Sexual Exploitation, Pornography and Prostitution of, and Trafficking in, Children and Young Adults.* Recommendation No. R (91) 11, Council of Europe.

Cowburn, M. (1992) 'Pornography in prisons'. In *Beyond Containment: The Penal Response to Sex Offending.* London: Prison Reform Trust.

Darke, J.L. (1990) 'Sexual aggression: Achieving power through humiliation.' In W.L. Marshall, D.R. Laws and H.E. Barbaree (eds) *Handbook of Sexual Assault: Issues, Theories and Treatment of the Offender.* New York, NY: Plenum Press.

Dellacoste, F. and Alexander, P. (eds) (1987) *Sex Work: Writings by Women in the Industry.* Pittsburgh, PA: Cleis Press.

Dempsey, R. (1995) *Creating Control.* Social Work Unit, HM Prison, Barlinnie.

Dhawan, S. and Marshall, W.L. (1996) 'Sexual abuse histories of sexual offenders.' *Sexual Abuse: A Journal of Research and Treatment 8*, 1, 7–15.

DiIulio Jr., J.J. (1989) *Governing Prisons: A Comparative Study of Correctional Management.* New York, NY: The Free Press, Macmillan.

Dworkin, A. (1979) *Pornography: Men Possessing Women.* New York, NY: Perigee.

Earle, J.H. (1998) *Polygraph as a Vital Component for Sex Offender Treatment.* Presentation to ATSA Conference, Vancouver, October.

Eldridge, H.J. (1992) *Relapse Prevention and its Application to Patterns of Adult Male Sex Offending: Implications for Assessment, Intervention and Maintenance.* Paper presented to the NOTA Conference, Dundee University, September.

Eldridge, H.J. (1994) *Report on Consultancy/Supervised Practice Jan–Dec 1993.* Head of Training, Gracewell Institute/Faithfull Foundation.

Eldridge, H.J. (1998) *Adult Female Perpetrators of Child Sexual Abuse: Patterns of Offending and Strategies for Effective Assessment and Intervention.* Appendix 2 of the response of the Lucy Faithfull Foundation to the 'Working Together' consultation paper.

Elliott, M. (1992) 'Images of children in the media: soft kiddie porn.' In C. Itzin (ed) *Pornography: Women, Violence and Civil Liberties: A Radical View.* Oxford: Oxford University Press.

Elliott, M. (1993) *Female Sexual Abuse of Children: The Ultimate Taboo.* Harlow: Longman.

Finkelhor, D. (1982) 'Sexual abuse: A sociological perspective.' *Child Abuse and Neglect 6*, 95–102

Finkelhor, D. (1984) 'How widespread is child sexual abuse?' *Children Today 13*, 18–20.

Finkelhor, D. and Russell, D. (1984) 'Women as perpetrators.' In D. Finkelhor (ed) *Child Sexual Abuse: New Theory and Research.* New York, NY: Free Press.

Fisher, D., Grubin, D. and Perkins, D.E. (1998) 'Working with sexual offenders in psychiatric settings in England and Wales.' In W.L. Marshall, Y.M. Fernandez, S.M. Hudson and T. Ward (eds) *Sourcebook of Treatment Programs for Sexual Offenders.* New York, NY: Plenum Press.

Fisher, D. and Thornton, D. (1993) 'Assessing risk of re-offending in sexual offenders.' *Journal of Mental Health 2*, 105–117.

Foucault, M. (1977) *Discipline and Punish: The Birth of the Prison.* Harmondsworth: Penguin.

Freeman-Longo, R.E. (1996) 'Prevention or problem.' In *Sexual Abuse: A Journal of Research and Treatment 8,* 2, 91–100.

Gallagher, J.D. (1994) Letter to author from Director (Human Resources) of SPS, reporting on a 'What went wrong?' input to an English Prison Service Conference on *Effects of Close Contact Confrontation Programmes with Offenders on Prison Staff.*

Garland, D. (1985) *Punishment and Welfare: History of penal strategies.* England: Gower.

Garland, D. (1990) *Punishment and Modern Society.* Oxford: Oxford University Press.

The Glasgow Herald (1992) 'Study links majority of children with crime.' 23 October 1992.

Groth, N. and Burgess, A. (1979) 'Sexual trauma in the life histories of rapists and child molesters.' *Victimology 4,* 10–16.

Hanson, R.K. (1997) *The Development of a Brief Actuarial Risk Scale for Sexual Offence Recidivism.* (User Report 1997-04) Ottawa: Department of the Solicitor General of Canada.

Hanson, R.K. and Bussière, M.T., (1996) *Predictors of Sexual Offender Recidivism: A Meta-Analysis.* (User Report 1996-04) Ottawa: department of the Solicitor general of Canada.

Hanson, R.K. and Bussière, M.T. (1998) 'Predicting relapse: A meta-analysis of sexual offender recidivism studies.' *Journal of Consulting and Clinical Psychology 66,* 2, 348–362.

Hanson, R.K. and Harris, A.J.R. (1998) *Dynamic Predictors of Sexual Recidivism.* (User Report 1998-01) Ottawa: Department of the Solicitor General of Canada.

Hanson, R.K. and Slater, S. (1988) 'Sexual victimization in the history of sexual abusers: A review.' *Annals of Sex Research 1,* 485–499.

Harrison, H. (1993) 'Female abusers – what children and young people have told ChildLine.' In M. Elliott (ed) *Female Sexual Abuse of Children: The Ultimate Taboo.* Harlow: Longman.

Heil, P., Ahlmeyer, S. and English. P. (1998) *Maximising the Use of the Polygraph with Sex Offenders: Policy Development and Research Findings.* Presentation to ATSA Conference, Vancouver, October.

Hogue, T.E. (1992) *Sex Offence Information Questionnaire (SOIQ), and Individual Clinical Rating Form,* Psychology Unit, HMP Dartmoor.

Home Office (1977) *Prisons and the Prisoner: The Work of the Prison Service in England and Wales.* London: HMSO.

House of Commons Official Report, Parliamentary Debates (1996a) First Scottish Standing Committee, 19 November 1996, on the Crime and Punishment (Scotland) Bill.

House of Commons Official Report, Parliamentary Debates (1996b) First Scottish Standing Committee, 28 November 1996, on the Crime and Punishment (Scotland) Bill. Op. cit. November 1996.

Hunter, M. (1990) *The Sexually Abused Male: Prevalence, Impact and Treatment.* Lexington, MA: D.C. Heath.

Ignatieff, M. (1978) *A Just Measure of Pain: The penitentiary in the Industrial Revolution 1750–1850.* London: Macmillan.

Inter-Departmental Group on Child Abuse (1992) Sub-group on working with offenders (January) *A Strategic Statement on Working With Abusers.* London: Department of Health.

Inter-Departmental Group on Sex Offending (1994) draft paper on the *Strategy for Multi-Agency Co-operation in dealing with sex offenders sentenced to imprisonment: Guidance to agencies on the supervision of sex offenders before and after release from custody.* London: Home Office.

Itzin, C. (1992a) *Pornography: Women, Violence and Civil Liberties: A Radical View.* Oxford: Oxford University Press.

Itzin, C. (1992b) *Evidence of Pornography-Related Harm and a Progressive New Approach to Legislating Against Pornography without Censorship.* A paper presented to the Birmingham Anti-pornography Conference, October.

Jack, A.M. and Mair, K.J. (1993) *Evaluation of the STOP Programme, HM Prison, Peterhead.* Psychology Unit, Peterhead.

Jacobs, J.B. (1977) *Stateville: The Penitentiary in Mass Society.* Chicago, IL: University of Chicago Press.

Jenkins, A. (1990) *Invitations to Responsibility: The Therapeutic Engagement of Men who are Violent and Abusive.* Adelaide: Dulwich Centre Publications.

Jones, G., Huckele, P. and Tanaghow, A. (1992) 'Command hallucinations, schizophrenia and sexual assault.' *Irish Journal of Psychological Medicine 9*, 47–49

Kaufman, K.L., Wallace, A.M., Johnson, C.F. and Reeder, M.L. (1995) 'Comparing female and male perpetrators' modus operandi: victim's reports of sexual abuse.' *Journal of Interpersonal Violence 10*, 3, 322–333.

Kinsey, R. (1993) *Lothian Crime Survey* (report of research). Edinburgh: Edinburgh University.

Langevin, R., Wright, P. and Handy, L. (1989) 'Characteristics of sex offenders who were sexually victimized as children.' *Annals of Sex Research 2*, 227–253.

Laws, D.R. (1996) 'Marching into the past: A critique of Card and Olsen.' *Sexual Abuse: A Journal of Research and Treatment 8*, 4, 273–278.

Lewis, P.S. and Perkins, D.E. (1996) 'Collaborative strategies for sex offenders in secure settings.' In C. Cordess and M. Cox (eds) *Forensic Psychotherapy: Crime, Psychodynamics and the Offender Patient, Vol. 1.* London: Jessica Kingsley Publishers.

Mann, R.E. (1999) 'Cognitive behavioural treatment for imprisoned sex offenders in England and Wales'. In G. Deegener (ed) *Therapy of Sexual and Physical Violence.* Weinheim: Psychologie Verlags Union.

Mann, R.E. and Thornton, D. (1998) 'The evolution of a multisite sexual offender treatment program.' In W.L. Marshall, Y.M. Fernandez, S.M. Hudson and T.

Ward (eds) *Sourcebook of Treatment Programs for Sexual Offenders*. New York, NY: Plenum Press.

Mann, R.E., Thornton D., Ward, T., Hudson, S.M. and Laws, D.R. (1998) *Remaking Relapse Prevention: 1*. ATSA Conference, Vancouver, 1998.

Marshall, W.L. (1992a) 'The social value of treatment for sexual offenders.' *Canadian Journal of Human Sexuality 1*, 109–114

Marshall, W.L. (1992b) *Report to the Scottish Prison Service on the Implementation of a Treatment Programme for Sex Offenders*. Ontario: Queen's University.

Marshall, W.L. (1994) *Appraisal of the Sex Offenders' Treatment Program at Peterhead Prison*. Ontario: Queen's University.

Marshall, W.L. (1995) *Report on Current Status and Future Development of Sex Offender Program at Peterhead and Suggestions for a Scottish National Policy*. Ontario: Queen's University.

Marshall, W.L. and Barbaree, H.E. (1990) 'Outcome of comprehensive cognitive–behavioral treatment programs.' In W.L. Marshall, D.R. Laws and H.E. Barbaree (eds) *Handbook of Sexual Assault: Issues, Theories and Treatment of the Offender*. New York, NY: Plenum Press.

Marshall, W.L., Laws, D.R. and Barbaree, H.E. (eds) (1990) *Handbook of Sexual Assault: Issues, Theories and Treatment of the Offender*. New York, NY: Plenum Press.

Mathews, R., Hunter, J.A. and Vuz, J. (1997) 'Juvenile female sexual offenders: clinical characteristics and treatment issues.' *Sexual Abuse: A Journal of Research and Treatment 9*, 3, 187–199.

Mathews, R., Matthews, J.K. and Speltz, K. (1989) *Female Sex Offenders: An Exploratory Study*. Orwell, VT: Safer Society Press.

Matthews, J. (1983) *Forgotten Victims: How Prison Affects the Family*. London: NACRO.

Matthews, J.K. (1998) 'An 11-year perspective of working with female sexual offenders.' In W.L. Marshall, Y.M. Fernandez, S.M. Hudson and T. Ward (eds) *Sourcebook of Treatment Programs for Sexual Offenders*. New York, NY: Plenum Press.

McGuire, J. and Priestley, P. (1995) 'Reviewing "what works": past, present and future.' In J. McGuire (ed) *What Works: Research and Practice on the Reduction of Re-offending*. Chichester: Wiley.

McIvor, G., Campbell, V., Rowlings, C. and Skinner, K. (1997) *The STOP Programme: The Development and Implementation of Prison-Based Groupwork with Sex Offenders*. Occasional Paper, No. 2/1997. Edinburgh: Scottish Prison Service.

Morrison, T. (1996) 'Emotionally competent child protection organisations: Fallacy, fiction or necessity?' In J. Bates, R. Pugh and N. Thompson (eds) *Protecting Children: Challenge and Change*. Aldershot: Arena.

Murphy, W.D. and Barbaree, H.E. (1988) *Assessment of Sexual Offenders by Means of Erectile Response: Psychometric Properties and Decision Making*. Washington, DC: National Institute of Mental Health.

N., J. (1995) 'STOP the Myth.' article by prisoner at Peterhead Prison. In *The Grapevine*, a magazine by inmates of Peterhead Prison, Easter 1995, Issue 3.

NOTA (1995) 'Working with adults and adolescents who exhibit sexually abusive behaviours: The use of sexually salient and pornographic materials.' *NOTANews 13*, 4–12. The National Association for the Development of Work with Sex Offenders.

O'Brien, M. (1992) 'Issues in Treating Adolescent Sex Offenders.' Address to NOTA Conference, Dundee, 2nd October 1992.

O'Connell, M.A., Leberg, E. and Donaldson, C.R. (1990) *Working with Sex Offenders: Guidelines for Therapist Selection.* Newbury Park: Sage Publications.

Osborn, C.A., Abel, G.G. and Warberg, B.W. (1995) *The Abel Assessment: Its Comparison to Plethysmography and Resistance to Falsification.* Paper presented at the 14th annual meeting of the Association for the Treatment of Sexual Abusers, New Orleans, USA.

Peart, K. and Asquith, S. (1992) *Scottish Prisoners and their Families: The Impact of Imprisonment on Family Relationships.* Scottish Forum on Prisons and Families. Edinburgh: Save the Children Fund.

Pfäfflin, F. (1996) 'The out-patient treatment of the sex offender.' In C. Cordess and M. Cox (eds) *Forensic Psychotherapy: Crime, Psychodynamics and the Offender Patient, Vol.1.* London: Jessica Kingsley Publishers.

Pithers, W.D. (1990) 'Relapse prevention with sexual aggressors: A method for maintaining therapeutic gain and enhancing external supervision.' In W.L. Marshall, D.R. Laws and H.E. Barbaree (eds) *Handbook of Sexual Assault: Issues, Theories and Treatment of the Offender.* New York, NY: Plenum Press.

Pithers, W.D., Marques, J.K., Gibat, C.C. and Marlatt, G.A. (1983) 'Relapse prevention with sexual aggressives: A self-control model of treatment and maintenance of change.' In J.G. Greer and I.R. Stuart (eds) *The Sexual Aggressor: Current Perspectives on Treatment.* New York, NY: Van Nostrand Reinhold.

Prentky, R.A. and Burgess, A.W. (1991) 'Rehabilitation of child molesters: A cost-benefit analysis.' *American Journal of Orthopsychiatry 60*, 108–117.

Prison Service (1998) *Prisoner Communications.* Order Number 4400, Prison Service Instruction Ref. No. 41/98. HM Prison Service.

Quinsey, V.L. (1990) *Strategies for the Assessment, Treatment and Management of Sex Offenders.* A report submitted to Correctional Services, Canada. Ontario: Queen's University.

Robertson, J. (1998) Review of *Assessing Men who Sexually Abuse: A Practice Guide. NOTANews 27*, 36–37.

Ross, R.R., Fabiano, E. and Diemer-Ewles, C. (1988) 'Reasoning and rehabilitation.' *International Journal of Offender Therapy and Comparative Criminology 32*, 29–36.

Rush, F. (1980) *The Best Kept Secret: Sexual Abuse of Children.* New York, NY: McGraw-Hill.

Russell, D.E.H. (1984) *Sexual Exploitation: Rape, Child Sexual Abuse and Workplace Harassment.* Newbury Park: Sage.

Salter, A.C. (1988) *Treating Child Sex Offenders and Victims: A Practical Guide*, Newbury Park, CA: Sage.

Salter, A.C. (1989) 'Epidemiology of child sexual abuse.' In W. O'Donohue and J.H. Geer (eds) *The Sexual Abuse of Children: Volume 1: Theory and Research*. Hillsdale, NJ: Lawrence Erlbaum.

Saradjian, J. (1993) 'Female perpetrators of child sexual abuse – an emerging perspective.' In M. Cardozo, D. Fisher and B. Print (eds) *Sex Offenders: Towards Improved Practice*. London: Whiting and Birch.

Saradjian, J. (1996) *Women Who Sexually Abuse Children: From Research to Clinical Practice*. Chichester: Wiley.

Saradjian, J. (1997) 'Factors that specifically exacerbate the trauma of victims of childhood sexual abuse by maternal perpetrators.' *The Journal of Sexual Aggression 3*, 3–14.

Secretary of State for Scotland (1996) *Crime and Punishment*. Cm 3302. The Scottish Office Home Department. Edinburgh: HMSO.

Seghorn, T.K., Prentky, R.A. and Bouchier R.J. (1987) 'Childhood sexual abuse in the lives of sexually aggressive offenders.' *Journal of American Child and Adolescent Psychiatry 26*, 262–267.

SHHD (1989) *Parole and Related Issues in Scotland*. Report of the Review Committee (Chairman: Lord Kincraig). Cm 598. Scottish Home and Health Department. Edinburgh: HMSO.

Silbert, M.H. and Pines, A.M. (1981) 'Sexual child abuse as an antecedent to prostitution.' *Child Abuse and Neglect 5*, 407–411.

Spencer, A.P. (1982) 'The age of responsibility.' *The Journal of the Association of Scottish Prison Governors 2*, 24–29.

Spencer, A.P. (1994a) *Containment and Treatment of Sex Offenders: In Prison and in the Community*. Paper presented to SACRO Conference 'Sex Offenders: Options for Change'. Edinburgh.

Spencer, A.P. (1994b) *Draft Strategy Document – Shaping SPS Policy on Sex Offenders: Proposals for an Integrated Approach to the Management of Sex Offenders within SPS and in the Context of the Scottish Criminal Justice System*. Peterhead.

Spencer, A.P. (1997) 'I'm not alright, Jack. Looking after our professionals: an invitation to management to accept responsibility and minimise harm.' *NOTANews 21*, 3–8.

SPS (1990) *Opportunity and Responsibility: Developing New Approaches to the Management of the Long Term Prison System in Scotland*. Edinburgh: Scottish Prison Service.

SPS (1992) *Sentence Planning Scheme: Development Files*. Edinburgh: Scottish Prison Service.

SPS (1994) 'Prisoners convicted of offences against children.' Circular No 60/1994, 7 October 1994. Edinburgh: The Scottish Office.

SPS (1996) *Scottish Prison Service Corporate Plan, 1996–1999*. Edinburgh: The Scottish Office.

SPS and Social Work Services Group (1990) *Continuity Through Co-operation, National Framework of Policy and Practice Guidance for Social Work in Scottish Penal Establishments.* Edinburgh: Scottish Prison Service.

Still, J. (1990) 'Personal issues to be considered when working with sex abuse.' Training Material, Gracewell Clinic, Birmingham.

Summit, R. (1983) 'The child sexual abuse accommodation syndrome', *Child Abuse and Neglect 7,* 2, 177–193.

SWSG (1991) *National Objectives and Standards for Social Work Services in the Criminal Justice System.* Social Work Services Group. Edinburgh: The Scottish Office.

SWSG (1994) *Child Protection: The Imprisonment and Preparation for Release of Prisoners Convicted of Offences Against Children.* Circular Instruction SW/11/1994, 6 October, 1994. Social Work Services Group. Edinburgh: Scottish Office.

SWSG (1997) *Implementation of the Sex Offenders Act 1997: Implications for Local Authorities.* Circular Instruction SWSG/11/1997, 11 August 1997, Social Work Services Inspectorate. Edinburgh: The Scottish Office.

SWSG (1998) *Crime and Disorder Act 1998: Section 86 (Extended Sentences – Interim Social Work Guidance).* Circular Instruction SWSG/14/1998, 12 November, 1998. Social Work Services Group. Edinburgh: The Scottish Office.

SWSI (1997) *A Commitment to Protect, Supervising Sex Offenders: Proposals for more effective practice.* (The Skinner Report) Social Work Inspectorate for Scotland. Edinburgh: The Scottish Office.

The Prisons and Young Offenders Institutions (Scotland) *Rules 1994, No. 1931* (S.85). London: HMSO.

Thornton, D. (1997) *Developing Systematic Risk Assessment for Sex Offenders.* Address to NOTA Annual Conference, Southampton, September.

Toch, H. (1995) 'Inmate involvement in prison governanace.' *Federal Probation Quarterly 59,* 2, 34–39.

Toch, H. and Grant, J.D. (1982) *Reforming Human Services: Change through Participation.* Newbury Park: Sage

Walker, A.R. (1992) Letter from Deputy Chief Executive of SPS to Dan Gunn, Governor of HMP Greenock and to Strathclyde Social Work Department.

Waterhouse, L., Dobash, R. and Carnie, J. (1994) *Child Sexual Abusers.* Report to Social Work Services Group. Central Research Unit. Edinburgh: The Scottish Office.

Watkins, B. and Bentovim, A. (1992) 'The sexual abuse of male children and adolescents: A review of the current research.' *British Journal of Child Psychology and Psychiatry 33,* 1, 197–248.

Webster, C.D., Harris, G.T., Rice, M.E., Cormier, C. and Quinsey, V.L. (1994) *The Violence Predictions Scheme.* Toronto, Ontario: Centre for Criminology, University of Toronto.

West, J. (1995) 'Governor takes the zero option.' *The Scotsman.* 15 June 1995, p.15.

Wolfenden Committee Report (1957) *Report of the Committee on Homosexual Offences and Prostitution.* Cmnd. 247. London: HMSO.

Wozniak, E. (1996) *Programme Delivery in North America.* Occasional Paper, No. 1/1996. Edinburgh: Scottish Prison Service.

Wozniak, E., Dyson, G. and Carnie, J. (1998) *The Third Prison Survey.* Occasional Paper, No.3/1998. Edinburgh: Scottish Prison Service.

Wyre, R. and Swift, A. (1990) *Women, Men and Rape.* Sevenoaks: Headway, Hodder and Stoughton.

Subject
Index

Abel Screen 76
abuse
  effects of 36–9, 68–9
  incidence *see* prevalence
  was I abused? 35
accreditation
  programmes 108, 114,
    115, 204
  staff 120, 126
acute risk factors 87
adapted programme
  (SOTP) 202
addressing offending
  behaviour 55, 59
admission to prison 46,
    50, 194, 195
aetiology of offending
    22, 40, 41
agencies
  communication
    between 16, 62,
    130, 135, 145, 156
  cooperation 135, 138,
    159
  information sharing
    135, 137
  meetings and case
    conferences 139,
    144, 167, 180,
    196,197, 198, 199
  multi-agency model
    194–200
  policy objectives 136,
    137

secondments 139, 140
services available 139,
    140
six Cs 144–5
value systems 135, 139
aims of STOP
    programme 77
allocation to prisons 45
anger diary 108
anger management 47,
    58, 110–11
Apex Trust 186
arousal *see* deviant sexual
    arousal
assessment 78–88, 116,
    118, 156
  mentally disordered
    offenders 30, 31,
    32
  multi-disciplinary 46
  phase of programme
    46, 77
  risk *see* risk assessment
  veracity 85
ATSA 122n, 125
attitude
  to offence 79, 84, 143
  to victims 78–9, 143
attribution of
  responsibility *see*
  blame

Barlinnie prison 15, 49,
    105, 138, 162, 183
Barony Housing 186
blame 28, 63, 72, 79,
    88, 147, 148
Boath, A. 123
booster programme
    (SOTP) 202–3

causes of offending
    21–3, 40, 41
case conference 144,
    180
case studies 205–32
censorship *see*
    pornography
child
  best interests of 62, 64,
    141, 145
  burden of 146
  compulsory measures
    of care 157, 167
  forgiveness 63, 147,
    149
  physical contact with
    62, 63
  pornography 69, 70,
    76
  protection 46, 64, 120,
    135, 142, 155–9,
    160, 162, 184,
    187, 195, 197, 198
  issues 155, 156, 157
  strategy 158
  rights 64, 69, 92, 141,
    148
  social worker of 142,
    143
  visitor to prison 61–4
ChildLine 24
children as victims
  bribed or threatened
    94, 95
  effects 36–9
  leading to offending
    40
  offences against 46
  survival techniques
    34–5
  was I abused? 35
Children First 186

children, sexual
    exploitation of 72–3
Childrens Hearings 136,
    142, 143, 157–8,
    185, 188
    reporter 136, 157, 196
classes see education
cognitive based
    programmes 54
cognitive distortions 24,
    28, 63, 73, 84,
    88–90
cognitive restructuring
    78
cognitive skills 47, 48,
    50, 55, 58, 107–8,
    202
community
    concern 65, 66, 143,
        197
    notification see public
        notification
    supervision 16, 135
completing programmes
    86, 87
conditions imposed 18
conferences 125, 129,
    160
confidentiality
    breaches 14
    in groups 53, 57
    of information 51
consent 78, 91–2
control groups 116
control over others 23
core programme 16
core workers see staff
court ordeal 43
courts 44, 133, 141,
    156, 162, 184–5,
    187, 194, 195, 196

'Creating Control' 49,
    138, 162
Crime and Disorder Act
    49, 142n, 162, 182
Crime and Punishment 115
Crime and Punishment
    (Scotland) Act 49,
    54, 162, 164, 182,
    183
Criminal Procedure
    (Scotland) Act 46,
    134, 182
criminal records office
    184
criticism of psychiatrists
    31
Crown Office 44, 132,
    184
culture of society 68, 92,
    179
'cycle of abuse' 40
cycle of offending see
    offence cycle

dance and drama 57,
    112
dangerousness 66, 67
date rape 92, 96
debriefing 126
denial 19, 32, 48, 60,
    63, 64, 72, 73, 79,
    80, 81, 84, 88–90,
    104, 116, 130, 132,
    147, 202
deviant sexual arousal
    73, 74, 75
Duncan, J. 123

Edinburgh prison 15,
    166, 183
education

classes 57, 107,
    111–13
    staff 46, 111–13, 187
effects of abuse 35,
    36–9, 68–9, 146
efficacy of 'treatment'
    117
Eldridge, H. 122, 129
empathy see victim
    empathy
equal opportunities 56,
    121
erectile response see
    deviant sexual
    arousal
evaluation 47, 50, 114,
    115, 116–18, 204
extended programme
    (SOTP) 202
extended sentence 48,
    142n, 162, 164,
    183, 195

Fabiano, E. 48
facilities for groups 19,
    53
family 142, 143
    contact 47, 61, 65, 67,
        120, 196
    home leave/visits
        65–6, 197
    leaving home 146
    reunification 16, 45,
        90, 141–55, 197
    issues 141–2
    letter 148–9
    proposed meeting
        143, 150, 150–1
    returning home 142,
        152–5
social worker 142
stigmatisation 173

fantasy 10, 42, 67, 73, 74, 93, 94, 95, 96, 100, 102, 148
fantasy rehearsal 93, 94, 95, 102
feelings 94, 95, 102
feeling-thought-action chain 93
female sexual offenders 23–9
  categories 25–6
  characteristics 24–5
  coerced by males 25–6
  prevalence 17, 24
  victimisation 24, 25
  victims of 26–7
female socialisation 23
feminists 22
fixated paedophile 96

gender issues 57, 92, 111
Glasgow Herald, The 20
governor 128, 129, 160, 186, 192, 203
Gracewell Clinic 122
'graduates' of programme 48, 49, 78, 103, 106
grooming victims 26, 52, 61, 62, 67, 78, 83, 93, 94, 95, 100, 102
group approach, the 52–54
groups
  challenges within 52
  confidentiality 53, 57
  disclosure of information 54
  female offenders 29
  heterogeneous 55, 90

high risk 47, 50
low risk 47, 50
maintenance 16, 47, 48
mixed gender groups 29
pre-intervention 48
relationships 92
rules 54
run by prison staff 18–19
rooms see facilities
self-help 48, 103, 104
sessions 78
why groups? 52–3
guilt 94, 95, 96

Hamish Allan centre 165
harm reduction 43
homework 91, 102
hostels 155–6, 166, 185
human rights 34, 132, 173
humiliation of women 22, 23, 71, 92

incentives 42
identification of sex offenders
  admission to prison 46, 50, 194
  in prison 43, 44, 45, 63
information
  about offender 130–4, 167
  admission to prison 138, 195
  analysis of 80
  disclosure by offender 130

how offender operates 43, 78, 130–4, 147
  see also witness and victim statements
personal history 79–80, 83
previous offending 45, 130–4
sharing and exchange 44, 131, 138, 197
'intervention' term defined 17
interventions see programmes
interviewing techniques 80, 81
intimacy 25, 27, 37, 79
'irrelevant' decisions 94, 96, 99, 100, 101

judiciary 44, 164, 181, 185, 187
justifications 28, 40, 70, 79, 80, 88, 90, 93, 94, 110

Lady Chaterly's Lover 161
letter to victim 63, 91, 102, 148–9
leisure time 92, 109
licence 163, 168, 180, 181, 182, 187, 198
life sentence 180, 181
local forums 166
Lothian Crime Survey 20

maintenance
  programmes 16, 47, 48, 78, 97, 103
male sexual offenders
  prevalence 17

victimisation 24
management, prison
  advice for 120, 129
  hard time 14
  home leave issues 66,
    142
  policy 114, 129
  support 51, 55, 120,
    121, 126
  visits 61–5
management of sex
    offenders, phases 16
manipulation by sex
    offenders 14
Marshall, Prof. W. 18,
    101, 122, 129, 161
masturbatory
    reconditioning 73,
    74–5, 76
Megan's law 169, 170
mentally disordered
    offenders 29–33
  assessment 30, 31, 32
  criticism of
    psychiatrists 31
  difficulties 32
  illness or offence? 30,
    32
  pharmacology 33
  prevalence 30
  programmes 30, 31,
    32, 33
  psychopathy 30, 33
  release 30, 31, 33
Mental Health Acts 29,
    30
minimisation 25, 26, 27,
    32, 34, 36, 37, 38,
    72, 79, 81, 84, 88,
    104, 130, 202
monitoring

of programmes 47, 50,
    114, 115, 204
  of progress 114
mothers who abuse see
    female offenders
mother, relationship with
    86–7
multi-agency approach
    see agencies
multi-disciplinary
    approach 105, 156
  mentally disordered
    offenders 32
  assessment 46

national induction unit
    46, 47, 50, 138
National Standards in
    Social Work see social
    work
networking 119, 120,
    123, 125, 160
non-offending mother
    61, 63, 147
normality, state of 94–5
NOTA 122, 125, 126

objectification 33, 34,
    64, 68, 69, 70, 76,
    91, 92
offence
  attitude to 79
  cycle 78, 84, 93–7, 98,
    100, 101, 104,
    110, 116, 130,
    147, 164, 181
  continuous 94, 96
  inhibited 94, 96, 97
  linked 97
  process description
    94
  short circuiting 97

one-to-one work 52
one-way mirror 19, 53

paedophile networking
    46
parallel work 77, 103,
    107–13
'para professionals' 126,
    203
parole 47, 76, 164, 195
  board 45, 142, 163,
    180, 181, 182,
    183, 187, 198
  conditions 16, 180
  role of psychiatrists 31
  video material 54, 114,
    180–1, 183
participation in
    programmes 84, 86,
    87
pattern of offending 78
penile plethysmograph
    (PPG) 73, 75, 76,
    86, 201
personal development see
    sentence planning
personal history 79, 83
personal officer 13, 18,
    56–7, 58, 59,
    108–10, 114, 121,
    142, 197
Peterhead Prison 15, 18,
    34, 47, 48, 49, 53,
    55, 56, 59, 60, 65,
    71, 104, 105, 106,
    107, 108, 121, 122,
    125, 126, 127, 129,
    130, 181, 189, 193
phallometric assessment
    see PPG
pitfalls 13–14, 15, 17
Playboy 56

plea bargaining 43, 173
pleading guilty at court 43
police 109, 142, 162, 184, 187, 197, 198
  information 20, 44, 54, 130, 131, 134
polygraph 81–2
  countering deception 81
  uses 82
pornography 14, 33, 56, 68–73, 92, 93, 184
  child, use of 69, 70, 72–3, 76
  definitions 70–1
  ethical questions 76
  media 68–9
  pornography-free 17, 18, 57, 59, 71, 72, 73
  staff view 71, 72
Porporino, F. 48
Portuguese 14
post supervision support 16
power 21, 22, 23, 25, 62, 69, 92, 94, 95, 111
PPG 73, 75, 76, 86, 201
precognitions 133, 134
prediction 40, 75, 83, 85–7, 117
pre-release 113
prevalence
  difficulties of identification 43, 44, 45, 63
  females 17, 24
  males 17
  in prison 15, 17, 44

of sexual abuse 20, 39, 40, 68
  in prison population 41
Prisoners and Criminal Proceedings (Scotland) Act 48, 162, 164, 182
Prison Officers Association 14, 127
prison officer's role 51, 52
prison staff running groups 18–19
prison management see management
prison population 15, 17, 44
Prisons Minister, Scotland 54–5, 115
Procurator Fiscal 131, 132, 133, 134, 157
'professional accommodation syndrome' 128
Programme Development Section 203, 204
programme manager 114, 128
programmes
  effects 84
  in isolation 16
  intervention process 88–102
  for females 28–9
  length 104–5
  low-risk 47, 48, 103–4
  maintenance 16, 47, 48, 78, 97, 103

mentally disordered offenders 30, 31, 32
  pre-intervention 48, 83, 103, 104
  response 85
  stages 16, 104
  SOTP 117, 201–4
  STOP see under STOP
  throughput 105
prostitution 35, 38, 39, 72, 193
psychiatric services 29, 156, 195
psychiatrists 31, 32, 46, 187
psychologists 46, 58, 74, 76, 114, 116, 122, 128, 156, 162, 187, 195
psychology role 50
psychopathy 30, 33
  PCLR score 85, 201
public notification 168–78
  advantages 171–2
  disadvantages 172–6
  driving underground 177, 178
  harassment 168, 171, 174
  human rights 173
  issues 169
  is there a balance ? 177–8
  levels of risk 171
  Megan's law 169, 170
  system in USA 171

RAPID system 52
rationalisations 88

recidivism, predictors 83,
    85
regime, supportive 56
regional secure units 29,
    33
registration of sex
    offenders 142, 162,
    164, 166, 174, 178,
    184, 195
  disclosure of
    information 167,
    168, 169
  duties of police 167,
    169
  provisions 166
  risk assessment 167
relapse 94
relapse prevention 47,
    78, 84, 97–102,
    103, 104, 105, 116,
    143, 145, 154, 155,
    165, 196, 198, 199,
    202, 203, 204
  high risk situations
    98–9, 100, 101
  lapse 97–8, 98, 99,
    100
    avoidance 100
    defined 97–8
    reduction 100–1
  maintenance manual
    101, 102
  new approaches 102
  relapse 94, 97, 98
    defined 97
  reminder cards 100,
    101
  self-management 98,
    99
  strategies 45, 98, 100,
    138, 164
relationships 92–3, 110

in group 92
  staff/prisoner 14, 57
  with mother 86–7
release arrangements 143
'relevant part' 181
religion 14
response to programme
    85
responsibility 19, 36, 37,
    46, 63, 77, 78,
    88–90, 116, 147,
    149
reunification of family see
    family
'ripple' effect 90
risk
  assessment 16, 45, 46,
    50, 79–80, 82–8,
    103, 130, 143,
    162, 167, 194,
    198, 203
  factors 86–7
  levels 83
  'low' risk 16
  predictors 83, 85
  RRASOR scale 86

SACRO 165, 186
safe environment 9, 29,
    36, 47, 57, 59, 60
Salter, A. 159
SASD 188
Salvation Army 186
Save the Children 186
Schedule One offenders
    46, 134, 162, 183
Scottish Courts
    Administration see
    courts
Scottish Forum on
    Prisons and Families
    186

Scottish Prison Service
    (SPS) 15, 18, 44, 48,
    54, 55, 108,
    109–10, 115, 117,
    130, 131, 184
Secretary of State 163,
    181
security category 'B' 67
security category 'D' 66
self-esteem 25, 28, 37,
    57, 59, 84, 110,
    112
self help group 48, 103,
    104
sentence planning
    10–11, 18, 45, 47,
    50, 56–7, 59,
    108–10, 121, 194,
    195, 196
sentences, short 48–9,
    164, 182–3
sequencing 115
Sex Offender
    Registration see
    registration
Sex Offenders Act 142n,
    162, 166, 177, 187,
    199
sexual knowledge 92
Sexual Offences
    (Scotland) Act 46,
    134
sexual offending
  acts 94, 95, 102
  a definition 21
  causes 21–3, 40, 41
  females 23–9
  feminist explanation
    22–3
short-term prisoners
    48–50,
Shotts prison 15

Skinner Report 130, 165, 188
smoking cessation 112
social enquiry report (SER) 162, 195
social skills 57, 111
social work
  aptitude 161
  departments 162, 167, 168–9, 185–6, 187,
  duties 160, 163, 164, 165
  information sharing 44, 131, 156
  in prison 18, 46, 58, 91, 114, 120, 128, 130, 138, 142, 160, 162, 187, 194–9
  legislation 162
  National Standards 162, 164
  practitioner stance 161–2
  role in visit 61
  resources 160, 162, 164 166
  sex offender registration 167
  support 160
  training 160, 161, 164
SOTP 117, 201–4
special hospitals 29, 30, 32
specialists 'falling out' 14
SPIN project 44, 184
stable risk factors 87
staff
  alienation 13

attitudes 33, 119, 120, 123
awareness training 55, 56, 120, 121
  also see training
collusion 13, 52, 57, 59, 60, 120, 121, 127
core workers 51, 54, 55, 57, 58, 91, 114, 119, 120, 121, 126, 127, 128, 138, 142, 181
dangers for 119–20
effect on 119
elitism 13, 57
motivation 17, 19, 51, 192, 193
negative attitudes 13
networking 119
personal problems 13
pornography 55–6, 71, 72
Prison Officers Association 14, 127
resilience 119
respite 104, 125
shift systems 14, 105, 127
stress 126, 128
supervision 122, 124, 127, 128
support 119, 120, 126–9
standards 114
static risk factors 87
steering group 114, 128, 129
STEP 3 report 204
STOP programme 15, 46, 48, 51, 56, 77–8, 98, 103, 104,

106, 110, 113, 116, 117, 121, 123, 124, 128, 129, 149, 189, 201, 202
  its name 17
stress management 93
Structured Anchored Clinical Judgement 85, 203
substance abuse 58, 112
success rates 116–18
supervised release order 48, 164, 182, 183
supervision
  community 16, 101, 162, 164
  indicators of risk 87–8
  non-parole 182
  practical approaches 165
  post-supervision support 16
supervising officer 138, 142, 154, 168, 180, 182, 195
  voluntary 16, 101, 162, 196
supportive environment see therapeutic
SWSG 162, 167, 168–9, 185

'talk the talk' 105, 138
targets for agency 55
target victims 26, 52, 62, 67, 78, 93, 94, 95, 96, 100, 102
Tay project 162
team approach 50–2
temporary release 67, 68
therapeutic environment 55–9

thinking errors 88–90
throughcare 45, 135, 137–40, 159, 180, 203
timing of interventions 47–8
training
  core workers 58, 119, 120, 122
  group working 122, 123
  interviewing 122, 123, 124
  library 124
  'osmosis' 124
  pornography 122
  psychiatrists 31
  sex offender issues 123
  staff awareness 55, 56, 120, 121
  unit, staff training 121
  victim awareness 123
  videoing sessions 53–4
'treatment' defined 17, 19
'treatment' effects 84
trauma see effects
triggers 92, 93, 94, 95, 102
trust 50, 52, 134, 135, 136, 147

underground, driving 155, 177, 178

'vampire syndrome' 40
victim
  to abuser 40–1, 87
  attitude, offender's 78–9, 143
  context 34, 192–3
  disclosure 20

effects on 26–7, 36–9, 68–9, 90, 146
empathy 78, 84, 90–91, 104, 116, 138, 149, 204
of female offenders 26–7
letter to 63, 91, 102, 148–9
prevalence 20, 39, 40, 41
public notification impact 174
rights 132
statements 130, 131, 132, 133, 184
support groups 145, 186
survival techniques 34–5
voice of 141, 142
was I abused? 35
video recording 19, 53–4
snapshots 54, 114
violence, domestic and 'battering' 34, 65, 79, 110, 111
Violence Risk Appraisal Guide (VRAG) 85, 87
visits
  to prison 61–5
  guidelines 63–4
  issues 62–3
  play facilities 62
voluntary support 16, 101, 162, 196
vulnerability of sex offenders 46, 187

warrants, marking of 134, 184, 194
witness statements 131, 132, 133, 134, 184, 187
women, men and society 57, 111, 123
women's rights 33, 69, 92

Author Index

Abel, G.G. 39, 52, 76
Adshead, G. 24
Ahlmeyer, S. 82
Aitken, D. 156, 161
Alexander, P. 35n
Andrews, D.A. 15
Asquith, S. 64, 186
ATSA (Association for the Treatment of Sexual Abusers) 76, 81

Barbaree, H.E. 11, 15, 73, 75, 116, 117
Barker, M. 30
Bass, E. 34–5, 35, 36n
Beckett, R. 52
Beech, A. 117, 204
Bentovim, A. 24
Berliner, L. 146, 169n
Blake, J. 90
Bouchier, R.J. 41
Bowlby, J. 27
Brown, A. 50
Brownmiller, S. 22
Burgess, A.W. 7, 24
Bussière, M.T. 40, 75, 85, 86
Butwell, M. 30

Cameron, J. 155
Carnie, J. 17, 51n, 52, 53
Chaney, E.F. 98

Chiswick, D. 32
Colorado (Department of Public Safety) 82
Condy, S. 24
Cooke, D.J. 164
Cooklin, S. 90–1
Cooper, C.L. 41
Council of Europe (Committee on Crime Problems) 34, 69, 70, 72–3
Cowburn, M. 71

Darke, J.L. 22–3
Davis, L. 34–5, 35, 36n
Dellacoste, F. 35n
Dempsey, R. 105, 138, 147, 156
Dhawan, S. 41
Diemer-Ewles, C. 48
DiIulio, Jr., J.J. 9
Dobash, R. 17, 52, 53
Donaldson, C.R. 21
Dworkin, A. 22
Dyson, G. 51n

Earle, J.H. 82
Eldridge, H.J. 24, 29, 94, 96, 97, 105
Elliott, M. 27, 70
English, P. 82

Fabiano, E. 48
Finkelhor, D. 21, 24, 26
Fisher, D. 30, 31, 32, 85
Foucault, M. 9
Freeman-Longo, R.E. 169n, 172, 173

Gallagher, J.D. 13–14
Garland, D. 9
Gibat, C.C. 98

Glasgow Herald, The 20
Grant, J.D. 9
Grapevine, The 189
Groth, N. 24
Grubin, D. 30

Handy, L. 41
Hanson, R.K. 40, 75, 85, 86, 87, 88
Harris, A.J.R. 87, 88
Harrison, H. 24
Haynes, M.R. 41
Heil, P. 82
Hogue, T.E. 117
House of Commons (Official Report) 55
Howett, M. 24
Huckele, P. 30
Hudson, S.M. 102
Hunter, J.A. 24
Hunter, M. 40

Ignatieff, M. 9
Inter-Departmental Group on Child Abuse 135, 136–7
Inter-Departmental Group on Sex Offending 131, 135–6, 139
Itzin, C. 71

Jack, A.M. 117
Jacobs, J.B. 9
Jenkins, A. 80–1
Jones, G. 30

Kaufman, K.L. 28
Kinsey, R. 20

Langevin, R. 41
Laws, D.R. 11, 76

Leberg, E. 21
Lewis, P.S. 32

Mair, K.J. 117
Mann, R.E. 102, 126, 201, 203, 204
Marlatt, G.A. 98
Marques, J.K. 98
Marshall, W.L. 7–8, 11, 15, 18, 41, 47, 48, 49–50, 57, 58, 73, 79, 83, 84, 104, 116, 117, 125, 127, 130, 133, 192
Mason, F. 24
Mathews, R. 24, 25, 28
Matthews, Jill 91
Matthews, J.K. 25, 28
McGuire, J. 15
McIvor, G. 117
Morgan, R. 30
Morrison, T. 128
Murphy, W.D. 41, 73

NOTA (National Organisation for the Treatment of Abusers) 70–1

O'Brien, M. 40
O'Connell, M.A. 21, 22, 75, 148, 150–1, 152–3, 153–4
O'Leary, M.R. 98
Osborn, C.A. 76

Peart, K. 64, 186
Perkins, D.E. 30, 32
Pfäfflin, F. 32
Pines, A.M. 193
Pithers, W.D. 98, 99
Prentky, R.A. 7, 41

Priestly, P. 15
Prison Service (Home Office) 10, 64, 75,

Quinsey, V.L. 44–5, 130, 192

Robertson, J. 31
Ross, R.R. 48
Rush, F. 22
Russell, D.E.H. 22, 24

Salter, A.C. 20, 68, 81, 88n
Saradjian, J. 25, 26
Scotsman, The 192
Secretary of State for Scotland (Scottish Office) 115
Seghorn, T.K. 41
SHHD (Scottish Home and Health Department) 164
Silbert, M.H. 193
Slater, S. 40
Speltz, K. 25
Spencer, A.P. 10, 11, 128, 192
SPS (Scottish Prison Service) 10–11, 55, 66n, 67n, 108–10, 137, 160, 185
Still, J. 36n
Summit, R. 128
Swift, A. 179
SWSG (Social Work Services Group) 137, 162, 164, 166, 167, 168, 169, 185, 187, 196, 199
SWSI (Social Work Inspectorate for

Scotland) 131, 134, 165, 182, 183, 188

Tanaghow, A. 30
Thornton, D. 85, 102, 126, 203, 204
Toch, H. 9

United Nations 64

Vuz, J. 24

Walker, A.R. 44
Warberg, B.W. 76
Ward, T. 102
Waterhouse, L. 17, 40, 52, 53
Watkins, B. 24
Webster, C.D. 85
Wolfenden Committee 161
Wozniak, E.51n, 54, 72
Wright, P. 41
Wyre, R. 179